The New Manager Guidebook

Second Edition

Steven M. Bragg

AccountingTools®

For more information about AccountingTools® products, visit our Web site at www.accountingtools.com.

ISBN-13: 978-1-64221-070-5

Printed in the United States of America

Table of Contents

Preface

Management is a unique occupation, where success is defined by the ability to persuade others to get work done. Someone newly promoted to the role may find management to be quite difficult, and has little time to learn through trial and error. *The New Manager Guidebook* greatly increases a new manager's odds of success by dealing with every management essential, including how to organize work, motivate employees, and monitor outcomes. The *Guidebook* also shares insights into the best ways to recruit, coach, and train employees, as well as give them useful performance appraisals. In addition, it delves into the details of how to manage teams, run projects, and oversee start-up operations.

You can find the answers to many questions about management in the following chapters, including:

- What kind of organizational structure should I use?
- What methods can I use to motivate my employees?
- What steps should I follow to make changes in my area of responsibility?
- What kinds of variances should I review to see how the business is performing?
- What general principles should I follow when looking for job candidates?
- How can I coach my staff to be better employees?
- How can I be more efficient in making decisions?
- How do I deal with conflicts within a team?
- What tools are available for scheduling a project?
- What are the main pitfalls to avoid when managing a start-up business?
- How can I influence employees so that they'll follow higher ethical standards?

The New Manager Guidebook is designed for anyone who has just been promoted into a management position. It can be used as a reference tool for dealing with many issues that new managers are likely to encounter.

Centennial, Colorado
July 2021

About the Author

Steven Bragg, CPA, has been the chief financial officer or controller of four companies, as well as a consulting manager at Ernst & Young. He received a master's degree in finance from Bentley College, an MBA from Babson College, and a Bachelor's degree in Economics from the University of Maine. He has been a two-time president of the Colorado Mountain Club, and is an avid alpine skier, mountain biker, and certified master diver. Mr. Bragg resides in Centennial, Colorado. He has written more than 250 books and courses, including *New Controller Guidebook*, *GAAP Guidebook*, and *Payroll Management*.

Steven maintains the accountingtools.com web site, which contains continuing professional education courses, the Accounting Best Practices podcast, and thousands of articles on accounting subjects.

Buy Additional AccountingTools Courses

AccountingTools offers more than 1,250 hours of CPE courses, with concentrations in accounting, auditing, finance, taxation, and ethics. Related courses that you might like include:

- Accounting for Managers
- Activity-Based Management
- Business Strategy
- Effective Innovation
- Effective Leadership
- Revenue Management
- Understanding Organizational Behavior

Go to accountingtools.com/cpe to view these additional courses.

AccountingTools®

Chapter 1
Introduction to Management

Introduction

A manager is a person who is in charge of one or more tasks, usually with several employees reporting to him. How managers handle their responsibilities can have a profound impact on a business, in either a positive or negative manner. Because of a manager's position of responsibility, all actions taken are magnified, rippling out through the organization. This book is intended to show how one can be an effective manager, minimizing negative impacts and providing a great deal of value to a business.

For many people, being an effective manager is a dark art. They do not understand how a person can work through others to achieve outstanding results. A newly-appointed manager is especially befuddled when it becomes apparent that one cannot act like an Egyptian pharaoh and simply issue a few commands and then watch the work being performed. Instead, the manager has to find a way to motivate employees and persuade them to work together. Thus, management can be defined as getting work done through others. More specifically, management involves the following activities:

- Planning
- Organizing
- Leading
- Controlling

By engaging in these activities, a manager will be able to improve the efficiency and effectiveness of an organization. *Efficiency* involves the completion of a task while wasting a minimum amount of time and effort. *Effectiveness* is the extent to which an objective is attained. Thus, completing an objective quickly while using minimal resources is the essence of being efficient and effective.

In this chapter, we provide an overview of the key management activities (which are expanded upon in later chapters), along with several related topics.

Core Management Activities

As noted in the introduction, the core management activities are planning, organizing, leading, and controlling. A manager needs to develop her skills in all four areas in order to be truly effective.

Planning involves setting targets for where an organization should go, as well as how to get from here to there. This is a multi-level process, requiring the formulation of a mission statement, strategic plan, and tactics. These plans are based on an analysis of the environment in which a business operates. Depending on the situation, it may be useful to also engage in scenario planning to model a few alternative courses of action. This topic is covered in more detail in Chapter 3, *Planning Activities.*

A business needs to be properly organized in order to achieve its plan. This calls for the second management activity, which is developing an organizational structure that is tailored to support the organization's strategy. There are many organizational choices available, such as a tightly-organized, top-down structure where senior management makes the bulk of the decisions, or a much flatter structure in which decision making is pushed down into the organization, or somewhere in between. Within these overall systems, the manager needs to design individual jobs, aggregate these jobs into departments or teams, create lines of authority, and set up systems to coordinate activities. This topic is covered in more detail in Chapter 4, *Organizational Structures.*

Once there are plans and an organizational structure in place, the manager needs to persuade employees to engage in the necessary work. Doing so requires one to inspire employee trust, which is covered in Chapter 5, *Leadership.* It also requires the use of various types of reward systems to encourage employees to engage in those areas where the firm needs them to work the hardest, as discussed in Chapter 6, *Motivating Employees.* The task of motivating staff is made much easier if there is a favorable corporate culture that already has a positive impact on the business, as noted in Chapter 7, *Corporate Culture.* And in those cases where systems need to be replaced or revised, the manager can follow a structured process for doing so that greatly increases the odds of success, as described in Chapter 8, *Change Management.*

To see how well a business is achieving its goals, the management team should continually monitor and evaluate all aspects of the business. This involves the use of a budget, financial statements, and variance analysis, as described in Chapter 9, *Management Control Activities.*

In addition to these core management activities, an effective manager needs to locate and develop a great supporting cast. This means paying attention to the recruiting process to zero in on the best possible candidates, as noted in Chapter 10, *Employee Recruiting and Appraisal,* as well as providing effective coaching for them, as noted in Chapter 11, *Employee Coaching.* And finally, a targeted system of training should be used that identifies employee weaknesses that need to be corrected through training programs, as noted in Chapter 12, *Employee and Manager Training.*

A manager will be judged based on how well he can make decisions, especially those that involve significant risks and rewards for the business. There are a number of decision making tools available, as well as a structured process for making decisions, as described in Chapter 13, *Manager Decision Making.*

At some point during his career, a manager may be called upon to manage in more unusual circumstances, such as a team, project, or start-up business. We cover these situations in Chapters 14 through 16. Of most interest is Chapter 15, *Project Management,* which describes many project management tools, including estimating, Gantt charts, the critical path method, and the program evaluation and review technique (PERT).

Managers set the tone for how employees behave, so a key consideration is setting up an ethical infrastructure that makes employees more aware of the ethical practices that management wants to promote. We deal with ethics extensively in Chapter 17, *Manager Ethics*.

And finally, Chapter 18, *7 Habits of Effective Managers*, addresses several key habits that will make a new manager significantly more efficient and effective, addressing both short-term and long-term considerations.

Essential Areas for a Manager to Emphasize

When a person is working in a non-management role, he is probably valued most for his technical skills and his ability to get along with other employees. For example, a software programmer is valued for his coding skills, while a salesperson is valued for her ability to interact with customers. These priorities change when a person is promoted into a management role. As a new manager, technical skill becomes much less important, since the manager is not expected to directly assist employees with their work. Instead, the manager needs to maintain or increase his ability to interact with others, becoming more sensitive to their personalities, quirks, needs, strengths, and weaknesses. This higher level of sensitivity is needed to gain insights into how employees can be persuaded to work with each other and complete assigned tasks. These interpersonal skills can cover many topics, such as:

- Communicating with others
- Employing enhanced listening skills
- Coaching employees
- Fostering teamwork
- Empowering employees to make their own decisions
- Monitoring the personal well-being of employees

In addition, a much greater awareness is needed of how one's area of responsibility fits into the organization, how the organization is impacted by market changes, and how this impacts decisions.

EXAMPLE

A new department manager is responsible for granting credit to customers. She is aware of how incorrect credit decisions can increase bad debt losses. In addition, she is aware that a gradual decline in general economic conditions could accelerate bad debt losses, so she recommends that the firm's credit policy be tightened until economic conditions improve. This recommendation shows that the credit manager has a strong awareness of how her department fits into the organization.

Beyond the basic human relations and conceptual skills just noted, a manager also needs the more specific technical skills associated with her specific position. For example, a company controller needs to have a thorough understanding of how payables, receivables, and payroll are processed, as well as the accounting standards that apply to her company, in order to manage the accounting department properly. In addition, a controller should understand the problem-solving skills that apply to accounting issues, such as how to analyze the financial statements or locate an error in the accounting transactions. However, the need for technical skills tends to decline as a person advances into more senior management positions, since a senior manager has mid-level managers and supervisors with the requisite technical skill sets. For example, if a company controller is promoted into the chief financial officer slot, she no longer has to understand exactly how the company processes its payables, receivables, and payroll, since someone else is now responsible for these activities.

Essential Management Behavior

A range of management styles may prove to be effective. However, no matter which style a manager may have, there are a number of behaviors that can assist in coaxing a group of employees into their most productive mode. Consider the following behaviors:

- *Be calm.* A group environment can be fraught with tension, especially when there are "A" team high performers with large egos battling each other. The manager should convey an air of calmness through this turbulence, which can go a long ways toward settling the entire group.
- *Listen.* There may be several dozen issues within a group that could potentially crater its performance. The only way for the manager to understand all of these potential problems is to listen to what employees say, and watch them for changes in body language. The discerning manager can then arrive at conclusions regarding the true state of affairs. In order to observe, this also means that the main form of communication for the manager is face-to-face, not e-mail. See the following Listening Skills section for more information.
- *Push out information.* The manager should be a distributor of information. Most information reporting systems are geared to accumulate information for the sole use of management. An excellent supervisory activity is to put this information into the hands of those people who need it the most – employees. This information should literally include *everything* – the costs incurred to date, performance measurements, key metrics in the industry that can impact operations, and so forth. The best management behavior of all is to find out what other information the group needs, and then obtain it.
- *Push down planning.* A manager does not solely engage in planning – employees do it. They will not buy into a project unless they have thrashed out amongst themselves what the goal will be, the roles of each person in the group, and who is responsible for what. Also, requiring a group to plan eliminates one of the reasons that naysayers could otherwise use to backstab the group, which is that "we were not consulted."
- *Push up at management.* If the group has a problem, the manager should take on the burden of forcing senior management to resolve the issue. Problem resolution might require obtaining additional funding, materials, or personnel,

or perhaps changing policies and procedures that are getting in the way. The manager is the only person who is empowered to do this.

- *Push back at performance issues.* When someone in the group is performing below expectations, push back at them at once. These issues may sometimes be dealt with by others in the group, but the manager has the extra authority to give additional emphasis to the message.
- *Follow through.* When the manager commits to take action on any issue, she must *always* follow through on this commitment. This means writing down the issue so that it is not forgotten and taking action promptly. By doing so repeatedly, employees will realize that she is completely reliable, and so will trust her in their other interactions with her.

Once a manager consistently exhibits the preceding behaviors, employees will realize that her core values are deeply aligned with them, and so will trust her more as their leader.

Listening Skills

A manager should have listening skills that are well above the average. The best listeners are able to not only understand the words being spoken by someone, but also their tone of voice and the body language they use while delivering it. This means that the full attention of a person must be directed at someone in order to receive the full message being conveyed.

The first step in achieving proper listening skills is to encourage the other person to communicate. This means stopping whatever else the listener is doing, facing the speaker, and maintaining a consistent level of eye contact. In addition, maintain an expression of wanting to hear what the person has to say. This means not fidgeting, checking voice mail, texting, frowning, and so forth.

The second step in listening properly is to strive for the most active possible listening mode. The following are a number of levels of listening skills, starting with the best (active listening) and declining to the worst (passive listening).

1. *Active listening.* The listener pays complete attention to every communication channel being used – words, tone, and body language. The listener understands every aspect of the message being conveyed, and responds with cogent questions that focus on the key issues. When a speaker encounters an active listener, there is a high probability that the speaker will take the extra time to flesh out all aspects of the message.
2. *Attentive listening.* The listener pays close attention to the words being spoken, and is likely to have excellent retention of the words conveyed. He may also ask questions to clarify points being made, and comment on certain issues. However, he does not expand his perceptions to include the tone and body language of the speaker, and so may not understand the entire message being conveyed.
3. *Selective listening.* The listener only retains what he wants to hear, and ignores the remainder of the message. This approach can trigger substantial

misunderstandings and conflict, since only part of the message is being conveyed.

4. *Passive listening*. The listener sits quietly, making no indication that a message was received, and not making any positive or negative gestures. When passive listening is used, the speaker receives no feedback at all, and so gradually "runs out of steam" and stops speaking.

There is an enormous difference between the volume and quality of information transferring to an active listener and a passive listener. When a manager is an active listener, there are far fewer misunderstandings between her and her team.

Coaching Skills

A manager must engage in a considerable amount of coaching in order to squeeze the maximum amount of performance out of his employees. In order to engage properly as a coach, the manager must first understand that this new role is not the classic manager role to which he may be accustomed. Being a coach does not mean being a firefighter, jumping in to resolve every crisis. Instead, a coach realizes that the real value generated by the position is to enhance the effectiveness of the entire group on an ongoing basis, so that there are fewer fires to fight. This can be accomplished by engaging in the following activities:

- *Meet with employees*. An accomplished coach circulates through the group, spending a lot of time engaging with each person. By doing so, one can determine whether anyone is beginning to diverge away from the departmental work plan, and implement a minor correction to bring them back on track. These meetings also allow the manager to spot instances in which additional resources are needed, and then take action to obtain them.

- *Conduct meetings*. The manager routinely brings the group together to discuss progress, issues found, and any new information obtained. These meetings keep the group aligned, and can also bring the thinking of everyone to bear on a particular problem.

- *Link people to plans*. The manager must always be aware of every aspect of the group's action plan, and refers to it whenever meeting with them. Doing so reminds everyone of what they are supposed to be doing, and the deadline for the current work activity. This constant level of attention to the plan also allows the manager to make micro-adjustments to the plan on a continual basis.

- *Assign responsibility*. One of the main differences between a classic manager and a coach is that a coach pushes responsibility down into the group, rather than retaining it. This means that each employee is made well aware of what is expected of them, and how they are performing against that standard.

- *Give feedback*. When meeting with employees, the manager routinely gives feedback regarding how people are doing in comparison to expectations. This feedback is highly focused, noting exactly which performance or behavior was lacking, and what is expected. By giving feedback constantly, employees know exactly how they are doing at all times.

- *Recognize success*. Departments typically have concrete goals, so celebrate them when they are achieved – along with all of the sub-goals and individual accomplishments that occurred along the way. Doing so gives positive feedback to the entire group.
- *Mentor employees*. A coach that has a long-term view of the success of employees will mentor them. This means discussing with them their strengths and weaknesses, career plans, training needs, and so forth.

When engaged in coaching activities, keep in mind that the goal is not to make employees a fun group to work with. The goal is to achieve the target set for them, which may require pushing employees harder than they would like. The outcome may be a situation in which the group views the coach as a hard taskmaster, but also as one who inspired them to achieve a major accomplishment.

The Sources of Power

An effective manager needs to influence others in order to maximize her impact on a business. Doing so requires a certain amount of *power*, which is the ability to make things happen. There are several types of power available to a manager. A manager is more likely to be effective if she can tap multiple sources of power. These sources are:

- The power associated with a specific position. Thus, the position of chief operating officer confers a substantial amount of power on the holder of that position.
- The power to reward employees. When a person is able to hand out pay raises or other benefits, this tends to confer a certain amount of power. For example, the human resources director tends to have more power than the title itself would imply, because this person advises management about pay raises and promotions.
- The power associated with being an expert. When a person has a highly specialized skill, people tend to follow her recommendations. This type of power can be distributed throughout an organization. For example, an information technology expert will have substantial power over the choice of software that a business purchases.
- The power associated with personal characteristics. People who are admired have a certain amount of power to influence others. For example, an unusually empathetic manager who has earned a solid reputation for fair dealings with her subordinates will likely gain power through their loyalty to her.
- The power of networking. When a person is deeply embedded in a network of interpersonal connections within (and outside of) a business, this position can confer a significant amount of power. Networkers can strongly influence

the opinions of others, even when they are located in odd corners of the official corporate hierarchy.

Truly powerful managers probably combine several of these sources of power. The most likely combination is the power associated with having a specific position and the power derived from being a strong networker. Weaker managers only rely on their ability to reward or coerce employees, which tends to drive the best performers out of a business in short order.

How to Influence People

To a great extent, management is about getting work done through others, which can involve a substantial amount of persuasion. Some of that persuasion capability comes from the use of power, as discussed in the last section. However, there are subtler ways to influence people, including the following techniques:

- *Present a logical argument.* One can marshal facts and supporting analyses to build a persuasive case for a particular direction. This approach is especially useful when the manager is a recognized expert in the field under discussion.
- *Build a favorable opinion.* People are more likely to help someone they like, so an effective manager should constantly be building a favorable impression by treating others fairly and with a high level of respect.
- *Swap favors.* People are more likely to be of assistance when a manager has already helped them, perhaps by allocating some time or monetary resources to them, or by providing support in another decision area. Thus, a manager can be constantly providing support everywhere in a business, in expectation of benefiting from this assistance in the future.
- *Cultivate partners.* A manager can search for and build ties with others in the organization who have similar interests and needs. These partners then support each other in accomplishing goals that they all believe in. This can mean that a manager cultivates different groups of allies, where each group is targeted at a different set of goals.
- *Gain senior management support.* When softer approaches do not work, it may be necessary to gain the support of someone who has more authority, perhaps someone in the executive suite. This use of raw power is generally used quite rarely, only after all other forms of persuasion have failed.

The best managers are able to switch among several types of persuasion, depending on the circumstances, and usually with little need to impose any coercive power. People tend to work harder when they have truly been persuaded to engage in an activity, rather than being forced to do so.

Networking

Networking is the creation and active maintenance of a group of acquaintances for the mutual benefit of the group. The use of a network is an essential criterion for a manager, especially a more senior manager. A network provides a manager with support, feedback, advice, and resources. For example, an acquaintance can provide insights into what characteristics to look for when hiring a new marketing manager, or can act as a go-between to arrange a meeting with a possible recruit, or is available as a sounding board when dealing with a difficult union contract renewal. The members of a network have differing experiences and skills, which can be drawn upon to expand a manager's capabilities.

Networking can appear to be a formidable problem for someone who has just been promoted into management, since the basis for that promotion was quite possibly a high level of technical skill, not people skills. Nonetheless, the aspiring manager should reach out to the following groups to form a network:

- *In-house personnel.* The manager should engage in regular discussions with direct reports, superiors, and peers scattered throughout the organization, since these people have the most direct impact on ongoing projects within the firm. A deep network in this area helps to complete work more efficiently.
- *Business partners.* The manager may be deeply involved with suppliers, customers, regulators, and joint venture partners, all of which call for in-depth, on-going relations with their representatives to deal with day-to-day issues.
- *Personal connections.* The preceding groups are inherently obvious, since they involve ongoing contacts related to daily tasks. A manager should also develop a network of personal connections outside of work, which results in a broader base of contacts with far-ranging experiences. This group can be useful for providing access to an entirely new set of contacts, as well as information not readily available within the company.
- *Strategic connections.* As a manager moves into more senior roles within an organization, it becomes more important to build a network that encompasses the managers of other business units within the firm as well as other stakeholders that allow her to gain input into the future direction of the business and how resources are allocated in relation to that direction.

A manager can identify the likeliest candidates for an in-house network by identifying those people who could potentially support or block a project. Outside of the firm, possible network candidates can be targeted by attending the meetings of professional associations, alumni groups, and similar organizations.

Many new managers elect not to establish networks because they do not believe there is enough time to do so. However, the support of a strong network can make a manager more effective, so it is essential to block out enough time for networking activities. One method for doing so is to delegate more work to subordinates, thereby freeing up time and also giving the subordinates valuable experience in dealing with new activities. Managers may also avoid networking because they are uncomfortable with the idea of making connections with people they barely know. There is no easy way around this issue – the only solution is to block out the time to make connections with other people on an ongoing basis. One may gradually feel less discomfort from the process, while gaining some benefits from networking activities that will make the cost-benefit tradeoff more favorable over time.

Managing Upward

A good manager does not just manage her subordinates – she also managers her boss. There are several reasons for doing so. First, the manager needs to secure adequate resources for her areas of responsibility, and her boss is involved in the allocation of those resources. Consequently, the boss has to be fully aware of the need for those resources, so that he can more effectively argue in favor of their allocation with other members of the senior management team. Second, the boss can provide a manager with contacts throughout the organization, which may be needed in cases where co-operation is needed from a number of functional areas within the firm. Third, the manager is closer to the action than her boss, and so can provide well-justified opinions regarding the future direction of the company that her boss may not have considered. This implies a certain amount of bottom-up planning in the setting of strategic plans. And finally, the boss may have strengths in areas where the manager is weak, and so can be a terrific source of advice for how to deal with specific situations.

Managing upward requires an understanding of the work style of one's boss. The individual might have certain preferences in regard to the frequency of updates and whether they are written or oral. Perhaps the boss prefers discussions over a meal, or at the start of the day. The boss may prefer detailed discussions, or only a short set of bullet point summaries. He may have a tendency toward conflict, or perhaps conflict avoidance. Or, the boss likes to be deeply involved in daily operating decisions, versus someone who only wants to hear about operations when there is a problem. Given these differences in style, it can be useful to have a frank discussion about it up front, so that the manager can ascertain the best way to proceed.

Managing upward also requires a firm grasp of the boss' goals. After all, one definition of a quality employee is one who helps a manager to succeed. Consequently, a manager should discuss with her boss the boss' most critical goals, and how she can help to achieve them. This analysis can extend to any pressures being imposed on the boss, which drives how he deals with his subordinates. Only after a manager has a clear understanding of a boss' situation can she structure a plan for managing upward. Further, the manager needs to keep asking questions, since her boss' situation will likely change over time.

Tactics for Management Efficiency

There are many techniques available that can assist an overburdened manager in coping with the ongoing flood of demands on his time. Consider the following possibilities:

- *Review the day*. Before the work day begins, review what needs to be done and adjust plans to ensure that key tasks are completed.
- *Maintain a task list*. Keep a running list of every task that needs to be completed today. This can be an effective reminder list for the most immediate issues.
- *Prioritize*. Within the preceding task list, identify which items are the most important, and which *should* be done but which have minor consequences if they are not done. All other items on the task list can be delayed or delegated.
- *Focus on individual tasks*. Avoid splitting up tasks and dealing with them in pieces throughout the day, since this is less efficient than focusing solely on a single task and completing it in one pass.

Common New Manager Mistakes

There are several areas in which new managers can be relied upon to make mistakes. One is being unable to let go of their old job. They persistently retain the tasks that used to be their responsibility, while also trying to layer management activities on top, resulting in a massive amount of work overload. This problem occurs because they are most familiar with their old job, and are scared to let go and launch into the great unknown of management.

Another new manager mistake is wanting to do all of the work themselves, rather than delegating it. They are deeply uncomfortable with handing off work, especially when the recipient is relatively inexperienced, since they assume that any failures by the recipient will reflect back on the new manager (which is true). A new manager also believes that he can do a better job himself (quite possibly true). What the new manager does not understand is that management involves almost total delegation of *all* tasks, along with a commitment to develop the abilities of the people to whom work has been delegated. By engaging in delegation, decisions are pushed down to the level of the organization at which employees have the best visibility into the likely outcome. In addition, employees are given more control over their jobs, which not only improves their morale, but also gives management insights into which employees are ripe for promotion.

How to Delegate

In the preceding section, we noted the need for delegation. Delegation is an essential task for any manager, and yet many people have only a poor concept of how to delegate work in such a manner that the outcome will be positive. Consider using the following best practices when delegating work:

- *Centralize responsibility*. When delegating work, give responsibility for task completion to just one person, rather than to a group. Doing so keeps responsibility from being diffused, while also giving the targeted person considerably more incentive to make sure that the task is completed.
- *Assign authority*. Assigning responsibility will not work unless the person on the receiving end of a task is also given the authority to make whatever decisions are needed to ensure that the task is completed properly.
- *Inform fully*. Delegation only works when the person receiving a task is fully informed about all aspects of the task. This includes instruction about what needs to be done, when it must be completed, what results are expected, and what resources will be made available. It is best to write down these instructions, to reduce errors.
- *Follow up*. The manager should make it clear that he is available to answer questions about the delegated task. This may involve manager-initiated follow up with a newer or less experienced employee, to ensure that the person is on track.
- *Evaluate results*. The manager should review the results turned in by the employee, and provide advice and/or praise, depending on the outcome. This feedback loop is essential, both for improving employee performance and for deciding the nature of any other tasks that could potentially be delegated to the person.

A Day in the Life of a Manager

Managers work in a wide variety of roles, so it is impossible to create a detailed timeline for what one can expect over the course of a day. However, it is quite possible to generalize the nature of the work, such as:

- *Quiet time*. A manager cannot expect to be alone during the day – at all. Given the demands of meetings, phone calls, chats with subordinates, other managers, and business partners, there is essentially no time left to sit quietly and think.
- *Communications*. A manager will spend a large part of the day talking to other people, both within and outside of the business. This can involve acquiring information, as well as passing it along to others.
- *Multi-tasking*. A manager can expect to deal with many topics over the course of a day, quite possibly dozens of them. One can expect to have crises, phone calls and e-mails pile up during a meeting, which must be dealt with in the interval before diving into the next meeting.

- *Travel*. Depending on the type of position, it is quite common for managers to spend an inordinate amount of time traveling. This is especially common in multi-division companies where managers may be given responsibility for employees, if not entire business units, located far away from the home office.
- *Hours worked*. There is no such thing as an eight-hour day for a manager. Instead, there seems to be an unending flood of issues that need to be addressed for as long as the person wants to continue addressing them.
- *Scheduling*. A large number of meetings are normally included in a manager's schedule, possibly for months into the future. In addition, there will be many unscheduled meetings happening every day, usually jammed in around the scheduled meetings.

Work may not stop when a manager goes home, since there are always phone calls and e-mails to return. Unfortunately, this means that managers frequently have to address business issues on weekends. To deal with the pressures of the job, the best managers periodically block out time to decide whether they are making the best use of their time. For example, they may elect to shift certain activities over to an administrative assistant or a staff person, or they may decide to exit certain activities that are no longer important to them.

Having dealt with the nature of the work, what about the types of activities that a manager is likely to encounter? Though these tasks are widely varied, they tend to fall into the following classifications:

- *Allocate resources*. Decide who receives funding and personnel through ongoing scheduling and budgeting activities.
- *Collect information*. Seek out information throughout the business and from outside the firm.
- *Disseminate information*. Decide which information items are important, and disseminate them to targeted individuals both within and outside of the business.
- *Handle crises*. Investigate problems as they arise and take corrective action.
- *Initiate improvements*. Begin new projects to enhance the business.
- *Lead*. Motivate employees and provide coaching in various skill areas.
- *Negotiate*. Represent the department in negotiations with other departments, as well as with outside entities, such as suppliers, customers, and unions.
- *Network*. Maintain a strong network both within and outside of the business.

The Effectiveness of Managers

Many of the discussion topics in this book might give the impression that a manager can have a profound impact on a business. Is this really the case? There is an argument that external forces can have a major impact on an organization, either positive or negative, that has nothing to do with any actions taken by a manager. For example, a rapidly expanding market will likely trigger massive sales increases for all firms lucky enough to be situated in that market at the right time, irrespective of the quality of its management team. Conversely, a rapidly declining market will reduce the sales of the best-managed company in the world. Examples of other outside forces that can impact a business and yet are beyond the control of managers are:

- A major customer goes bankrupt
- Interest rates increase on the debt held by a highly leverage company
- The stock market declines sharply, so that customers are less inclined to sell their shares and spend the proceeds
- The government imposes new regulations that severely hamper company operations
- A competitor launches a technologically superior product
- The business cannot get out of a long-term supply contract that commits it to pay above-market prices for a key raw material for the next decade

Under this viewpoint, the existence of strong outside forces can greatly limit the effectiveness of managers.

Contravening this "external forces" viewpoint is the view that canny managers can foresee changes in market conditions, alter resource allocations to exploit opportunities, and shed poorly-performing business units for a good price, before anyone else realizes that they have lost value. There may be a few managers who are actually this good, with an almost omnipotent view of the market that allows them to routinely beat competitors. However, a great many managers are so involved in the day-to-day minutiae of running their businesses that they do not see broad changes in their relevant markets, and so are constantly in a reactive mode, dealing with problems as they appear.

When the board of directors believes that top managers have a profound effect on the performance of a business, they are more likely to swap out old managers for new ones as soon as corporate performance declines, in the belief that a fresh viewpoint will trigger an immediate turnaround. If the board instead has an appreciation for the impact of outside forces on corporate performance, they may be more willing to let managers stay on for a longer period of time.

Summary

In this chapter, we have provided an overview of the general activities of a manager. The essential takeaway from this discussion is that a manager's day is entirely different from that of a non-managerial person. Rather than engaging in a specifically defined set of tasks, which is the case with most employees, managers need to sharpen their listening skills, formulate plans, persuade others to take action, and delegate work. These activities may seem entirely foreign to a new manager. In the following chapters, we will delve into more detail regarding how to become an effective manager. But first, Chapter 2 provides some background information about the theory of management.

Chapter 2
Management Philosophies

Introduction

It can be useful to gain an understanding of why management practices exist in their current form. In this chapter, we present a selection of the different viewpoints on how a business should be managed, which have been developed over the past 150 years.

Scientific Management

One of the earliest techniques used to improve the productivity of a business was scientific management, which focused on the careful study of a job to determine the best possible procedures for conducting it. The emphasis was on finding the best combination of movements, coupled with equipment, to achieve the highest possible amount of output. It involved the following activities:

1. Develop a standardized approach for performing a task.
2. Select workers who have the correct skills to follow the new standardized approach.
3. Train these workers in the use of the standardized approach.
4. Eliminate work disruptions so that workers can focus on their assigned tasks.
5. Provide wage inducements to incentivize higher output levels.

One method for finding this ideal work method is the *time and motion study*. Such a study involves the analysis of the exact motions required by a person to complete a task, as well as the amount of time required to do so. After collecting this information, an analyst can devise a more efficient approach by stripping away certain actions and replacing others. These studies are most cost-effective when applied to highly repetitive tasks, so that the gains achieved can be leveraged through many iterations of the task. Time and motion studies are useful in situations where a business wants to drive down its costs to become the low-cost, high-volume producer in a market. Conversely, time and motion studies are not cost-effective when applied to tasks that are not repeated on a regular basis, since the cost to conduct such a study exceeds the resulting efficiency improvements.

Despite its contributions to corporate efficiency, scientific management suffered from several flaws. Most critically, it did not provide for inputs from workers, assuming instead that an expert would be in the best position to create optimal work processes. This made workers feel unimportant. In addition, the system made no provision for the higher needs of workers, who might want to advance beyond their current positions. These issues fueled the rise of organized labor. Consequently, scientific management is no longer followed as a discrete discipline, though some aspects of its teachings have continued to the present day, mostly in regard to devising work standards and holding employees to them with variance measurements.

General Administrative Theory

Henri Fayol, a French mining engineer and executive, developed a set of 14 foundational principles for management that are still highly relevant today. He believed that the following principles could be applied to any business:

- *Division of work.* By having employees specialize in just a few tasks, they can become much more efficient than having employees engage in every possible task. Though quite correct, this principle resulted in deeply uninteresting jobs; employers have subsequently added back tasks to make jobs more interesting.
- *Authority.* Managers must be vested with authority, which gives them the right to give orders. This principle has held up, though a general trend toward pushing decision making deep down in the organization has shifted authority to more and more people.
- *Discipline.* Employees must obey the governing rules of the organization. This principle is still true and remains relevant.
- *Unity of command.* Each employee should only receive orders from one supervisor. This principle has largely held up, though matrix organizations involve the use of two supervisors (see the Organizational Structures chapter). Also, teams are more likely to operate with reduced levels of supervision, instead tackling issues as a group.
- *Unity of direction.* There should be one plan of action to guide employees. This principle is inherently obvious; there cannot be multiple, possibly conflicting plans tugging employees in different directions.
- *Subordination of individuals to the group.* The interests of a single employee do not override those of the entire organization. If this principle were to be violated, employees could refuse to work on essential but uninteresting tasks.
- *Remuneration.* Employees must be paid a fair wage. Though obvious, this principle points out that employees will work harder if they are properly compensated for their work. Subsequent research has found that remuneration only forms a part of the rewards that employees tend to value.
- *Centralization.* The amount of decision making should be properly balanced throughout the organization, and not just at the top. This was a quite forward-thinking principle, and foreshadowed the ongoing trend to empower employees well down in the organizational structure.
- *Scalar chain.* There should be a direct line of authority from the top of the corporate hierarchy to the bottom, so that any employee can contact a manager in the line of authority if an issue arises that needs a decision. This concept is still largely operable.
- *Order.* Employees must have the correct resources available to complete their jobs properly, which includes a safe and clean workplace. Managers still

spend an enormous amount of their time ensuring that resources are properly organized.

- *Equity*. Employees should be treated fairly and well. This statement was for-ward-thinking when it was first promulgated, and has become more relevant as the value of retaining top-grade employees has become more of a concern.
- *Stability of tenure*. There should be minimal employee turnover, which can be assisted by proper personnel planning, so that new hires can be brought in in an orderly manner.
- *Initiative*. Employees should be allowed to express their ideas, which make them more involved in the organization and increase the competitiveness of the business.
- *Esprit de corps*. Managers should continually try to improve employee mo-rale, which enhances the mutual trust of employees and creates a more har-monious workplace.

Nearly all of these principles appear to be painfully obvious today, but were consid-ered quite leading-edge when they were developed in the late 1800s.

Bureaucracy Model

Sociologist Max Weber theorized that the bureaucracy model would be the ideal way to organize and run a business. This model requires an intensive level of organization throughout a business, where jobs are clearly defined, there is a clear hierarchy of authority, and there are rules and regulations that govern how decisions are made. Though the term has since come to imply the existence of an oppressively rigid deci-sion making process, the underlying concept is a good one – that a structured network of relationships among specialized positions would result in a more efficient organi-zation that generates consistent results.

The bureaucracy model works best in larger organizations, where a business can succeed not by relying on any particular individual, but rather by following a standard set of rules. These larger organizations need to deal with many products and custom-ers, possibly with operations spanning the planet, and so require a high level of stand-ardization to bring order to what might otherwise be a chaotic situation.

The bureaucratic model is not needed and may even be harmful in a smaller or-ganization that prides itself on a loose culture that can respond quickly to shifts in the marketplace, altering its products, customers, processes, and so forth on short notice.

Mintzberg's Managerial Roles

Another way of looking at the role of management was developed by Henry Mintzberg, who found that managers engaged in three broad areas, which were inter-personal, informational, and decisional. *Interpersonal roles* involved being a figure-head (a source of inspiration) for one's group, acting as their leader, and engaging in liaison activities between the group and other groups. Information roles involved mon-itoring the flow of external information to see which items pertain to one's group, monitoring the status of the group, and disseminating that information, as well as controlling the flow of outbound information as a spokesperson for the group. Finally, decisional roles involved the allocation of resources, engaging in negotiations on behalf of the group, settling disturbances, solving problems, and generating new ideas.

At the highest possible level, Mintzberg held that an effective manager was one who got things done. A manager could take action directly, such as by managing projects or negotiating contracts. A more indirect approach would be to manage those who take action, such as by using one's figurehead role to inspire others to action. And finally, a manager could indirectly trigger action by organizing and issuing information that convinces others to take action. In summary, by any of several possible means, a manager propels a business forward.

Theory X and Theory Y

Early management theories took polar-opposite views of how one should deal with employees. The *Theory X* style of management held that employees must be coerced to engage in work, because they dislike it and will engage in work avoidance behavior unless closely monitored at all times and threatened with punishment. This essentially negative view of employees held that most people prefer to be told what to do, do not want to be held responsible for their actions, and have minimal ambition for advancement.

The *Theory Y* style of management essentially reverses the description of Theory X. Under Theory Y, employees do not dislike work, and so are capable of being self-directed in accomplishing tasks. Furthermore, given their interest in doing a good job, employees will seek out responsibility. In addition, many employees can be relied upon to come up with imaginative solutions to problems.

Use of the Theory Y style can result in massive productivity improvements within a business, since management is tapping the potential of the entire workforce to come up with new ideas. Conversely, Theory X relies upon just the management team and a group of efficiency experts to make improvements, which may result in only a small fraction of the gains experienced under Theory Y.

Employee Empowerment

The inverse of scientific management is employee empowerment, which is the practice of giving employees an increased amount of information and decision-making responsibility. By doing so, employees can take action to enhance an organization's performance. The main concept is to allow those closest to a problem to solve it, rather than delaying judgment until a management person can address it. Empowerment allows a firm to make better decisions more quickly, thereby making the organization more responsive to changes in the marketplace. Empowerment can represent a major competitive advantage over competitors that are tied to a more rigid decision-making philosophy. It can also improve employee satisfaction, since they have much more control over their jobs than would have been the case if scientific management had been used instead.

Employee empowerment significantly changes the role of the manager, who now becomes a facilitator, assisting employees in the management of their daily work and advising them on additional training that may be of assistance.

Management by Walking Around

One of the best ways for a manager to collect information is simply by walking around the business, observing operations and talking to people. This frequent, informal approach to data gathering allows a manager to keep current on workplace issues. By doing so, one can respond more quickly to problems while they are still small. In addition, employees tend to appreciate such constant contact and responsive action, since it deals with their concerns more promptly. Also, there tends to be much less conflict between employees and management in this environment.

This concept can be improved upon by positioning manager offices in the midst of company operations. By doing so, employees have easier access to managers, and managers find themselves in the center of the most critical company activities, instead of hidden away in a distant suite of offices.

Total Quality Management

Total quality management (TQM) refers to the ongoing elimination of process errors, as well as the streamlining of operations. Doing so results in a system that contains only a small number of non-value-added elements, so that it produces results with very few errors. TQM should be tightly focused on the customer, so that the business is continually trying to discern what customers want; with this information, systems can be adjusted to meet customer needs and expectations.

There are four steps in the TQM process, which are continually revisited to achieve ongoing improvements. The steps are:

1. *Plan*. Determine the problem to be targeted. Collect information pertaining to it, and then discover its root cause.
2. *Do*. Choose the best way to fix the root cause, complete the fix, and start measuring the results of the change.
3. *Check*. Review the measurement using before-and-after testing; to decide whether the root cause has actually been eliminated – or at least reduced.
4. *Act*. Report on the results of this cycle. Also, issue any recommendations needed to further address the problem as part of the next iteration of the cycle.

The acronym for these steps is the PDCA cycle.

A business that is committed to TQM will likely have either ad hoc or permanent committees that operate PDCA cycles throughout the organization. The extent of this effort depends on the circumstances and management's commitment to the overall improvement of company operations.

A TQM system calls upon the skills of many employees throughout an organization, which makes this approach very much a group effort. Because so many people are involved, essentially the entire organization is held accountable for TQM results.

Constraint Analysis

Constraint analysis focuses on the bottlenecks within an organization. Under this viewpoint, a manager should only focus on maximizing the utilization of a bottleneck, since the bottleneck controls the overall profitability of the business. Focusing on any other aspect of the business has no impact on profits. This is an important concept, since bottlenecks can be found anywhere within (or even outside of) a business. For example, if sales require a high degree of technical knowledge and all salespeople are fully utilized, then a business will not achieve an incremental increase in sales unless it can somehow hire and train additional salespeople. Similarly, a company will not be able to produce any additional units of a widget if a key part is only available from one supplier, and that supplier is operating at its maximum capacity level.

Summary

While many of the preceding concepts may appear obvious, it is useful to understand them in the context of business conditions when they were originally developed. There simply were no management principles in place, resulting in a certain amount of flailing by company owners to find the best way to run their organizations. Since then, management concepts have been refined to a considerable extent through ongoing research, resulting in the management discussions that appear in the following pages.

Chapter 3
Planning Activities

Introduction

As noted in the Introduction to Management chapter, one of the four key management activities is planning. This means setting targets for where the business should go, as well as how to get from here to there. Without a planning process, it is quite likely that managers will simply focus on the demands of daily activities, so that a firm does not progress in any meaningful way. In this chapter, we work through the various levels of planning activities, as well as several related topics.

The Mission Statement

The planning process begins with the mission statement, which is a written statement of the core purpose of an organization. This statement should clearly identify the market that will be served, thereby focusing the attention of the organization in the desired direction. Here are several examples of mission statements:

> To be earth's most customer-centric company; to build a place where people can come to find and discover anything they might want to buy online. [Amazon]

> To provide high value-added logistics, transportation and related business services. [FedEx]

> We build cars, symbols of Italian excellence the world over, and we do so to win on both road and track. [Ferrari]

> To enhance the lives of our customers by creating and enabling unsurpassed vacation and leisure experiences. [Marriott Hotels]

> Saving people money so they can live better. [Walmart]

In all of the preceding cases, the mission statement can also be used to prevent management from adopting a strategy that clearly heads off in an unusual direction. For example, the Amazon mission statement is clearly targeted at online activities, so it is difficult see the company entering the mining business. Similarly, the Walmart mission statement is focused on saving customers money, so the company is unlikely to adopt a strategy that has it manufacturing high-end race cars. And finally, the quite specific mission statement for FedEx could result in it operating almost any form of commercial transport, but would not allow it to expand slightly into building or operating the underlying infrastructure, such as airports and toll roads.

The strategy adopted by a business is designed to follow the core purpose laid out in the mission statement.

Strategy and Tactics

Plans can be divided into strategy and tactics. *Strategy* is a plan of action that is targeted at achieving a major aim, while *tactics* are the detailed means by which strategy is carried out. Strategic plans tend to be longer-term, and may extend multiple years into the future, depending on the business. For example, the strategic plan for a power company may need to extend a decade into the future, since its plans must encompass the development of electricity-generating facilities and an electrical grid for its customers. Conversely, the strategic plan for a company situated in an entirely new industry may not extend more than one year, since the market is still developing and could branch off in unexpected directions. Examples of several highly simplified strategic plans are:

- *Retail chain.* To develop an online store, serviced by regional warehouses that can deliver to any customer in North America within two days.

- *Automobile manufacturer.* To enter the sport utility vehicle market with a mid-sized offering within three years, to be sold in the European and Asian markets.

- *Hotel operator.* To double the number of properties within ten years, focusing primarily on vacation destinations around the world.

- *Utility company.* To increase the proportion of renewable energy sources to 40% of the total amount of electricity provided within 10 years.

Tactical plans define what specific functional areas of a business must do in the short-term (usually one year) to ensure that the strategic plan is achieved. Tactical plans are much more voluminous than strategic plans, since they must identify the specific operational changes that must be implemented in order to achieve strategic goals. For example, if a strategic plan calls for an increase in sales of $10 million in the next year, the related tactical plan may need to include the following topics:

- A recruiting plan to find a sufficient number of prospective sales candidates to achieve the sales goal.
- A training plan to make the new salespeople sufficiently familiar with company products to be able to sell to customers.
- A salesperson partnering program, so that new salespeople can shadow more experienced salespeople for a period of time.
- The development of two new products to fill holes in the company's product line.

- Expansion into two new sales territories in order to access new customers, as well as the construction, staffing, and stocking of a warehouse in each of these regions to service new customers.
- The creation of new performance metrics and bonus plans to incentivize employees to achieve the preceding goals.

Tactics may be translated into a yet more detailed set of plans, which are *operational plans*. These plans are created by front-line managers, and focus on those specific processes and tasks needed to achieve the tactical goals created by middle management. For example, the preceding goal to create two regional warehouses may call for the following goals in an operational plan:

- Acquire warehouse lease by November 15.
- Complete warehouse layout plan by November 20.
- Place orders for racking systems by November 23.
- Conduct warehouse recruiting campaign by November 25.
- Complete assembly of racking systems by December 20.
- Complete the designation of racking locations by December 23.
- Install warehouse management system by January 5.
- Conduct picking system tests through January 20.
- Begin accepting inventory on January 7, with expected completion by February 15.
- Begin delivering orders on February 16.

Strategy is most commonly developed by the senior management team, with the approval of the board of directors. Tactics are developed by middle managers, based on the strategy given to them by senior management. Ideally, there is a strong communications flow between senior and middle managers in the development of strategy and tactics. For example, middle managers could point out that certain resources are not available to achieve a strategic target, which triggers a strategic revision by senior management.

EXAMPLE

The senior managers of Epic Launch Systems want to expand the firm's satellite launch service into the heavy-lift market, where its rockets can boost 20-ton payloads into orbit. Accordingly, they set a corporate target of launching ten of the firm's BBR (Bloody Big Rocket) rockets into orbit, with commercial payloads, in the next year. However, middle management points out that the approval process for the rockets with several governments is delayed, so that these governments are not issuing permits for anyone to buy satellite space on the BBR. They advise that the permits will probably be issued by the middle of next year; based on this information, senior management cuts its launch goal in half, to five rockets in the next year.

The development of strategy and tactics inevitably results in some level of disagreement within the management team. This is because there are usually diverging opinions about the best course to pursue. Consequently, the planning process will involve a great deal of discussion, both across the management team, down into the employee ranks, and with outsiders, such as investors, customers, and suppliers. A final strategy is only settled upon after an operating coalition has been built within the organization, which can take a considerable amount of time when there are many stakeholders to bring into the conversation.

Criteria for Effective Goals

Goals must be carefully defined, to ensure that the organization has a reasonable chance of achieving them. Consequently, a goal should have the following characteristics:

- A goal should be clear, such as "reduce overdue receivables by 10% within the next quarter," rather than "reduce overdue receivables."
- A goal should be measurable, such as "reduce scrap rates by 50%," so that one can ascertain when it has been reached.
- A goal should be realistically attainable. When a goal is assigned that is clearly beyond the abilities of an organization to achieve, employees will probably ignore it.
- A goal should be relevant to the vision of the firm. Thus, creating a goal to develop an electric version of a lawn mower is relevant to a company that has a vision of producing environmentally friendly lawn care products.
- The goal should be achievable within a reasonable period of time. For example, employees are more willing to get behind a goal that can be achieved within one year than in supporting a goal that may require 20 years of effort.

In general, management should not adopt too many goals at one time, since employees will not know which ones are the most important, possibly resulting in their ignoring everything. A better approach is to focus attention on a small number of the most essential goals, and then replace them with new goals once the initial goals have been achieved.

High-Level Planning

The part of planning that managers must get right is high-level planning. This involves determining the grand strategy of the business. If management fumbles this direction, or ignores it entirely, all other aspects of planning will not matter, since they will not be based on an effective overall strategy. There are multiple ways in which high-level planning can go wrong, as described in the following examples:

- A cereal company wants to expand its production for the South American market, and so decides to centralize its production facilities in Venezuela – where they are later expropriated by the government, wiping out the company's production capabilities in the region. In hindsight, a better plan would have been to reduce the risk of expropriation by spreading out the production facilities across several countries in the region.

- A clothing company decides to shift its clothing production work to several contractors located in Bangladesh, to take advantage of low labor rates. A few years later, the company is blindsided by a Spanish retailer that sources its goods much closer to its stores, in order to greatly accelerate the time to market. In hindsight, the company was focusing too much on costs and too little on the advantages of rapidly churning out new styles.

- The managers of a mapping business acquire firms that engage in security consulting with the federal government, customer service software, and range finding equipment for golfers. The company is unable to sell shares, because its strategic direction is too muddled to excite investors. In hindsight, the company should have focused its attention on a single market, to create a more tightly-focused message for investors.

To avoid such mistakes, managers have to constantly re-evaluate how the business fits into its various markets, the nature of the trends impacting the company, how its relationships with customers will change over time, and other factors. The outcome of this analysis will be a set of decisions about how to better position the company in relation to its competitors, preferably in a way that gives it a distinct and sustainable competitive advantage[1]. To arrive at this enviable place, managers should investigate the following issues:

- *Identify core customers.* The typical business is designed to service a particular set of customers. It may end up servicing customers outside of this core group, but it should always maintain a tight focus on its core customers. For example, an audit firm located in northern California decides to service the accounting, audit, and tax needs of vineyards and wineries. There are certainly other industries in the area, but the firm's managers decide that every function of the business will be targeted at this specific group of customers. Or, the managers of a vehicle maintenance firm decide to focus on the ongoing maintenance of large fleet operations, so it builds service centers wherever large fleets are located; it is not designed to service the needs of individual automobile owners.

- *Create intellectual property.* Intellectual property is knowledge that has commercial value and which can be legally protected from infringement. For example, a concrete manufacturer develops a new form of concrete that vastly reduces the amount of carbon dioxide emitted during the production process. When patented, the manufacturer will be the sole provider of this product, and can market it as an environmentally responsible construction material. Since no one else can legally copy the formula, the firm will not experience pricing pressure until the patent expires.

---

[1] A competitive advantage is a condition that puts a business in a favorable business position, allowing it to generate more sales and/or superior margins.

- *Build upon core competencies.* A core competency is a defining advantage that distinguishes a business from its competitors. A core competency should not only be unique and difficult to replicate, but also something that provides real financial and operational value to the business. For example, a pharmaceuticals firm develops an exceptional skill at efficiently working its way through the drug approval process, so that the time to market is greatly reduced. Or, an airline selects and trains its employees so well that they become renowned for the best customer service in the industry.

- *Acquire for synergies.* When looking for other businesses to acquire, look for entities with special features that, when combined with the parent company, can provide a positive effect much greater than their impact on just the target company. For example, a potential acquiree has an extensive network of distribution warehouses throughout Europe. This would allow the acquirer to more rapidly build out a network of retail stores in Europe, serviced by those warehouses. Or, a small regional airline owns the leases on an unusually large number of gates at several major airports, which are quite valuable to a large international carrier that could exploit those gates with many additional flights.

- *Deliver exceptional customer value.* Combining core competencies with the right set of customers can result in an exceptional value proposition that will generate a high proportion of repeat customers. For example, a retail chain becomes a master at cutting costs out of its distribution system; by combining this competency with the selection of low-income people as its primary customer group, the firm is able to generate massive amounts of repeat business with customers who are deeply concerned about saving money. Or, a regional home builder partners with a highly skilled architectural firm to produce semi-custom designs that delight customers, and which draw upon the builder's expertise to construct these homes within a relatively short period of time. What customers see is distinctive home styles, created to their specifications and completed within a reasonable period of time.

- *Understand weaknesses.* It is useful to have an understanding of where a firm's weaknesses lie, in order to avoid strategies that rely on these areas. It is not always necessary to spend resources to enhance areas of weakness, since doing so may direct attention (and shift resources) away from existing core competencies that are already providing a competitive advantage. For example, a computer company has a distinct competency in driving down its costs, so that it has an ongoing cost advantage over its competitors. Conversely, its weakness is undistinguished product design. However, design is not essential to the firm's customers, who are primarily interested in low-cost equipment.

Even the most perfectly-designed strategy will decline in effectiveness over time. For example, power companies used to be perfectly positioned in monopoly markets, distributing electricity from massive power generating stations – and then home-based solar power came along. Consequently, managers should constantly evaluate whether the original strategic vision is beginning to weaken. If so, adjusting the strategy will call for a significant amount of detailed investigation into the causes of the weakness, and debate about what to do next.

SWOT Analysis

One of the most common tools used in the formulation of strategy is SWOT analysis, which is short for the Strengths, Weaknesses, Opportunities and Threats associated with a business. By going through a SWOT analysis, managers will gain valuable background information that can be used in the formulation of a strategy.

A SWOT analysis is used to see if there are strengths that an organization can build upon to improve its competitive position, minimize any weaknesses, pursue opportunities, or guard against potential threats. The strengths and weaknesses relate to the internal capabilities and structure of the business, while the opportunities and weaknesses relate to the environment in which it operates. In short, SWOT analysis informs management of the potential actions that can be taken to improve the competitive position of a business. Examples of each element of the analysis are as follows:

- *Strengths*. Having a powerful brand, patent or copyright protection, a well-designed distribution network, a low cost structure, and locked-in access to a rare raw material can all be considered strengths.
- *Weaknesses*. Having no patent protection, a poor order fulfillment rate, a high product failure rate, excessive overhead costs, and a facility that is subject to seasonal flooding can all be considered weaknesses.
- *Opportunities*. An expected new technology that can be used to improve the reliability of products, an impending change in regulatory approvals, and a possible new market that is not being addressed by competitors are all potential opportunities.
- *Threats*. The appearance of lower-cost substitute products, the signing of a trade deal that opens a market to foreign competition, and a possible decline in demand due to changing customer demographics can all be considered threats.

A more detailed list of strengths and weaknesses appears in the following table.

Possible Strengths or Weaknesses for a Business

Process Related	Customer Related	Finance Related
Constraint management	Customer service quality	Breakeven point
Equipment replacement program	Distribution channels	Cash flow
Field service capabilities	Employee capabilities	Cost structure
Information technology effectiveness	Employee relations	Credit rating
Machinery maintenance effectiveness	Employee turnover	Leverage
Manufacturing efficiency	Management capabilities	Profitability
Research and development effectiveness	Organizational structure	
Quality control systems	Sales force effectiveness	

Tip: Managers should use every possible resource to obtain information about opportunities and threats, which can include business associations, customers, suppliers, lenders, investors, consultants, professional journalists, and government reports.

SWOT analysis is usually conducted along with the same analysis for competitors. By doing so, one can visualize how a business is positioned in relation to other entities, which can suggest certain actions to improve the firm's comparative competitive standing.

The outcome of a SWOT analysis can be a redirection of company resources. By doing so, management is focusing increased attention on just a few opportunities, thereby concentrating resources on the most essential issues. Ideally, an existing strength can be aligned with a perceived opportunity. Some weaknesses may be left alone, on the grounds that the payoff from enhancing them will not be worth the resources expended, especially when those resources can be more profitably employed elsewhere.

A problem with SWOT analysis is that it only describes a firm's standing in relation to the existing competitive environment. It does not provide an indication of new directions that a business might take in order to uncover entirely new markets where there are no resident competitors.

Competitive Strategies

Once the management team has completed a SWOT analysis, it has a good idea of the competitive landscape and the nature of its capabilities. With this information in hand, it can choose from one of the following competitive strategies:

- *Differentiate.* The company can clearly differentiate itself from the competition. This can be achieved through a series of unusual marketing campaigns, spectacular service levels, excellent product development work, and so forth. When following this strategy, businesses can usually charge a premium, but must also invest more in order to maintain a high level of differentiation. For example, a coffee shop differentiates itself by only using the highest-grade coffee beans, offering free high-speed Internet access, and an extremely comfortable sitting area. To make this strategy work, management needs to focus on a supportive culture, hiring practices that search for the most innovative candidates, an effective product development department, and a well-funded branding effort.

- *Low-cost provider*. The company is continually searching for ways to reduce its costs, so that it can deliver the lowest-cost goods and services in the industry. By doing so, it can offer the lowest prices in the industry while still earning a profit. This can lead to the departure of competitors from the industry, leaving the low-cost provider with an ever-increasing share of the market, which in turn allows it to reduce its costs even more. For example, a producer of cell phones targets low-income markets where a low price is valued more than any other feature, and sells a reasonably priced phone with a modest number of features. Doing so captures a massive share of these markets, blocking high-end phone makers from gaining any meaningful market share. To make this strategy work, management needs to concentrate on high levels of process standardization and efficiencies, relatively few products, and distribution through as many channels as possible.
- *Narrow markets*. The company targets its offerings at a narrow slice of the market. It reorients its products, services, and processes around servicing this highly-defined market, which it can do better than other firms that have a more generic offering. For example, an insurance company decides to concentrate solely on farmers, and does such a good job on its crop insurance product that farmers use it to the exclusion of all other insurers. To make this strategy work, management should follow the practices already mentioned for the differentiation strategy.

The competitive landscape in an industry typically includes one low-cost provider, with everyone else following either a differentiation or narrowly-defined (niche) market focus. In addition, there will be any number of companies that have never attempted to define their competitive strategies, resulting in mixed strategies that probably yield lower profits.

Strategy for a Multi-Unit Business

The planning process for an organization with a number of disparate business units is complicated by the multitude of markets in which the firm operates. When planning at the level of the parent company, the business units can be viewed as pieces in a chess game that may be advanced (given resources) or withdrawn from the playing field (sold or shut down). At this level, the planning effort may encompass one or more of the following strategy perspectives:

- *Portfolio strategy*. Under this planning view, managers within the corporate parent strive to achieve a balanced portfolio of business units, where some units are considered to be low-risk and others high-risk, and where the corporation as a whole gains some competitive advantage by having assembled this specific group of subsidiaries.

EXAMPLE

Calories International is a holding company that focuses on pre-packaged meals that are sold ready to eat. To achieve this overall strategy, it buys a company that prepares pre-packaged sandwiches for sale in convenience stores, along with a chain of taco food stands that operates in stadiums, a pre-packaged sushi preparation firm that sells through airport shops, and a pre-packaged vegetarian meal company that sells its products through health clubs. By assembling this particular set of subsidiaries, the company is able to diversify its holdings across a variety of food types, so that it will still generate reasonable sales growth even if there is a decline in the popularity of any one type of food.

- *BCG matrix.* The BCG[2] matrix classifies organizations in terms of how rapidly their industry is growing and their market share within that industry. The four quadrants in the matrix cover low growth – low market share, high growth – high market share, low growth – low market share, and high growth – low market share. Businesses are then divided into the dog, star, cash cow, and question mark classifications on the matrix. A dog business is in a low-growth market and has a minimal market share. A star business is growing rapidly in a high-growth market, and so should be strongly supported. A cash cow earns significant profits but is situated in a low-growth market. And finally, a question mark business has a relatively modest market share in a rapidly-growing market, so it could potentially become a dog or a star. From the perspective of the corporate parent, dogs are to be divested, while the cash generated by a cash cow should be redirected toward supporting the star and question mark businesses. Other characteristics of these matrix designations are:

  - *Dog.* A dog business, as the name implies, does not perform well. It generates minimal profits in a low-growth sector and represents a poor allocation of funds.
  - *Star.* A star business has the potential to be a dominant player in its industry that can earn outsized profits even after the industry growth rate begins to level off. To get there, it needs heavy investments in branding and infrastructure.
  - *Cash cow.* A cash cow business is fully developed and already has the infrastructure to maintain its positive cash flows for the foreseeable future.
  - *Question mark.* A question mark is a highly risky business, since it is balanced between success and failure. Managers need to decide whether to take the chance on further investments to see if they can push it into the star classification.

---

[2] The Boston Consulting Group devised the matrix.

EXAMPLE

Amalgamated International owns four subsidiaries, each operating in a different market that is associated with the visual sciences. Its Pisces Telescopes company has been the dominant business in the amateur astronomy market for years, and now requires little investment to keep churning out significant profits. It is classified as a cash cow. Its Golf Rangefinder company owns a small niche in the rapidly-expanding field of laser rangefinders for golf courses. Since its niche is small, the company is classified as a question mark. The Owl Binoculars company has been battered by cheap Asian imports, and is now a money-losing proposition in the binoculars market. It is classified as a dog. And finally, the OverView company sells miniature cameras that fasten to drones for aerial video recordings; it is the largest company in a rapidly-growing market, and so is classified as a star.

Knowledge of the BCG strategy can be used to attack a competitor. For example, if the cash cow of a competitor can be identified, it may make sense to mount a concerted attack on the market share of that business; defending against the attack will require cash that might otherwise have been diverted to the competitor's star and question mark businesses.

Decentralized Planning

A valid concern about planning is that it can be *too* centralized, where senior management formulates plans with comparatively little input from front-line managers and employees. The result can be planning that is seriously out of touch with the marketplace. To combat this, senior management can limit its planning to just setting a general strategic overview for where the business should go, and pushing all other planning deep down into the organization. This means giving front-line personnel the ability to shift company resources to meet customer needs and to pursue market opportunities. In this environment, senior managers only provide advice to those developing plans lower in the organization, and will not step in to make changes unless they see resources being allocated outside of the strategic direction of the business. This approach can be quite effective when competitive conditions are changing rapidly, since front-line employees are in the best position to experience and react to these changes.

Decentralized planning calls for a highly educated, experienced, and responsible workforce that is deeply committed to the business, so it can be difficult to implement in an environment in which there is a high level of employee turnover. However, when done right, it can result in a deeply satisfying workplace and a business that earns a reputation for pivoting quickly to meet marketplace opportunities.

Planning for Individual Functions

A major problem for many functional areas of a business is that there is too much work to do. While this workload may stem from having too few people or too little equipment to process the normal stream of transactions, it is also possible that the workload comes from ongoing requests to implement any number of changes within the business. This may involve such projects as rolling out a distribution system in a new sales region, installing an automated invoice scanning system, or implementing a new production flow system. In these situations, it can be extremely useful to have a department-level strategy that is used to screen proposed projects. Using this strategy, a department's management team can decide which requests to prioritize, which ones to ignore, and where to invest cash. Without a strategy, a department manager is essentially choosing *not* to choose between projects – instead, everything is thrown into the work queue, resulting in employees being saddled with multiple projects at once and nothing being completed on time. Under this approach, a department is merely accepting all requests made by a firm's business units, without any attempt to sort through them. There are several negative effects associated with accepting all requests from all parties, which are as follows:

- *Staffing loss.* Employees are perpetually under pressure to grind through an unending series of demands from business unit managers, which can result in an unusually high level of employee turnover.
- *Ineffectiveness.* Since the department is overwhelmed with work, the business unit managers are constantly frustrated with the slow pace at which their demands are being met. A common outcome is for the business unit managers to bring some of the departmental functionality in-house, where they can have greater control over the work that gets done.

Given these issues, the essential task for an individual department is to determine the implicit strategy of the department right now (in terms of how it sets priorities) and the strategy of the business as a whole. By comparing the two, one can determine whether a disconnect exists; this may result in a change in the priorities of the department, so that the work accepted is more supportive of what senior management wants to do with the business.

A further refinement of the concept is to determine which business units are the primary customers of a department (based on which ones are most essential to the strategy of the entire organization), and specifically how the department serves these business units. This analysis can reveal new areas in which services can be provided that are more strategically important for the business as a whole.

It is quite possible that a department's priorities will inadvertently drift over time, perhaps due to the work preferences of the department's manager or other employees. This means that a comparison to the organization's overall strategy should be conducted at regular intervals, to see if the departmental strategy needs to be tweaked to make it more responsive.

Tip: Have an in-house consultant conduct this analysis, since department managers tend to be quite supportive of the status quo, and so will be less inclined to identify issues requiring attention.

Planning Alignment Issues

It is quite possible that the initial iterations of a business plan will contain conflicting goals, so that achieving one goal makes it less likely that another goal will be reached. Middle-level managers need to sort through these conflicts and coordinate with each other to bring the issues to the attention of senior management. Here are several examples:

- Senior management wants to set aside $100 million for a prospective acquisition of a competitor, but doing so leaves little available funding to create a new production facility, which is also part of the plan.
- A cost-reduction component of the initial plan calls for a 10% reduction in headcount in the human resources department, which conflicts with the need to hire several hundred employees for a new division of the company.
- A cost-reduction campaign forces the purchasing department to source goods with very low-cost suppliers whose quality is somewhat suspect. A likely outcome will be an increase in product returns from customers, leading to a decline in customer satisfaction levels.

If a final plan is produced that still contains alignment issues, it is quite possible that the plan will fail in short order. Consequently, managers need to take the time to run the plan through a few iterations to make sure that these problems have been identified and resolved.

Scenario Planning

Scenario planning involves the derivation and examination of a set of distinctly different future viewpoints. The intent of scenario planning is to build several plausible future outcomes that vary from the most commonly-accepted scenario. This planning process can be quite useful to senior management, so that it can evaluate alternative courses of action.

A business may maintain a set of plans for how to deal with several alternative futures, usually ones that are considered to be relatively likely to occur. These plans are developed at a high level in a workshop setting by the senior managers of a business, sometimes in conjunction with outside experts who can contribute additional information concerning the industry, competitive pressures, recent inventions, and other factors that could lead to alternative scenarios. The resulting plans can have the following benefits:

- Once managers have discussed alternative futures, they are more likely to spot the warning signs associated with these futures as they unfold at a later date. Thus, awareness of warning signs is enhanced.
- Managers can develop summary-level plans for the actions to be taken if one of these scenarios actually occurs.
- Managers can face their own ingrained prejudices regarding why they consider certain outcomes to be more or less likely to occur.

The general process flow for scenario planning is as follows:

1. Arrive at an agreement about the time period over which the analysis will be made.
2. Enumerate the key factors driving competitive advantage in the market.
3. Identify the primary uncertainties in the market that could trigger major changes.
4. Discuss the likely ranges within which these uncertainties are likely to vary within the designated future time period.
5. Construct a matrix of scenarios that is derived from the interaction of the uncertainties that have been identified.
6. Translate the most likely outcome of each scenario in the matrix into financial terms.
7. Create a general strategy for how to address each scenario in the matrix.

The information developed in such a planning session can be used as the starting point for future planning sessions.

EXAMPLE

An airline's management team determines that a key uncertainty is the price of aviation fuel over the next ten years. The team agrees that the most likely price range is anywhere from a 25% increase to a doubling of prices over the 10-year period. Any of these price increases will have to be passed through to the ticket prices paid by customers, which will reduce their demand for seats. As a result, the team decides on a plan to gradually sell off or sub-lease all of the firm's jets that have low-efficiency jet engines and replace them with planes using the most fuel-efficient models. In addition, the team wants to experiment with the use of a fuel surcharge.

Contingency Planning

A variation on the concept of scenario planning is the development of plans to deal with emergencies, such as a fire that destroys key company records, or a flood that impacts a production facility, or perhaps an earthquake that destroys a key supplier. These plans are specifically targeted at worst-case scenarios for situations that can have a severely negative effect on the business.

A contingency plan is highly tactical in nature, since it contains action items that are intended to mitigate the damage from a specific event. For example, the plan may call for the development of a backup IT center that can be started up on short notice, in the event of damage to a company's primary IT center. Or, the purchasing department decides to maintain contacts with several backup suppliers, placing modest orders with them, so that they will be available to pick up orders if the primary supplier is put out of action by a natural disaster.

Planning Iterations

A major complaint about planning is that it cannot keep up with ongoing changes in the competitive environment. This problem arises because most planning is conducted by senior management, which may not be in touch with the most recent competitive positions taken by rivals. The solution is not to avoid planning, but rather to improve the linkages between senior management and those people most involved with the market (typically the sales, customer service, and product development personnel). Those in charge of planning need to continually review the front-line information being sent to them and decide when a change in strategy is warranted. In most cases, only tactical changes are needed, so that the overall strategy is preserved, with only subsidiary-level changes being made. When *any* changes are contemplated, run them past a selection of the front-line personnel, who are in the best position to see if the changes make sense. This type of planning process will likely result in ongoing alterations to parts of an organization's business plan, but will not call for a complete revision of the plan.

The number of planning iterations will vary based on several factors, not least of which is the maturity of the market. In a well-developed market that is difficult for new players to enter, and which is not being impacted much by technology changes, it is likely that an annual plan will rarely have to be changed. In this environment, the same industry players are behaving in predictable ways and there are few opportunities for breakout products that would upset anyone's planning processes. The situation is entirely different in relatively new industries, where competition is intense and companies are battling to establish market share by continually throwing new products, marketing ploys, and sales approaches into the fray to see what works. In the latter case, plans may need to be reviewed every few days to see if they still apply to market conditions; if not, it may be necessary to conduct a pivot to a different strategic direction that will require the deployment of new tactics.

Level of Goal Challenge

When developing goals, one should consider just how challenging they should be. When a plan is essentially a copy of the current year's actual results with a slight increase in the required performance level, employees are not being stretched, and so are more likely to loaf through the year; the firm may very well achieve its goals, but will not reach its full capabilities. Conversely, setting up very difficult stretch goals may trigger fraudulent behavior in order to falsely meet the goals, or else it may cause employee apathy when they realize that the goals are just too difficult. The trick is to find a balance between these two extremes, where the plan includes challenging goals, but ones that are achievable if employees are properly supported and adequate resources are supplied. When deciding how difficult a planning challenge to pose for employees, one should consider the following additional factors:

- *Proportion of new employees.* When a business has recently hired a large number of employees, management should scale back the aggressiveness of its planning targets, since the new employees may not reach their peak effectiveness for many months. This is a particular concern when there are many new salespeople, since it takes time for them to develop relationships with customers.

- *Market growth.* If the market is growing at a rapid rate, the plan needs to call for an equivalent amount of sales growth, just to maintain the same market share over time. Otherwise, what appears to be a moderately aggressive plan might actually result in a business shrinking in size compared to the competition.

Plan Execution

How does a manager convert a plan into reality? There needs to be a way to convince the organization to implement the actions required by the plan, as well as for the manager to monitor the progress of the implementation activities. We describe two ways to do so in the following sub-sections.

Management by Objectives

Management by objectives (MBO) is a methodology for achieving the goals outlined in a plan. It requires managers and employees to jointly agree to specific objectives, and then follow through on the implementation of those objectives by using a standardized reporting system. Any number of rewards may be tied to the reported outcomes. By including employees in the objective-setting process, the theory assumes that employees will increase their efforts to achieve the stated objectives.

The main benefit of MBO is that a company no longer focuses only on handling the current workload, but rather on improving the state of the business. Examples of typical objectives are on reducing costs, increasing capacity levels in bottleneck areas, minimizing scrap rates, and reducing equipment setup times.

MBO requires a well-defined measurement system, where all parties agree about which measurements to use for progress monitoring, as well as how those measurements will be calculated. If the measurement can impact the amount of any compensation tied to the completion of objectives, employees will likely have a deep interest in it. This concept will have an especially strong impact on employee motivation if MBO results are included in annual employee appraisals.

Before anyone agrees to an objective, it should meet the following requirements to the greatest extent possible:

- *Compatible with other objectives.* One objective should not conflict with another objective. Thus, reducing the amount of inventory by 40% while increasing sales by 25% could represent conflicting objectives; normally, more inventory is needed to support an increase in sales.
- *Quantifiable.* The objective should be measurable. Thus, reducing the scrap rate by 8% is a quantifiable objective. Conversely, improving employee morale is quite difficult to measure.

- *Realistic*. An objective should be achievable, within the resource constraints of the organization. Thus, it may not be possible to triple sales if the firm cannot afford to triple the number of salespeople.

MBO can produce demonstrable results. However, it may suffer from the following problems:

- It can become mired in the large number of meetings needed to discuss objectives, so that more time is spent on the development process and less on achieving the desired outcomes.
- There is a tendency for MBO not to place enough emphasis on the quality of the underlying products and processes.
- Employees may be tempted to report fake results in order to meet their objectives.

Despite these issues, MBO can be effective when managers build MBO discussions into their ongoing interactions with subordinates.

Performance Dashboards

A performance dashboard is a data presentation, usually available through a computer terminal, that shows the key performance indicators and measurements that are essential to the accomplishment of an organization's plan. The dashboard is usually configured to the needs of the user, so that the dashboard viewed by the chief executive officer (CEO) will differ from the one viewed by the marketing manager or production manager. For example, the performance dashboard viewed by a production manager might include the number of failed quality inspections per hour, while the marketing manager might see the conversion rate for the company's latest promotional mailing.

The most comprehensive dashboards allow a user to drill down through the data, to access real-time information from around the company regarding what is causing high-level performance information to change.

Performance dashboards are quite useful for the rapid identification of problem areas, so that managers can take action to remedy them as soon as possible. This approach is especially useful when managing by exception, where the system draws the manager's attention to outlying conditions that are well outside the norm. Dashboards are quite useful for the CEO, who normally relies on highly summarized data, but who can now drill down deep into the data to obtain more precise information about specific problem areas.

Other Plan Execution Activities

MBO programs and performance dashboards are vital tools in the effort to execute a plan. However, they will not be sufficient unless the management team is constantly cajoling employees to implement the plan. This means meeting with people throughout the company on an ongoing basis to discuss their progress, listen to their concerns, and find a way to propel the business forwards.

In addition, responsibility for every part of the plan must be assigned to someone. At a minimum, this means assigning responsibility to department managers. However, the process may be more pervasive, with specific tasks assigned to individual employees, or to specially-assigned teams that exist only to carry out certain tasks. There needs to be a progress measurement and feedback loop, to ensure that all responsible parties are made aware of their progress (or lack thereof). It is entirely possible that problems with the plan will arise as implementation proceeds, in which case management needs to encourage open lines of communication, so that employees will not feel that they will be pounced on if they raise concerns. Otherwise, the business may pour resources into an initiative that will ultimately fail or deliver sub-standard results.

Another area that deeply affects plan execution is to closely align the human resources function with the plan. This means only hiring employees who would be a good fit for the type of business outlined in the plan, training them to understand the processes being created or updated in the plan, and compensating them based on how well they carry it out. For example, an old clothes manufacturing business wants to concentrate more specifically on outdoor wear for hikers, so the human resources department focuses on hiring people who are deeply interested in the outdoors, trains them in design techniques, and promotes them based on their ability to design products that succeed in the chosen niche.

Planning Benefits and Concerns

There can be considerable benefits associated with the planning process, though it can also cause a few problems. The main benefits are as follows:

- *Performance measurement.* Employee performance can be measured against the goals outlined in the plan, which can be integrated into employee appraisals. These goals can also be used for variance reporting, to spot instances in which actual results are not meeting expectations.
- *Resource allocation.* A plan can be used as the basis for assigning employees to specific tasks, as well as to allocate funding toward those aspects of the business considered to be the most critical to the plan.
- *Sense of direction.* The planning process focuses the attention of everyone on what is important to the business, and what can be ignored.

Despite these benefits, some managers tend to avoid the use of plans, for the following reasons:

- *Bureaucratic stagnation.* When following the plan is deeply ingrained within an organization, there is less room for quirky, innovative thinking that might otherwise result in unique solutions to problems. This can result in the rapid departures of the most innovative thinkers in the company, who feel too constrained by the corporate bureaucracy.
- *Implied certainty.* Once a plan has been constructed, it can convey a false sense of security that it *will* be achieved, when in reality the assumptions underlying the plan may turn out to be incorrect.

- *Operational rigidity*. When an organization tightly follows its plans, it may be ignoring opportunities that have arisen since the plan was first developed. This is a particular concern in fast-moving markets that may call for rapid reactions by management.

To mitigate the concerns just noted, management can obtain ongoing feedback from front-line employees, who are the most cognizant of changes in the market. Also, the sheer volume of the planning process can be reduced, thereby making it easier to produce planning updates as conditions change.

Summary

Planning is essential to the long-term viability of a business. A manager needs to consider the long-term direction of the firm in order to orient resources in the correct direction. Despite this need, many managers do not engage in an adequate amount of planning. A common complaint that keeps managers from planning is the amount of time required, which takes away from dealing with day-to-day concerns. A good way to handle this complaint is to focus the plan quite tightly on the most critical areas of the business, and to avoid an excessively detailed plan that will require too much time to update over the course of the year. Ideally, the plan should have a high cost-benefit ratio, where the cost to maintain it has a large payoff in generating an actionable plan.

Chapter 4
Organizational Structures

Introduction

Businesses are structured in a variety of ways, based on the inclinations of their founders and subsequent managers. They may opt for a high level of centralized control, more dispersed decision making, or a solution that lies somewhere in between. These structures may change over time to match changes in the corporate strategy. Here are several examples:

- Competitors are devising new products at an accelerating rate, so a company has to restructure its organization around a number of product teams, with the rest of the organization subordinated to the needs of those teams.
- A company has numerous distribution channels and a separate marketing team to market products into each one. For efficiency, marketing coordinators are hired to synchronize the efforts of these marketing teams.
- A bank wants to push decision making down into its employee ranks in order to improve customer service, so it changes the roles of its middle managers to be coaches, with most decisions being made by front-line supervisors and personnel.

In this chapter, we cover the many types of organizational structures and the circumstances under which they are most effective.

Organizing as a Management Function

In the preceding chapter, we noted how planning is one of the core management functions. Another core function is organizing, which is the process of assembling resources in such a way that specific objectives can be achieved. This could be seen in the introduction, where businesses had specific problems and rearranged their organizational structures in order to more effectively deal with those problems. Organizing a business involves the following activities:

- Organizing work into specific jobs
- Aggregating jobs within departments or teams
- Establishing lines of authority
- Ensuring the effective coordination of employees across departments

The organization of work into specific jobs is designed to introduce a high degree of specialization into the workplace. Specialization greatly increases efficiency, since it allows employees to learn a few key tasks through ongoing repetition. For example, within the accounting department, a collections person spends her entire day contacting customers about late payments; this task is highly specialized and only certain people are good at it, so only a few people engage in it. The concept is most obvious on an assembly line, where a person might engage in just a single task.

An excessive degree of specialization can make jobs boring, which leads to minimal job satisfaction and high turnover. To combat these negative effects, businesses can engage in periodic job rotations, where employees work their way through the various positions within a functional area, which has the beneficial side effect of having a thoroughly cross-trained staff that can fill in for each other when someone cannot work. Another option is to conduct more work as teams, so that small groups are formed to deal with specific problems. Teams provide a better social environment for employees, and also tend to result in better solutions to problems, since a group can devise a broader range of solutions than just one person.

Any work that is conducted on a repetitive basis is usually organized within a department, while work that must be completed just once is typically assigned to a team. The bulk of all work is completed within departments. These departments are separated by function; thus, within a manufacturing company, there are separate departments for accounting, human resources, information technology, investor relations, maintenance, materials management, marketing, production, and sales. The types of departments will vary, depending on the type of business. Thus, a casino would have a significantly different set of departments than would a mining company or a distributor. The functions handled by each department are so specialized that employees typically earn a special college degree to work in each one. This level of specialization certainly contributes to a high level of efficiency within each department, but there is also a high risk that this structure will introduce the *silo mentality*, where there is very little information sharing between departments. Silos contribute to a sharp reduction in efficiency, since employees are more likely to be working with outdated information and may be discouraged by their bosses from working with other departments.

There should be a clear *chain of command* within the organization. This is the official order in which authority is delegated down from top management to employees, stating who is in charge and from whom one must obtain permission to engage in certain activities. For example, a billings clerk reports to an assistant controller, who reports to the controller, who reports to the chief financial officer, who reports to the chief executive officer. Problems can arise when there is not a clear chain of command, since employees do not know who they should ask before they can engage in an activity. The result is usually a much less effective organization.

The chain of command is based on several underlying concepts. One is *authority*, which is the power to give orders, make and enforce decisions, and commit resources. Authority is associated with a specific position, rather than a person. Thus, authority is associated with the vice president of manufacturing; once the person occupying that role shifts to a different position, the authority associated with that vice president position shifts to the next person assigned to the role. Also, senior managers are vested with more authority than their subordinates, so that those at the bottom of the corporate hierarchy tend to be vested with quite small amounts of authority.

Another underlying concept for the chain of command is *responsibility*, which is the obligation to perform a task. Authority and responsibility should be paired, so that authority gives someone the force to achieve a task. When a person has authority but is not held responsible for his actions, there is a strong risk that the person will act in a tyrannical manner. When a person has responsibility but no authority, the person must rely on persuasion to get work done, which may yield minimal results.

The final concept underlying the chain of command is *accountability*, which is the obligation of a person to account for his actions to the people above him in the chain of command. Accountability is an especially useful concept when someone is using his authority in an irresponsible manner, since a more senior person with more authority can curtail the person's activities.

The chain of command becomes more efficient when managers vested with authority and responsibility are willing to delegate it to positions lower in the corporate hierarchy. By doing so, decision making is shifted into the customer-facing positions of a business, which greatly empowers employees to do whatever it takes to improve customer satisfaction in their dealings with the company, as well as to design and deliver products that are more closely aligned with customer needs. Delegation also means that managers only have to deal with a smaller number of more critical issues, making them more effective. However, because managers are still responsible for any delegated authority, they may be uncomfortable with the concept.

Ensuring the effective coordination of employees across departments can be accomplished with a line and staff arrangement. *Line and staff* are the two broadest categories within which employees are organized in a firm. Line personnel are directly involved in the core operations of a business, such as production, distribution, sales, and marketing. The line functions also generate revenue for the organization. Staff personnel facilitate the activities of line personnel with advice and recommendations. For example, people working in the accounting, internal auditing, human resources, public relations, and risk management areas are usually considered staff personnel. Thus, an internal auditor can conduct a review of the control systems in the materials management department, and can advise the manager of the department about ways to improve those controls. Line personnel are directly involved in attaining the goals of the business; staff people are only indirectly involved, since they are facilitating the work of the line personnel.

There can be conflict between line and staff positions. Line personnel tend to resent staff personnel for interfering with their activities, while staff personnel complain that they are being ignored by the line personnel. The situation can be exacerbated when staff personnel become excessively involved in line work, to give the appearance that they are justifying their positions. Ideally, there should be just enough staff personnel to create a net gain in the performance of the business as a whole. Too many staff personnel will increase costs, while at the same time reducing the efficiency of the line personnel.

Organizational Structure

Organizational structure is the set of rules used to describe how tasks are controlled within a business. These rules describe the reporting relationships between positions, as well as how work is delegated and controlled. Another definition is that organizational structure is the formal arrangement of jobs within a business. The two general types of organizational structure are:

- *Centralized*. Decision making is concentrated at the top of the business, with lower levels of the firm being told how to implement those decisions. This structure is more common in larger organizations operating in markets that do not experience much change, and especially where there needs to be tight control over costs. This structure is also referred to as a *hierarchical structure*.
- *Decentralized*. Decision making is spread out in the organization, which results in fewer levels within the organizational structure. This structure works best when the organization needs to be more nimble in its decision making.

There is a trend away from centralization and toward decentralization, since doing so shifts routine decisions away from senior managers, while also allowing front-line staff the ability to make tailored responses to local conditions.

More specifically, an organization might adopt one of the following structures that are tailored to operate best within its specific business environment:

- *Functional structure*. This approach breaks up a company into departments, so that each area of specialization is run by a different manager. For example, there may be separate departments for accounting, finance, engineering, maintenance, manufacturing, purchasing, and sales. This is the most common organizational structure.
- *Organic*. This approach employs a flat reporting structure, in which the span of control (described later in this chapter) of the typical manager covers a large number of employees. Communications between employees tend to be horizontally across the organization, rather than vertically between layers of managers and those reporting to them.
- *Divisional*. This approach employs separate organizational structures to service different product lines or geographic regions. It is most commonly used in larger organizations. A division may have subsets of functional or organic structures within it.
- *Matrix*. This approach assigns multiple responsibilities to employees across multiple functional areas. When implemented correctly, it can result in a highly effective organization, but it is a confusing structure, and so is rarely used.

Organization Chart

An *organization chart* is a visual representation of the chain of command of an organization. The chart usually shows the highest management position at the top, and then works downward through the various levels of the corporate hierarchy. Each position, department, or functional area is depicted in the chart as a box. Lines linking the boxes show the flow of authority from one box to another. This chart can be used to depict the structure of an entire business, or it can be more narrowly focused to show just the structure of a single department or function. Though these relationships may be obvious to a corporate insider, the chart is useful for showing outsiders or new hires how a firm is organized. A sample organization chart appears in the following exhibit, showing the chain of command from the chief executive officer down to individual managers.

Sample Organization Chart

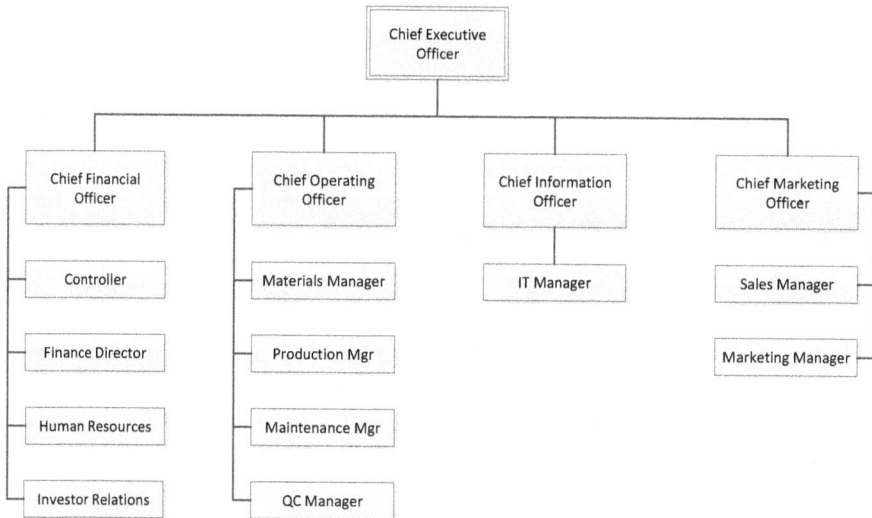

```
                        Chief Executive
                            Officer

   Chief Financial     Chief Operating    Chief Information    Chief Marketing
      Officer             Officer            Officer              Officer

    Controller        Materials Manager     IT Manager         Sales Manager

   Finance Director    Production Mgr                        Marketing Manager

   Human Resources     Maintenance Mgr

   Investor Relations     QC Manager
```

Elements of a business can also be organized by geographic region. This is most commonly found in the sales department, where there may be numerous sales regions. The intent behind this structure is to provide better sales and service support to customers. It tends to suffer from the duplication of functions in each region; for example, each region may be supported by a separate administrative staff. The concept is illustrated in the following exhibit.

Sales Department Organized by Region

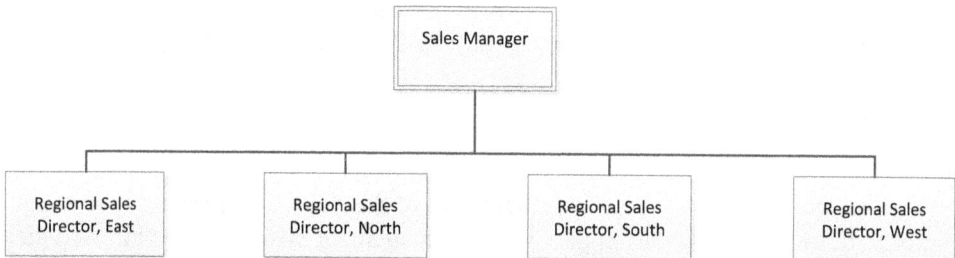

```
                        Sales Manager

  Regional Sales     Regional Sales     Regional Sales     Regional Sales
  Director, East     Director, North    Director, South    Director, West
```

A variation sometimes found in the sales department is to organize the department around customers, usually by type of customer. Thus, there may be different managers overseeing retail, wholesale, and government accounts. The concept appears in the next exhibit.

Sales Department Organized by Customer

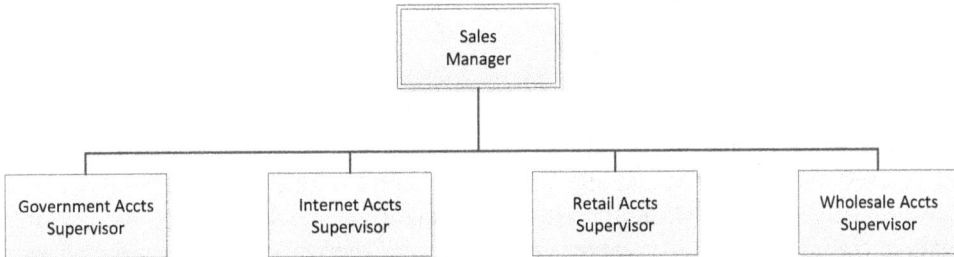

```
                          ┌──────────────┐
                          │    Sales     │
                          │   Manager    │
                          └──────┬───────┘
        ┌──────────────┬─────────┼─────────┬──────────────┐
┌───────────────┐ ┌──────────────┐ ┌──────────────┐ ┌──────────────┐
│ Government Accts│ │ Internet Accts│ │  Retail Accts │ │Wholesale Accts│
│   Supervisor   │ │  Supervisor  │ │  Supervisor  │ │  Supervisor  │
└───────────────┘ └──────────────┘ └──────────────┘ └──────────────┘
```

It is relatively common to organize individual departments by process, so that employees can develop specializations that make processes more efficient. The concept is shown in the following exhibit for a production department.

Production Department Organized by Function

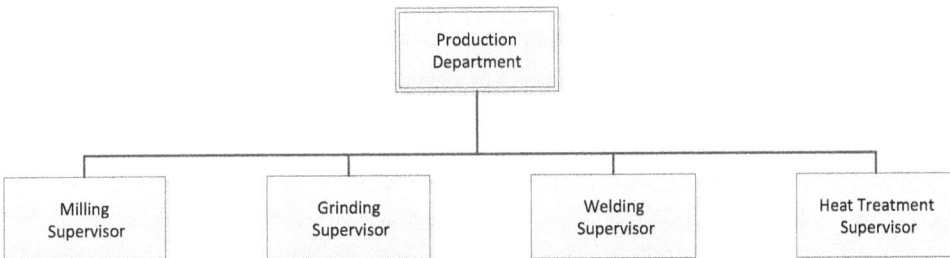

```
                          ┌──────────────┐
                          │  Production  │
                          │  Department  │
                          └──────┬───────┘
        ┌──────────────┬─────────┼─────────┬──────────────┐
┌───────────────┐ ┌──────────────┐ ┌──────────────┐ ┌──────────────┐
│    Milling    │ │   Grinding   │ │    Welding   │ │Heat Treatment│
│   Supervisor   │ │  Supervisor  │ │  Supervisor  │ │  Supervisor  │
└───────────────┘ └──────────────┘ └──────────────┘ └──────────────┘
```

Yet another variation is to organize a business by product group. This approach allows for a high degree of specialization by product, where every facet of an operating division is targeted at improving the customer experience with specific products. This structure can be used to support a strategy of constructing and defending a market niche. However, functions tend to be duplicated within each product group; for example, each group may have its own cost accounting staff. The concept is illustrated in the following exhibit.

Organization by Product Group

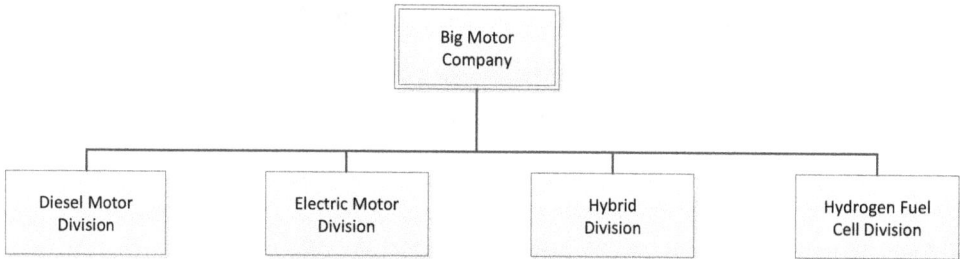

```
                          ┌──────────────┐
                          │  Big Motor   │
                          │   Company    │
                          └──────┬───────┘
        ┌────────────────┬───────┴────────┬─────────────────┐
  ┌───────────┐   ┌─────────────┐   ┌───────────┐   ┌──────────────┐
  │Diesel Motor│  │Electric Motor│  │  Hybrid   │   │Hydrogen Fuel │
  │  Division  │  │   Division   │  │ Division  │   │Cell Division │
  └───────────┘   └─────────────┘   └───────────┘   └──────────────┘
```

An organization chart depicts only the formal organizational structure of a business. Its informal chain of command may be quite different, with certain people low on the chart actually exercising a large amount of authority, and vice versa. An informal chain of command may be based on such factors as expertise, seniority, or networking ability.

Functional Organizational Structure

The functional organizational structure organizes the activities of a firm around areas of specialization. This approach involves a substantial amount of process standardization within the organization, with the real decision making authority focused at the top of the business. For example, there may be an engineering department that only designs products and production processes, a marketing department that only engages in publicity and promotion activities, and a sales department that only deals with prospective customers to land orders. This structure is the most common type of organization found in larger companies, since these businesses deal with such large production and sales volumes that no other form of organization would be anywhere near as efficient. The functional structure is especially effective in the following cases:

- Competition within the industry is mostly based on cost
- Processes are highly standardized and rarely change
- The company has a large fixed asset base that must be carefully managed
- There are few new product introductions, since they are not impacted by changes in fashion, taste, or technology
- There is a high volume of standardized product sales

In short, the functional organizational structure works well in a stable environment.

EXAMPLE

Grunge Motor Sports, which manufactures dirt bikes, has just passed $25 million in sales, and its president believes that this is a good time to restructure the business to enhance efficiencies through job specialization. Accordingly, he clusters employees into the following functional areas:

- Accounting department
- Corporate department
- Engineering department
- Human resources department
- Legal department
- Maintenance department
- Materials management department
- Production department
- Sales and marketing department

A functional structure can be useful for the following reasons:

- *Chain of command.* This structure employs a very clear chain of command, so every employee knows which decisions they can make, and which ones must be handed off to their supervisors.
- *Efficiency improvement.* When employees are directed at one specific functional area, they can achieve significant improvements in the efficiency of the business.
- *Promotions.* The process of creating career paths and monitoring employee progress toward the related goals is easier when those paths are confined within a functional area.
- *Specialization.* It is more cost-effective to hire a group of extraordinary specialists who can strongly impact specific activities within the business.
- *Training.* The training regimen is more standardized and easier to monitor within functional areas.

Despite the advantages just noted, the functional organizational structure can skew the fundamental processing and decision flow within a firm, with the following results:

- *Fast growth.* When a business is growing at a rapid rate, it needs to continually adjust its operations to meet changing conditions. The functional structure can reduce the speed with which the necessary changes are made, since requests for decisions must move up the corporate hierarchy to a decision maker and then back down to the person requesting a decision. If there are many levels in the corporate structure, this process can be quite time-consuming.
- *Queue times.* A process may cross over the boundaries of several functional areas; whenever this happens, queue time is added when a process step is

47

handed off to a new person. These queue times can greatly increase the time required to complete an entire transaction.

- *Responsibility*. When there are many specialists involved in a process, it is difficult to pin the blame for a malfunction on just one person, so process errors tend to proliferate.
- *Silos*. The people in one silo usually communicate amongst themselves fairly well, but less so with people in other silos. This issue can be mitigated by setting up cross-functional teams.
- *Specialist viewpoint*. Because most employees are clustered within functional silos, there is hardly anyone left who can see the total strategic direction of the business. This can result in a series of incorrect decisions that are designed to optimize operations at the silo level, but not for the whole company.

A special characteristic of the functional structure is a strong flow of information upward through the organization, where employees within a department report their results up to the department manager, who then reports it up to his or her manager, and so forth. Conversely, there is much less information flow *across* the organization, from one department to another.

Organic Organizational Structure

As noted earlier, an organic organizational structure is characterized by a very flat reporting structure. Because interactions are mostly among employees, decisions are more likely to be made by consensus among the employees, rather than by individual managers. Information sharing among employees also tends to increase, which differs markedly from the concentration of information with top management that occurs in a more traditional top-down reporting structure. This tends to result in more cooperation between departments and fewer instances of the silo mentality.

The singular advantage of the organic structure is that the widespread availability of information tends to result in better decisions, which can be especially useful in an unstable market environment where change occurs regularly. This structure calls for different hiring practices, since it tends to operate better with employees who have diverse skill sets and the ability to deal with and make decisions on many topics. These types of employees are self-starters who need little encouragement (or direction) from management.

There is a reduced need for a cluster of formal procedures in an organic structure, since procedures change as the business routinely adapts to variations in the business environment. Instead, it is more common to have a few relatively unchanged procedures related to core processes, and more fluidity among those procedures associated with other aspects of the business that tend to change regularly.

A downside of the organic structure is that the need to build a consensus reduces the speed of decision making. Consequently, this structure works best when there is time to churn through the alternatives, and works less well in a crisis environment where decisions need to be made at once. Another problem is that the organic structure can be difficult to implement in a union environment, where work rules enforce a higher level of rigidity in how operations can be conducted.

Divisional Organizational Structure

The divisional organizational structure is intended to organize the activities of a business around market, geographical, product or service groups. Thus, a business organized along divisional lines may have operating groups for North America or South America, or for its nonprofit customers, or for its red widget product line. Each of these divisions contains a complete set of functions. Thus, a North American division would be in charge of its own accounting, engineering, finance, materials management, production, and sales activities.

The divisional approach can be useful when the organizational structure is designed to react more quickly to local conditions. However, this approach will result in higher total costs due to the duplication of functions across the organization. It is also possible that the various divisions will quarrel with each other, rather than working together for the good of the entire business.

EXAMPLE

Mole Industries, maker of trench-digging equipment, has just exceeded $200 million in sales, so its CEO decides to adopt a divisional structure in order to provide better service to customers. Accordingly, he institutes the following structure:

- A commercial division that focuses on all commercial customers and which has its own product development, manufacturing, accounting, and sales departments.
- A retail division that focuses on all retail customers in Canada, and which has its own product development, manufacturing, accounting, and sales departments.
- An international division that focuses on all retail customers outside of Canada. It shares product development and manufacturing facilities with the retail division, and has its own accounting and sales employees.

The key points favoring use of the divisional structure are focused on placing decision making very close to the customer. In general, the advantages of the divisional structure are:

- *Accountability*. It is easier to assign responsibility for problem resolution, because a division is run by its own management group.
- *Competition*. This structure works well in markets where the competition level is high, since local managers can quickly shift the direction of their business units to respond to changes in local conditions.
- *Culture*. A separate culture can be created at the divisional level that closely meets the needs of the local market. For example, a division that operates retail stores could have a culture that is focused on providing high levels of service within stores.

- *Local decision*. This structure moves decision making away from corporate management and into the hands of divisional managers, which improves the ability to respond to local market conditions.
- *Multiple offerings*. When there are many disparate products being sold, a divisional structure can be used to aggregate the servicing and sale of these products in a more logical manner.

The essential issues going against the divisional structure involve the cost of duplicated functions across the company, as well as a reduced focus on the direction of the company as a whole. The disadvantages are:

- *Cost*. When each division has a complete set of functions, there will certainly be more employees in total than would be the case if the business had been organized under a functional structure. In addition, there will be the cost of a corporate staff, which is needed to oversee the divisions.
- *Economies of scale*. It is not possible to take advantage of some economies of scale, such as volume discounts on purchases, since there are fewer transactions at the functional level than there would have been if functions had been organized for the business as a whole.
- *Inefficiencies*. When functions are organized at the divisional level, the functions may not gain enough mass to be as efficient as would have been the case if there had instead been one central group for each function.
- *Rivalries*. Division managers may be incentivized to generate profits at the local level rather than for the organization as a whole, so there is little inducement for them to work together. They may even work against each other in order to gain more resources.
- *Silos*. Since skills are compartmentalized within each division, it can be difficult to transfer best practices across the divisions. Similarly, it can be difficult to cross-sell products and services across the various divisions.
- *Strategic focus*. Strategic planning is more likely to be focused on each individual division, rather than on the company as a whole. This can result in local strategies being at cross-purposes to the strategy of the parent company.

Matrix Organizational Structure

The matrix organizational structure requires that employees have more than one reporting relationship. This arrangement involves reporting to a manager within a functional organization, while also reporting to a project manager who is overseeing the work on a project that requires staffing from multiple functional areas. The following exhibit shows how this arrangement would work.

Sample Matrix Organizational Structure

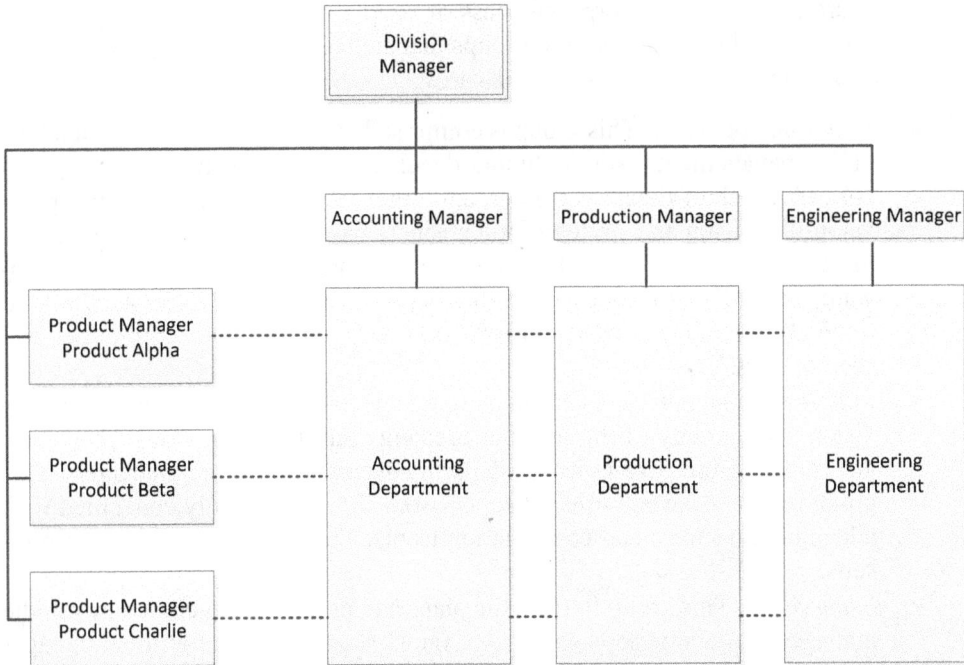

A matrix organization is designed to encourage cooperation across functional silos, so that work requiring input from multiple functional areas can be managed more effectively and efficiently. It is especially useful for generating a higher level of responsiveness to customers by bringing together information from across the organization to assist them. This is useful to some degree, but the primary reporting relationship for an employee is still his or her manager within a functional unit. For example, in the preceding exhibit, someone working in the engineering department and assigned to Product Alpha will still report to and be evaluated by the engineering manager. Another concern with this arrangement is that product or project managers have little power, and so must rely upon persuasion to obtain resources from the functional managers. A further concern is that functional managers can become frustrated with the demands of multiple product or project managers on their resources; a functional unit has a limited amount of resources, and most of those resources are likely to be targeted at the main responsibilities of the unit, not the special projects being advocated by product or project managers. Also, employees can be overwhelmed by the demands of the two bosses to whom they are assigned, resulting in ongoing meetings to resolve resource constraints. A final concern is that some employees will not be able to function well in this ambiguous organizational structure, and so will leave the firm. Because of these concerns, matrix structures are relatively uncommon.

Levels of Management

Managers are not a single, amorphous mass of people who all have the same skills. Instead, they can be broken down into groups that are based on their relative levels of skills and experience. These classifications are:

- *Senior management.* This group is comprised of the highest-ranking members of the management team, including the chief executive officer, chief operating officer, chief financial officer, and other vice presidents. This group develops the vision and strategy for a business based on how it views the external environment, and monitors how well the organization is progressing toward them. This group oversees the activities of middle management, and routinely communicates its vision for the organization to employees and stakeholders.
- *Middle management.* This group includes any manager who expands upon the vision and strategy of the top management team to create plans, processes, and organizations. Examples are department and business unit managers. This group oversees the activities of supervisors. They are mainly concerned with allocating resources and coordinating teams. Their focus is on near-term results.
- *Supervisors.* This group follows the plans and processes developed by middle management, and reports to them. Examples are a production line manager and a department manager in a retail store. This group is responsible for facilitating the performance of individual employees, as well as for the production of goods and services. Their focus is on day-to-day results.

A position that falls somewhere between middle management and supervisors is the project manager. This person is responsible for a short-duration project that may combine the services of people from multiple functional areas within a business, as well as from outside the corporation. Many project managers are uniquely talented for project management, and specialize in this area, rather than moving up into middle management.

Span of Control

The span of control is the average number of people managed by each supervisor in an organization. The span of control tends to be narrow when the nature of the work is highly complex and can vary substantially from day to day. Conversely, it tends to be much broader when jobs are routine and highly regimented, such as a production line. Other factors that can lead to a broader span of control are when employees are concentrated in one location, they are highly trained and need little management support, and there is plenty of documentation that shows employees how to complete tasks. The most effective span of control to use depends on the following factors:

- *Level of control.* If the senior management team wants to maintain tight control over the organization, then the span of control should be narrow, so that managers have sufficient time to closely follow the activities of their direct reports.

- *Level of experience.* If employees are lacking in experience, they will need more oversight, which calls for a narrower span of control. Conversely, a deeply experienced group requires little oversight, which allows for a wide span of control.
- *Level of empowerment.* If employees are being empowered to take control of their jobs, managers shift into the role of occasional coaches, which calls for significant amounts of initial coaching, which tails off over time. Eventually, the result is a wide span of control.

A highly efficient organization strives to achieve a broader span of control, since doing so calls for the employment of fewer managers. The span of control can differ radically, ranging from as few as five to more than 50 employees per manager.

There are significant cost and decision making reasons for having a broad span of control. First, a narrow span of control requires many more managers, as well as more managers to manage the managers, which adds up to a substantial expenditure. The following exhibit shows that the number of managers can be substantially reduced by broadening the span of control. In the exhibit, Company A is using a relatively narrow span of control of six employees for each manager, while Company B is using one manager for every twelve employees. Company A requires 201 managers to oversee the activities of 1,000 employees, while Company B requires 110 fewer managers to oversee the same number of employees.

Sample Calculation of Span of Control

Level	Company A	Company B
1	1 President	
2	5 senior managers	1 President
3	28 middle managers	7 middle managers
4	167 front-line managers	83 front-line managers
5	1,000 employees	1,000 employees
Total employees	1,201 total employees	1,091 total employees

Another cost issue is that employee turnover tends to be higher when employees are more closely supervised, so a narrow span of control tends to cost more in terms of employee replacement and hiring costs. There is also a decision making problem, which is that senior managers tend to take on more of the routine decisions when there is a narrow span of control. Broadening the span requires a business to push routine decision making down into the ranks, thereby giving senior managers more time to review only the most essential issues.

Summary

There are solid reasons why any organization would want to adopt, or at least consider adopting, the functional organizational structure. People usually obtain training that allows them to specialize in a certain functional area, so the education system itself is designed to produce people who are tailor-made for functional organizations. Further, the functional structure can be an efficient way to conduct work, since each department is filled with specialists who are very good at their narrowly-defined jobs. The problem is information sharing across departments, which can be close to zero. Consequently, we generally advocate the functional structure, but only when it has been modified to incorporate a high degree of communication and collaboration across departments.

Though the modified functional structure can work well for most organizations, it is not the best fit for certain types of business strategies. When the strategy calls for a rapid pace of innovation, an organic organizational structure is a better choice, since it encourages information sharing across the organization.

Chapter 5
Leadership

Introduction

Leadership is the act of inspiring others to engage in the tasks needed to achieve a goal. It is an essential part of management, since merely setting goals and providing the appropriate type of organizational structure will not convince employees to actually *do* anything. In this chapter, we cover the essential elements of leadership.

The Difference between a Manager and a Leader

A person may take on the role of a manager and yet not be able to perform as a leader. What is the difference? A manager promotes a stable, well-organized set of processes. For example, a manager will ensure that the production schedule is completed on time, that customer orders are picked and shipped in an orderly manner, and that customers are unfailingly billed in the correct amounts and in a timely manner. As part of these activities, managers try to mitigate risks wherever they are found. Many people can be trained to be excellent managers.

A leader promotes a vision for where the business should be in the future, which also involves making the changes needed to get from here to there. Since change increases the level of risk, leaders must balance the need for change with the increased risk of failure that accompanies those changes. There are far fewer great leaders than great managers, since it requires a truly unique skill set to lead an organization. We explore these skills through the remainder of this chapter.

Manager Introspection

In order to lead, a manager should go through a process of introspection, to be more aware of how he is perceived by others. Someone who might consider himself to be a friendly sort could be shocked to find that subordinates consider him to be domineering. To gain a better understanding of oneself, it is useful to go through a process of soliciting feedback from others. It is essential to ask others for their opinions, since most subordinates are not brave enough to offer unsolicited advice. When asking for feedback, be sure to make an open-ended offer, encouraging employees to continue to offer comments over an extended period of time. Otherwise, employees might get the impression that the request covers only a limited period of time, and will then be closed.

It can also be useful to engage in an ongoing process of self-assessment. This involves reflecting on how others have reacted to one's behavior, and how these reactions have altered employee behavior in the office. This should be a fairly frequent activity, perhaps during the commute home each night, or as part of an occasional period of meditation.

An issue that may make this process of introspection more urgent is the concept of *emotional contagion*, where one person's emotions and related behaviors trigger the same emotions and behaviors in others. This phenomenon occurs frequently when a manager's emotional response to an event rubs off on his entire staff. For example, an angry outburst at a missed deadline causes an entire department to be angry with each other. When a manager realizes that he can have such a forceful impact on others, he may be more interested in engaging in a process of introspection, to minimize the emotional contagion effect, as well as to interact more effectively with others.

The introspection process is more likely to result in a person who is less interested in stoking his ego and more concerned with doing what is right for the organization. This person realizes that it is in the best long-term interests of the organization to build a solid grounding in such core values as respect for others and excellent customer service than treading on others to gain a personal advantage. Ultimately, the result may be someone who can lead.

Emotional Intelligence

An effective leader is more likely to possess a high degree of emotional intelligence, which is the ability to recognize her own emotions and those of others, and to manage emotions to enhance performance. A person who has a high degree of emotional intelligence exhibits the following characteristics:

- *Perceives emotions*. This person is able to detect and interpret emotions, both in herself and others. This is the core skill in emotional intelligence, since it is needed to process emotion-related information.
- *Uses emotions*. This person is able to harness emotions to enhance her cognitive activities related to problem solving.
- *Understands emotions*. This person appreciates changes in emotions over time, however slight, and understands how they can alter a person's behavior. This skill includes a high degree of empathy, which is being able to understand and share the feelings of others. A person who understands emotions appreciates diverging viewpoints and can interact effectively with the holders of those viewpoints.
- *Manages emotions*. This person can regulate her own emotions, and is also able to manage the emotions of others. This skill can be used to control negative emotions that might otherwise cloud one's thinking, allowing for a reasonable degree of optimism even when there have been significant setbacks.

Emotional intelligence is an essential capability for a leader, who will be much more effective if he can relate to others on an emotional level. Conversely, a person with low emotional intelligence can quickly destroy employee morale, triggering low levels of organizational effectiveness.

Core Skills of Great Leaders

The best business leader is able to bring an organization through a difficult period, such as surviving a major industry downturn or shifting to an entirely new business model. Doing so requires the following activities:

- *Tells compelling stories.* A great leader is able to fashion a story that links the history of a firm to where it is going, so that employees are energized to follow along.
- *Works through others.* He or she searches for help throughout the organization, so that responsibility for the direction and achievements of the firm are spread everywhere in the business. Doing so spreads the workload and may find previously unrecognized talent within the organization.
- *Fosters innovation.* There is an ongoing pursuit of better performance within the business, setting goals that are linked to the strategy of the firm.
- *Links efforts to metrics and reward systems.* The entire system of performance measurements and rewards is closely aligned with the activities that the manager wants employees to complete.
- *Builds up talent from within.* The business is continually searching for talented people within the business and expanding their experiences and skills. Doing so makes it much easier to grow the organization from within. A great leader leaves behind a solid corps of leaders who can seamlessly take over the organization after she leaves.

In order to successfully complete these activities, a great leader must be willing to relentlessly push the organization to meet performance targets, to provide guidance to those who need it, and to remove some people who are not able to meet the firm's performance metrics.

One might think that the preceding activities can be conducted by *any* manager. However, there are significant differences between a manager and a leader, as noted in the following table.

Differences between a Manager and a Leader

Characteristics of a Manager	Characteristics of a Leader
Administers existing systems	Creates new systems
Focuses on processes and organizational structure	Focuses on people
Implements and maintains a system of controls	Inspires employee trust
Focuses on short-range goals	Focuses on a long-range vision
Imitates existing best practices	Creates new best practices
Works within the existing structure	Tears down the existing structure and builds a new one

Clearly, a leader is entirely different from a manager. A leader does not engage in detailed planning or organizational activities. Instead, a leader enacts change by knocking people out of their comfort zones and supporting them while they struggle through the resulting stress.

A leader may use multiple styles, depending on the demands of the current situation. The most effective leaders can survey a situation and select the most suitable style to yield the best possible outcome. These styles are as follows:

- *Coercive*. The person demands that his commands be followed. This approach is most effective in a crisis, when decisions have to be made quickly and employees need to be shocked into an alternative way of working. A coercive style is not helpful over an extended period of time, because it causes a high level of stress and resentment within the organization. Also, employees have no reason to think on their own, so the organization stagnates. Further, if the manager continues with the coercive style for a long period of time, it is likely that employees will leave the organization, possibly in large numbers.

  Example: A company has been losing money for years and will likely have to enter bankruptcy protection soon, so the board of directors hires a new CEO who terminates underperforming products, consolidates divisions, and conducts a large layoff. She uses the coercive style, since there is no time to engage in more participative approaches.

- *Bureaucratic*. The person develops an all-encompassing set of policies, procedures, and rules to govern the organization. This approach works best in environments where safety is paramount. However, employees are not energized by the clogging effect of so many rules, and so will either rebel against the system or lose all initiative.

  Example: The manager of an offshore oil rig wants to ensure the safety of the crew, while also minimizing the possibility of a blowout, and does so by imposed a set of rigidly-enforced safety rules.

- *Transactional*. The person creates performance plans for employees, where they are awarded bonuses if they meet performance targets that further the interests of the organization. Conversely, they may be punished if they do not meet their performance targets, such as by demoting them or terminating their employment. This approach can work in a top-down (hierarchical) organization where most decisions are made at the top, but fails in a more fluid environment where goals are likely to change on short notice.

  Example: A business is located in a stagnant market where its competitive position has been unchanged for a number of years. The firm operates under a hierarchical structure where the senior management team makes all strategic and most tactical decisions. It ensures that employees follow these mandates by setting up bonus plans with all mid-level managers and front-line supervisors, so that they have an incentive to meet specific performance targets.

- *Authoritative*. The person puts forward a strong vision for the direction of an organization, coupled with a high degree of enthusiasm for that vision. This approach works best when an organization is not performing well, and has not settled upon a future direction. This approach allows employees to come up with their own ways to fulfill the vision, and is highly participative.

Example: The marketing manager of a chain of retail stores realizes that Internet sales are stealing a large part of the company's sales, so she develops a new vision for producing and selling artisanal products that cannot easily be duplicated and sold on the Internet, which will result in a unique new value proposition for the business. Employees get to work on dozens of ideas for products that can be created in-house. The firm becomes a hotbed of innovation.

- *Affiliative.* The person uses positive feedback to build relationships with employees. This approach works well for establishing trust between parties that have not worked well together in the past. However, it focuses on high levels of praise, which leaves unanswered what to do about correcting poor performance. Also, there is no emphasis on the direction of the business, only on creating harmony within the firm.

Example: A subsidiary has just gone through a brutal period, during which its manager mandated long working hours and reduced pay in order to generate a large profit-based bonus for himself. Following his departure, a new manager is brought in who sees the collective damage wrought and decides to use the affiliative approach to heal the emotional scars from the prior reign of terror.

- *Democratic.* The person acts as a facilitator, helping a group to develop ideas and create plans. This approach works best when employees are experienced, and so can contribute at a high level. Employees also tend to feel more responsible for the direction of the company, since they were involved in setting that direction. It is especially useful for larger and more expensive decisions where it is critical to arrive at the most optimal solution. However, this approach calls for many meetings and a long time to settle upon a direction, and so is not useful in an emergency.

Example: A subsidiary is given a directive by its corporate parent to cut costs by 30%. The management team decides to convene a series of meetings with employees to figure out how the cuts can be achieved. Collectively, the company decides to eliminate an under-performing product line, as well as take a group pay cut. Because of the democratic nature of the proceedings, there are no complaints from employees about the nature of the cost reductions.

- *Pace-setting.* The person pushes the pace, demanding tight deadlines and high performance. This approach can yield results when employees are highly competent, but less-experienced staff may quit. Also, given the unrelenting pace, the organization as a whole can become exhausted over time, which means that employees are less likely to innovate. Further, a pace-setting manager has a tendency to step in everywhere and micro-manage, which leaves little room for personal initiative by employees.

Example: The leader of a product design team wants to complete a new electric bicycle design by the end of the year, so that the company will have a product in the market that can compete with a similar design already launched by a competitor. He sets a relentless pace, driving the team to work nights and weekends. The team makes the deadline, followed by the departure of several people who do not believe they will be able to tolerate the pace when the next project begins.

- *Coaching.* The person acts as a coach, advising employees in regard to how they should handle responsibilities and assisting them with obtaining new knowledge. This approach works particularly well when there is a gap between an employee's existing skills and what is needed. It is not an effective approach when employees resist changing their ways or when there is a large amount of employee turnover.

Example: A general ledger clerk has a history of missing or incorrect journal entries. The controller discusses with him the need for journal entry templates, which can be used to standardize recurring entries. As a result of the discussion, the clerk decides to attend a training session on journal entry templates. The two decide to meet again immediately after the training session to discuss what the clerk wants to do next.

- *Paternalism.* The person evinces great care for employees, taking on the role of father figure for the workforce. The effect of this behavior is that employees are more likely to remain with the firm for an extended period of time. Though this approach can create a highly committed team, the leader can undermine it by favoring a few people over the rest of the group.

Example: A software company is located in the hinterlands of a Midwestern state, where it is difficult to recruit qualified staff. To get around the problem, management adopts a paternalistic approach, including on-site health care, child care and workout facilities, as well as assistance with home loans. This comprehensive level of care is so great that employee turnover levels plunge.

Different management styles will work better in different situations. For example, a corporate restructuring may require an authoritative approach, while a process re-engineering situation may call for a more democratic style, and an unhappy workforce calls for the affiliative style. It is also quite possible that a leader will need to employ multiple styles over the course of a single day.

EXAMPLE

A manager is tasked with turning around a failing subsidiary, Creekside Industrial. He does so by holding an off-site meeting to discuss possible solutions (the democratic style) with Creekside managers, then rolls out a series of visionary messages to the Creekside staff to support these decisions (the authoritative style) and finally engages in forceful follow-up meetings with managers to discuss how well they are achieving the target set during the off-site meeting (coercive style).

The Introvert or Extrovert as a Leader

The classic view of a leader is a backslapping person who is comfortable wading into any crowd, and who feels energized by being around other people. This person can fire off speeches all day and spend time huddling with employees, thereby having many chances to pass along a vision for the company that others can follow. However, extroverted leaders also have significant failings. They spend less time considering the downsides of the positions they advocate, so they have a higher risk of failure. They also spend less time listening to others, since they are spending so much time passing along their message. There is also a risk that extroverted leaders will engage in self-aggrandizing behavior, where they become narcissistic and pompous. Extroverts tend to rely on a certain amount of charisma to get their way.

An introvert is very nearly the opposite of an extrovert, preferring to avoid the spotlight and engage with others on a one-on-one basis, away from the crowd. Introverts are far more likely to listen, since they have a minimal need to advance their own views. Being better listeners, they are inherently better at learning about problems and underlying causes, which can be a substantial benefit when formulating strategy and tactics. Also, introverts tend to be more deliberate in their actions, taking extra time to consider the ramifications of any proposed action. This level of deliberation tends to reduce the downside risk of any actions taken, since these risks have already been considered and actions taken to mitigate them.

Introverts tend to be *transactional leaders*. This means that they spend time defining the supporting structure beneath a vision, addressing such issues as required roles, tasks to be accomplished, schedules, and reward systems. A transactional leader is interested in keeping the organization running as smoothly and efficiently as possible during a period of change. A transactional leader is not afraid to hold people accountable, and to fire or demote them if necessary. This approach is too detailed for many extroverted leaders, who are more likely to focus on the vision, and less on how to get there.

In short, the introvert possesses many of the characteristics needed to be a great leader. However, the flip side of being an introvert is an inherent level of shyness that makes it difficult to mix with people. Consequently, extroverts tend to find their way into leadership roles far more frequently than introverts, which does not always bode well for the businesses they run. When an extrovert is in charge, it can make sense to pair up with an introvert as a partner, who monitors the business and provides advice as needed.

Summary

A final note on leadership is that it takes a significant amount of courage to lead a business in a new direction. The leader will have to fight through the barriers thrown up by adversaries, convince those who are doubtful of the new direction, reallocate resources, and possibly lay off employees – all in pursuit of a goal that may turn out not to be as profitable or competitively defensible as initially hoped. In short, a great deal of optimism and mental fortitude is needed to be a leader.

Chapter 6
Motivating Employees

Introduction

Motivation is any force used to stimulate the interest of people in achieving a goal. A properly motivated person will work much harder, so a manager needs to be attuned to what motivates each of her employees. In this chapter, we discuss several ways in which employee performance can be enhanced through motivation, as well as several ways in which they can be de-motivated.

Motivational Enhancements

An essential element of leadership is being able to motivate employees to perform in the most efficient and effective manner possible. There are many ways to do so, such as setting up a system of rewards that are targeted at specific employee needs, dealing with issues that cause employee satisfaction and dissatisfaction, altering jobs to make them more satisfying, and pushing authority and responsibility down into the organization. We cover these topics (and more) in the following sub-sections.

Intrinsic and Extrinsic Rewards

The most effective leaders find multiple ways to motivate their employees, where each method is tailored to the needs of the individual. These motivations fall into two general classifications, which are intrinsic rewards and extrinsic rewards. An *intrinsic reward* is the sense of satisfaction that an employee feels when performing a specific task, while an *extrinsic reward* is a tangible form of compensation or recognition given to an employee in exchange for achieving something. Intrinsic rewards are especially effective when one-off tasks are being completed, typically which are considered to be unusually challenging for an employee. As an example of an intrinsic reward, a person is assigned the task of developing a completely integrated warehousing solution for a company that has been suffering from using several separate warehousing software applications. Successfully completely this project represents a major accomplishment for the employee. Intrinsic rewards are an excellent way to motivate employees, especially because they are inexpensive or free. Here are several ways to promote the effects of intrinsic rewards:

- Set many short-term goals, so that employees get to experience an ongoing series of rewards as each successive goal is met.
- Maintain project staffing all the way to the end, so that employees can experience the satisfaction of a job well done at the end of the project.
- Thank employees for their efforts, especially when they are working through a rough patch. Doing so highlights the fact that they are appreciated.

- Break up the day with lighthearted events, such as the occasional beer bash, barbeque, movie, or oddball competition.
- Impose fewer supervisors on the workforce, so that employees can work with each other directly, without managers filtering the information coming and going through functional silos.

> **Note:** Assigning more difficult work to improve intrinsic rewards does *not* mean simply piling on more work, such as doubling the amount of paperwork that a clerk must process. Instead, it means adding *more interesting* work to a person's existing tasks, which may also involve subtracting out some of the less meaningful tasks to make way for the new tasks.

It can be difficult for some managers to design jobs that give their employees intrinsic rewards, since the result is a much more capable workforce that has less need for management oversight. Thus, some managers will resist the move toward intrinsic rewards on the grounds that it threatens their jobs.

Examples of extrinsic rewards are:

- Cash awards for cost savings
- Certificates of achievement
- Employee-of-the-month awards
- Post letters from customers that praise specific employees
- Promotion to a more advanced position
- Public praise
- Stock options
- Verbal thanks
- Written thanks
- Years-of-service pins

> **Tip:** Create an employee happiness committee that constantly dreams up new ways to recognize employee achievements.

Tips for how to give recognition or a reward are as follows:

- Link the reward to the behavior that triggered it. For example, an employee receives a reward specifically because she went out of her way to track down a missing shipment to a customer. When this is done in a public setting, employees are more likely to see the linkage, which may alter their future behavior.
- Give the reward in an entirely positive tone. Introducing a negative element into the discussion of a reward counteracts the positive impact of the reward. Thus, if a reward is being issued for an employee's help in getting an injured employee to the emergency room, do not also bring up the speeding ticket the person received while driving there (if anything, reimburse him for the ticket).

- Hand out rewards right after the triggering event. Always issue rewards as soon as possible after the behavior that management wants to reinforce. Immediate, positive reinforcement is great for locking in the desired behavior.

Tip: Include all rewards given in the monthly employee newsletter.

The type of recognition given will vary in effect, depending on the individual. One person might value having the manager come into his office and describe in detail why he is such a valuable performer for the company, while another person might place a higher value on being publicly praised in front of the other members of his team. The manager needs to explore how her direct reports respond to recognition, and adjust her methods accordingly.

Extrinsic rewards can be applied to virtually any situation, including tasks that are not of any particular interest to an employee. As an example of an extrinsic reward, an employee is offered a bonus if he can produce 100 widgets by the end of the day; the work may not be overly satisfying, but the bonus represents a significant motivation. Other examples of extrinsic rewards are piece rate pay (where compensation is based on the number of units produced), team-based compensation, and pay rate upgrades based on the number of new skills acquired. There can be a definite cause-and-effect relationship between extrinsic rewards and desired outcomes. However, these rewards can be overused, causing employees to become accustomed to them, which minimizes their motivational impact. To maintain their effectiveness, consider varying their nature and timing. For example, a positive reinforcement for meeting a sales goal could be a message from the president once every five or six months, while a reward could vary from a local vacation to business-class airfare to Las Vegas for a weekend of partying.

Another problem is that these rewards can trigger unexpected consequences, such as unethical employee behavior to record customer sales orders when customers have not actually ordered any goods or services. Consequently, it can make sense to regularly revisit these award systems to see if they need to be revised or adjusted.

Both the intrinsic and extrinsic approaches can be effective, since they have a positive payoff for the employee. An alternative approach is the use of threats, such as requiring that productivity must improve to meet foreign competition, or else a factory will be closed and everyone laid off. This approach can be highly effective when employees have few other choices for employment, such as in areas experiencing high unemployment, or when there is an economic downturn. However, it builds no loyalty – rather the reverse, where employees are constantly looking for new jobs, and will leave as soon as they can. Thus, positive rewards are better for long-term employee relations, while negative rewards can be used to ward off immediate problems, but will likely damage the firm over the long term.

The key difference between intrinsic and extrinsic rewards is that a business needs to continually apply extrinsic rewards in order to maintain the interest of employees. That is, they need a continuing stream of recognition, such as employee of the month awards, or rewards, such as a series of pay increases, to maintain interest in their jobs.

This is not the case with intrinsic rewards, where the nature of the work itself is the main reason why people come to the office each day.

Hierarchy of Needs

When designing a motivational system for employees, one would do well to examine the *hierarchy of needs*, as espoused by Abraham Maslow in his 1943 research paper, *A Theory of Human Motivation*. In essence, this concept states that the most essential need of a person is physiological, such as having enough food and housing – essentially the base minimum needed for survival. When the employee pay level is low, motivations need to target their physiological needs, such as monetary rewards that can enhance their income. It is not useful to target any higher-level employee needs until physiological needs have been dealt with[3]. According to Maslow, the second most essential need is for safety, which translates into job security and fringe benefits in the workplace. For example, offering health insurance to employees can be a powerful motivator, especially in places where it is too expensive to obtain health insurance. The third level of need is for belonging, which includes being accepted by fellow employees and being part of a group. This need can be met in the workplace by closely monitoring harassment and discrimination claims, and by fostering the development of work groups. The fourth level of need is for esteem, which involves the need for status, recognition, fame, prestige, and attention. A business can provide this by offering promotions, titles, and awards, as well as publishing the research results of employees or putting their names on patent applications. The final level in the hierarchy of needs is self-actualization, which is the realization of a person's full potential. In this case, the motivation is more varied, perhaps encompassing extensive training programs, the chance to work on personal projects of interest for a certain proportion of the work week, or a lengthy sabbatical after a certain number of years of service. In short, an effective leader needs to be aware of where her employees fall within the hierarchy, and develop motivations that address their specific needs. The hierarchy of needs is portrayed in the following exhibit.

---

[3] Needs listed in the hierarchy must be dealt with in sequence before it makes any sense to construct motivational initiatives that are targeted at higher levels. Thus, safety needs must be dealt with before belonging needs, while esteem needs must be dealt with before self-actualization issues can be targeted. Once a level in the hierarchy has been addressed, it declines in relative importance for the employee, who is now more concerned with the next level.

Maslow's Hierarchy of Needs

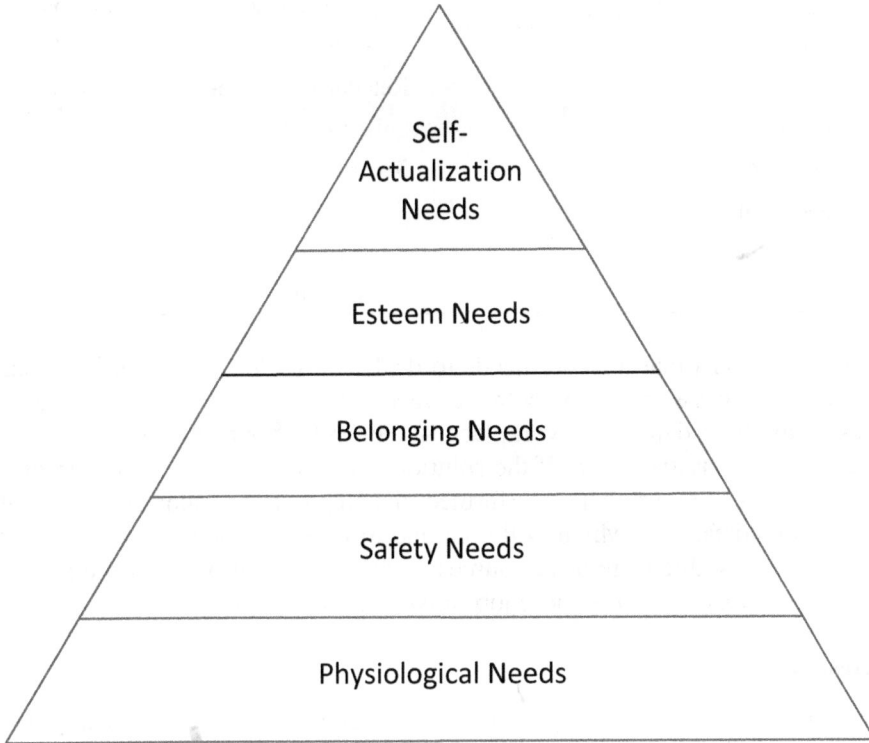

```
                    /\
                   /  \
                  / Self- \
                 /Actualization\
                /   Needs    \
               /--------------\
              /  Esteem Needs   \
             /-------------------\
            /   Belonging Needs    \
           /------------------------\
          /      Safety Needs          \
         /------------------------------\
        /       Physiological Needs        \
       /------------------------------------\
```

Two-Factor Theory

Another way to look at motivational systems is Frederick Herzberg's *two-factor theory*, which states that certain factors directly relate to employee satisfaction, while other factors relate to employee *dis*satisfaction, as noted in the following exhibit. Improving an issue that causes dissatisfaction does not increase job satisfaction – it merely removes the source of dissatisfaction. For example, improving a poor lighting situation removes an annoyance from the workplace, but it does not make employees any happier about working for the company.

Factors Relating to Employee Satisfaction and Dissatisfaction

Factors Causing Job Satisfaction	Factors Causing Job Dissatisfaction
Achievement	Company policies
Advancement	Relations with supervisor and peers
Growth	Salary
Recognition	Security
Responsibility	Status
The work itself	Supervision
	Work conditions

This concept means that a leader needs to deal with *both* factors, not just one. For example, employees are unhappy with management for a variety of reasons, including a series of layoffs, a dangerous workplace, and onerous work rules. These are all factors causing job dissatisfaction. If the solution is to issue pay raises to everyone and enhance the types of work being performed, the employer has addressed none of the causes of dissatisfaction, which will continue to rankle employees. Thus, the most effective leader is able to remove sources of dissatisfaction while at the same time creating motivators that cause more job satisfaction for employees.

Job Design

Yet another way to motivate employees is to design jobs that are specifically tailored to their needs and skills. The ways to do so are as follows:

- *Job enlargement.* Increase the number of tasks associated with a job, in order to increase the variety of work. This approach is most successful when the added tasks require an employee to increase her knowledge level. For example, a worker on a production line can also be tasked with conducting a quality review on her work.
- *Job depth.* Increase the level of authority and responsibility associated with a job, so that an employee has more control over how decisions are made and the manner in which work is performed. This approach is most successful when accompanied by ongoing feedback regarding a person's performance. For example, a production worker can develop alternative ways to manufacture a product.

When properly structured, a job can be designed to compensate an employee for routine activities that have no special attraction, while incorporating other activities that are inherently more satisfying. Ideally, a job should contain the following elements:

- Enough skills to be interesting
- The bulk of the tasks needed to complete a work product, so that the employee more closely identifies with what is being produced

- Activities that the employee considers to be important, as opposed to menial
- Some degree of independence in deciding how work is performed

This approach tends to result in significantly more complex jobs that span an array of activities. By developing more complex jobs, employees can become more invested in their work. A useful side benefit of improved job design is that employees are given more control over their work, which means that subsequent manager involvement tends to decline.

A variation on the job design concept is to leave the basic structure of each job alone, but to rotate employees through a series of jobs. Doing so broadens their experience level within the company, provides valuable cross-training so that employees can readily move among jobs, and also gives them a better view of how a series of jobs mesh with each other – which could trigger suggestions for improvements.

Empowerment

An issue related to job design is employee *empowerment*, which involves giving employees the authority and responsibility to get work done. Empowerment is really targeted at allowing employees to take the initiative, making decisions to solve problems and improve processes. To make empowerment as effective as possible, employees must be properly trained in every aspect of their jobs, given feedback about their performance, and rewarded based on how well they do. They also need to be given all of the information needed to perform their jobs, so there can be no information hoarding by management.

By shifting power down into the organization, employees are more motivated to accomplish tasks, since they get to decide *how* to do the work. Doing so gives them a greater sense of engagement with the organization. Further, they develop a sense of self-determination, since they now have a choice in regard to the methods and pace of their work. And finally, empowerment creates the opportunity for quick action, because front-line staff can detect and correct problems, as well as spot opportunities and take advantage of them immediately.

There can be short-term costs associated with an empowerment program, because employees may require training and will likely make some mistakes early on. However, their increased effectiveness should enhance the business within a short period of time.

Understanding Employees

In order to motivate, one must have an understanding of what drives others. Each employee views the world differently, has different priorities, prefers to engage in different types of work, handles challenges in different ways, and so forth. The effective manager needs to understand these differences in order to more effectively convince employees to work toward specific goals. In particular, one should attend to the following issues:

- *The job matches needs and interests.* An employee will be more productive if she *wants* to do the work, which is most likely when the job matches her needs and interests. This will likely mean that the manager should engage in some job tailoring. For example, if a retail clerk shows an interest in merchandising, it can make sense to include this activity in her job, even if the classic definition of a retail clerk does not include this activity.

- *The job matches personality traits.* Certain jobs are better for people who exhibit specific personality traits. For example, an extrovert is more likely to perform well in a sales position, while an unusually agreeable person would make a good project team member, and a conscientious person is more likely to fit into a clerical position.

- *The hours worked match employee requirements.* An employee may have conflicting work and personal requirements, such as being in the office at the same time that a child must be picked up from school. Fulfilling both needs (or not) represents an impossible conflict for a person that can lead to resentment of the employer. A manager can work with employees to identify these issues and devise workarounds that achieve a better work-life balance.

- *Training matches the person.* As just noted, job requirements may be adjusted to match the needs and interests of an employee. When this happens, the standard training regimen should also be adjusted, so that an employee's knowledge level is increased in those specific areas required for her to succeed in her job. Further, the manager should discuss training with employees on an ongoing basis, to see if there are any training holes to be filled that would make a person more proficient.

- *Working conditions are acceptable.* An employee will rarely be a high performer just because of excellent work conditions, but he is much more likely to leave if work conditions are substandard. Consequently, the manager should periodically collect opinions about this issue and make adjustments as necessary. For example, quality control inspectors are having a hard time seeing tiny flaws in products, so a reasonable upgrade is well-lit workstations with magnifying equipment to improve the situation.

- *There are positive relationships.* There should be good working relationships between employees and with the manager. If not, there is a high likelihood that squabbles will poison the operating environment, making the entire group less productive. These issues will not necessarily be brought to the attention of the manager, so spotting relationship issues calls for a high degree of sensitivity.

Ongoing Support

One of the more effective ways to motivate employees is to incrementally support their daily activities. This means that managers need to constantly visit their direct reports, make inquiries about any obstacles that are getting in the way of their work, and find ways around those obstacles. If this is not done, then employees will experience a large number of days when they are not making progress, which can significantly degrade their motivation to work. Unfortunately, *not* making progress tends to have a greater negative impact on employees than the positive effects associated with progress, so managers need to be especially careful to minimize these annoyances.

There are several tools available that can be used to motivate employees. For example:

- *Autonomy.* Give employees a sufficient degree of autonomy in conducting their work, so that they do not experience any oppressive management oversight.
- *Resources.* Make sure that employees have sufficient resources to engage in the work that motivates them. This does not just mean giving them funding; it also means giving them enough staff support and a reasonably uncluttered schedule.
- *Discussions.* Discuss issues with employees and brainstorm how they may be overcome. Draw upon lessons learned from previous activities, as well as how similar issues are being dealt with elsewhere in the company.

Tip: When employees are deeply engaged in a project, do not take it away from them, even if the reason for doing so is a promotion. They may be so invested in the project that taking it away will de-motivate them.

Capitalizing on the Uniqueness of Individuals

A manager should recognize that not every employee has the same skills or (more importantly) inclinations. They differ in terms of what drives them, what they consider to be a worthwhile challenge, how they relate to people, and how they think. Some people get along well with customers, others are great at long-term strategy, and others are wonderful nitpickers who can find any error in a document. These few examples show the massive range of inclinations among a group of employees. This represents an opportunity for the manager, who can mix and match responsibilities to maximize the unique attributes of each individual. Doing so builds a strong sense of interdependency within a group, since each one recognizes that he or she is a peak performer at a specific task, as are the others on the team.

Tip: The best way to determine an employee's inclination is to observe him in action. Another approach is to ask him what constitutes a good day or a bad day at work, and drill down into the factors influencing each state.

It can be useful to review the situation from the reverse perspective – what happens if a manager tries to impose identical training and work experience on every employee, so that they have (on paper) the same skills? Undoubtedly, there will be some improvement in those areas in which training was used to enhance an area of weakness. But (for example) will a deep introvert ever turn into a great salesperson? It is not likely. However, that same person might be a fantastic sales engineer, with deep knowledge of the product that a salesperson is demonstrating to a prospective customer. Thus, attempting to fit all employees into the same mold results in the severe under-utilization of their skills. Instead, identify their strengths and build upon them to develop the most robust team imaginable.

Persuasion Techniques

Management is about getting work done through others, so how does a manager persuade people to do things? There are several possible approaches, such as:

- *Be likeable*. Simply stated, people are more willing to engage in work for people they like. Therefore, a manager should search for the strengths of employees and praise them for their accomplishments in those areas. The manager can also look for areas of similarity between herself and her subordinates, since they are more likely to be supportive of people with similar interests. Conversely, this also means minimizing negative comments and avoiding bringing up dissimilar interests.

  Example: A new manager takes her new reports out to lunch individually and learns that she enjoys watching the same television show as one person, can chat about Thai cooking with another, and follows the same football club as a third person. She can use these shared interests to build rapport with her employees.

- *Give*. It is much easier to gain cooperation from other people when a manager has given to them first. Doing so creates an obligation that can be tapped at a later date, and which can open up a broad range of sharing opportunities over time.

  Example: The company controller learns that the production manager is having trouble compiling a capital expenditure request, so she offers to loan her financial analyst to the manager to help with the discounted cash flow calculations needed for the request. Later, the production manager is much more amenable to a request from the controller in regard to tracking the cost of scrap and spoilage in the production area.

- *Gain peer support*. A manager may not be able to exercise much direct authority over a group of recalcitrant employees, but can still succeed by gaining the support of an influential insider who is respected by the group. Thus, persuasion is not imposed from above, but rather from the sides – at the same level as the targeted employees.

  Example: A manager wants to alter the work rules related to the manning of a bottleneck machine in the production area, so that it is operated at all times. This initiative is met with deep suspicion by employees, who have a stormy relationship with management. The manager resolves the issue by walking a senior employee through the reasons for the work rules change, who then convinces his fellow employees to accept it.

- *Obtain firm commitments*. Employees are much more likely to follow through on their commitments when they are written down and made public, as opposed to verbal commitments that are made in private.

  Example: A manager has a discussion with a key customer service person about the need to be on time for work (he frequently oversleeps). The employee agrees to change his ways, but that has not worked in the past, so the manager also asks him to summarize the commitment in a letter, which the manager then circulates among the other people in the customer service department. This formalization of the commitment makes a noticeable positive difference in the employee's on-time attendance.

- *Build expertise*. A manager with strong expertise in an area is more likely to be persuasive if she is viewed as being an expert. However, employees will not know if the manager has expertise unless she finds ways to inform them, so some advance work is needed.

  Example: A new manager has just been hired. She is an expert in creating applications for the government approval of clean rooms for pharmaceutical manufacturing purposes. When a question comes up regarding how to deal with just such an application, she points out her expertise prior to making several suggestions for how to proceed.

The essential ingredient in all of these persuasion techniques is that they are all founded on the concept that both parties should gain from the experience. This is not a case of learning how to extract concessions from the other party, but rather to find ways in which to create mutual gain. Doing so forms the basis for fruitful, long-term relationships within a business.

Negative Motivation

There are numerous ways in which a manager can inadvertently demotivate employees, or achieve results through a motivational program that are bad for the business. In the following sub-sections, we address several of these effects.

The Effects of Incorrect Rewards

When setting up extrinsic rewards, be cognizant of the possibility that a reward will negatively impact the business. For example, issuing stock options creates a short-term incentive to raise profits and cash flow, thereby lifting the stock price and providing a cash-out opportunity for the employee. It does *not* provide an incentive to engage in longer-term activities that will generate a better competitive advantage for the business. Similarly, a bonus payment for producing a large number of units can be counterproductive when those hastily-manufactured goods turn out to have an unusually high proportion of quality problems. Or, a business pays a high commission rate to its salespeople for beating sales goals, so they sell large amounts of low-margin products that result in a decline in profitability. To avoid these issues, it can make sense to discuss proposed rewards with others to see if any downsides can be detected, as well as to revisit rewards at regular intervals to see if they are having the desired effects.

The Reactive Effects of an Initial Failure

A manager may inadvertently set up an employee to fail by engaging in a smothering amount of oversight as soon as the person falls short of initial expectations. For example, a manager might decide to meet with the person more frequently, check his work for errors, or monitor his performance in meetings more carefully. These steps might seem entirely reasonable to the manager, who wants to ensure that the employee's performance remains within the company's range of standards. However, this additional attention is usually interpreted as a lack of trust, resulting in the employee beginning to doubt his abilities. A likely outcome is that the employee withdraws from any attempts to improve himself, and instead operates in a reactive mode, constantly checking and re-checking his work for errors. Over time, this unhappy state of affairs results in the employee receiving a series of poor performance reviews that end in his departure from the organization. In short, the micro-management imposed on a person after an initial failure will likely be the cause of that person's eventual departure from the business, which means that the manager is – at least partially – at fault in the situation.

In this case, the employees who eventually leave the firm are not the only losers. In addition, the manager spends an inordinate amount of time supervising the supposedly errant employee; time which could be more profitably spent elsewhere. Further, as this obvious fracture appears in a work team, employees are more inclined to take sides between the employee and the manager, which interferes with team cohesion. If the manager is perceived to be acting unfairly in the relationship, other subordinates may think that the same behavior can be applied to them, which makes them more cautious around the manager. And finally, the employee being targeted by the manager will likely spend time discussing the issue with fellow employees, which wastes additional time.

When it appears that an employee is being set up to fail, the manager needs to ask herself several questions. First, do the facts of the situation actually indicate that there is a problem, or is the manager coming to a conclusion based on faulty assumptions? Second, if there *does* appear to be a problem, have an immediate and open discussion about it, focusing on the nature of the issue and how it can be corrected. Doing so focuses corrective action on just that one issue, thereby allowing for normal relations between the manager and the employee on all other topics. From this point forward, the manager needs to be on guard against typecasting the employee as being an underperformer in *all* respects, rather than in just one area.

The Effects of Disempowerment

We recently noted the positive effects of empowerment, where employees take more control over their work. The reverse situation is also quite possible, where employees are negatively motivated because decisions have been taken away from them or they have no input into decisions that directly impact them. For example, employees are not given a chance to interview a person who will be a co-worker. Or, employees make suggestions that are ignored or at least not acknowledged by their manager. Or, an employee is taken off a project and reassigned elsewhere with no explanation. These situations can all result in employees who make the minimum effort to retain their jobs, and provide no further assistance to the company. Clearly, soliciting the advice of employees and being seen to act on it can go a long ways towards minimizing disempowerment.

The Effects of Company Administration

The manner in which employees are impacted by company administration issues can have a noticeable negative impact on their motivation. In essence, they are less satisfied with their employer as the amount of bureaucracy increases (such as filling out forms or following policies that do not appear to have any point). There is no converse situation, where employee motivation improves with a reduction in the effects of company administration. Instead, the impact of administration on employees is purely negative, so the main point from a motivational perspective is to minimize the perceived amount of administration activities burdening employees. For example, a business could ensure that all paychecks are paid via direct deposit, so that employees do not have to manually cash the checks. Or, it can notify them that all existing benefit options will be automatically rolled forward into the next year unless employees want to make specific changes, thereby avoiding the need to complete any paperwork.

Dealing with Uncivil Behavior

Employees may engage in uncivil behavior towards each other, such as rude comments, undermining each other, and (perhaps the most common) checking e-mail and text messages during meetings. At worst, employees subjected to uncivil behavior are more likely to leave the firm. At a minimum, they are more likely to be distracted, because it affects their short-term memory. Given these concerns, one should engage in several activities that can minimize the effects of uncivil behavior. These actions are:

- *Pursue learning opportunities*. The brain can only focus on a few issues at a time, so actively engaging in learning opportunities can push instances of uncivil behavior out of short-term memory. For example, one might pursue a college degree after work hours. These opportunities do not have to be related to work, so other options are the pursuit of a new skills-based hobby or sport.
- *Work with a mentor*. A mentor can point out instances in which uncivil behavior is having a negative effect on a person, and can challenge the individual to break out of a negative cycle of rumination and recrimination by focusing more on his or her own performance.
- *Sleep*. A well-rested person is able to concentrate better and so is less likely to be distracted by uncivil behavior, or to react to it poorly.

- *Exercise.* A regular exercise program can massively reduce anxiety levels, while also minimizing instances of depression. The result is an ability to rebound quickly from negative interactions.
- *Engage in positive relationships.* Just one negative relationship has a much greater impact on a person than a number of positive ones, so be sure to build up close, positive relationships with a core group of friends that can offset the effects of the negative relationship.
- *Change jobs.* If the preceding factors do not work and the uncivil behavior continues to exact a negative toll, consider switching to a different job, with the intent of completely severing the relationship with the person causing the problem. Otherwise, there will always be a risk of running into the person again, which can be an ongoing concern that interferes with more productive behavior.

Uncivil behavior can be a massive demotivator, so a manager should be ready with the preceding advice whenever an employee is subjected to it.

Summary

In this chapter, we have outlined a number of ways to view motivation. No single approach can be applied to every employee. Instead, an insightful manager will tailor the available motivational tools to each employee. For example, one person may need to have a flexible work schedule in order to deal with children, while another person is more motivated by bonuses in order to pay off a mortgage, while a third wants recognition by being named on a patent. Though having individualized motivational systems will certainly be more complex for a manager, the payoff is much better employee performance.

Chapter 7
Corporate Culture

Introduction

Corporate culture is the group of beliefs, values, and norms that determine how employees interact with each other and process business transactions. Examples of the office culture are:

- *Belief structure*. Employees uniformly have faith in a common set of beliefs, such as "we look out for each other" or "the customer will be delighted" that underlies much of what they do. This belief structure could be summarized into a slogan, such as "The Few. The Proud. The Marines."
- *Bonus plans*. The bonus plan may be set up to disproportionately reward salespeople, thereby sending the message that boosting sales is the primary mission of the business.
- *Dress code*. For example, the office staff must adhere to a minimum standard every business day, with a business casual day on Fridays.
- *Office layout*. The office may be set up with manager offices on the floor above and staff offices on the main floor, thereby creating a certain amount of separation between management and employees.
- *Stated values*. A firm issues a list of its stated values to employees and posts them around the company, thereby placing a firm emphasis on certain behaviors.
- *Stories*. The company regularly tells stories that communicate the core beliefs of the business. For example, the story of a pilot buying pizza for everyone on a plane that was stuck on the tarmac tells employees that this action embodies the values of the airline.
- *Symbols*. The company shows its appreciation for employees by giving them something, such as a high-end suitcase (for traveling salespeople) or high-quality office chairs (for those working in the office all day).

Having a strong culture means that a group of employees at one company may come up with an entirely different way to deal with transactions than would a group at a different organization, sometimes with startlingly different results. For example, one culture focuses massively on pleasing the customer, making follow-up calls after an order is shipped to ensure that the customer is pleased, and providing whatever service is needed to make things right. Another company sells the same product, but its culture is focused on achieving the absolute lowest possible cost, which is passed along to the customer as a price reduction. There is no customer service. The result is that, in the first case, customers are thrilled with the level of support they received, while in the second case, customers are thrilled with the remarkably low price at which they bought the product. Neither approach is necessarily better than the other – they are simply the outcome of differing corporate cultures.

The Need for Corporate Culture

Culture is an essential element of competitiveness; when the culture meshes well with company strategy, the result can be a highly effective workforce. Ideally, a correctly designed culture boosts performance by guiding employee behavior, so that their actions are aligned with the strategic priorities of the business. Here are several examples:

- *Customer service culture.* A company is positioned within the retail sector, where there are many competitors. To rise above the crowd, management decides that the best approach is to create an extraordinary level of customer service. To this end, it fosters a culture where employees are given a great deal of slack in deciding how to deal with customers. There are few formal policies and procedures; instead, employees are given access to a modest pool of cash and encouraged to use it to assist customers. The corporate measurement system is focused on how likely customers are to recommend the company to their friends.

- *Design culture.* A company designs and produces jet engines. These engines must operate as trouble-free as possible, or else the company will be beset by expensive repair issues and the loss of customer confidence. Consequently, management fosters a culture that focuses on exceptional engineering and product safety. Design excellence awards are routinely handed out, along with bonuses for finding errors in engine designs.

- *Innovation culture.* A company develops consumer products that have extremely short shelf lives, typically just a few months. Employees must be able to collect information from the market and quickly convert these signals into new products, so management creates a culture that rewards creativity and risk taking. This includes rewarding new product development projects, even when the projects are cancelled; the intent is to develop a robust pipeline of ideas, from which a few winners will emerge.

- *Organized culture.* A company develops custom software for its clients. To ensure that designs are completed on time, management has developed a rigid process for system development, coding, and code reviews. By doing so, the company is able to avoid expensive cost overruns. The associated culture involves adherence to rules, consistent work schedules, and rewards for completing work on time and within budget.

- *Performance culture.* A company is intently focused on achieving specific performance targets in order to maximize its profitability. To support this orientation toward high performance, management creates a rewards system that pays large bonuses to just the top few percent of employees, while routinely counseling out those who do not achieve their goals. High performers are given increased status within the firm.

A well-designed corporate culture does not just support the strategy of the organization. It is also useful for attracting and retaining the types of employees who will be a good fit for each specific type of culture. However, this also means spending more time in the interviewing process to ensure that each new hire candidate would be a good fit for the firm's culture.

The Foundation of Corporate Culture

There are several ways in which management can form the corporate culture. The first step is to create a vision for what the company wants to be, such as "absolutely safe products," "discrete money management" or "the most unique camping equipment in the world." This vision needs to be stated over and over again and included on many corporate messages, both to employees and the outside world, until it becomes an overriding force within the organization. The second step is for management to back up the vision with every action they take. Employees are watching how management behaves, and so will only believe the vision if management truly supports it. For example, if the vision is to produce absolutely safe products and a customer complains of a faulty product, then a general product recall to pull all units from the shelves would be a powerful way to reinforce the message. And finally, the corporate reward system needs to support the culture, so that employees benefit from following the dictates of the culture. Thus, if an airline espouses the best customer service in the industry, a flight crew should be rewarded for buying pizza for everyone on a delayed flight.

Corporate culture needs to begin with the first person hired, since the existing base of employees transmits the culture to anyone hired after them. The longer management waits to develop a culture, the more difficult it is to impose it on the ever-increasing number of employees.

Once there is a corporate culture in place, new employees learn it by osmosis as they deal with various transactions on an ongoing basis. For example, a new employee in the customer service department is paired with another, more experienced employee. The new employee catches on to the company's standard approach for dealing with customers by watching the more senior employee in action. Or, employees see the culture in action during company events, such as a Friday afternoon beer bash, or perhaps during the traditional Wednesday barbeque lunch hosted by the company president. They may also be introduced to the company culture in a more formal setting, where it is discussed as part of new employee training. For example, the training class for flight attendants at a major airline could address the key priorities for dealing with customers, which are safety first, customer convenience second, and cost savings a distant third. A great reinforcement of the corporate culture is to explain to new hires that promotions are at least partially contingent upon adhering to the ideals of the business.

The process of developing and maintaining a solid company culture not only requires a great deal of effort, but also never ends. Without constant reinforcement, the culture will fade away, thereby eliminating one of a company's key competitive weapons.

The Downside of Corporate Culture

Thus far, we have intimated that corporate culture is a force for good. That is not always the case. When the top management team acts in an unethical manner, this can (and likely will) trickle down through the organization, resulting in a contaminated firm that is difficult to repair. For example, a software development firm is founded by a group of men who all come from the same college fraternity. They are accustomed to all-night programming binges, when they drink heavily and break for basketball viewing on a big screen television. Though the results of this culture are impressive, it also creates a poisonous atmosphere for any women hired into the firm. As another example, the senior management team encourages its sales staff to break the law by expanding into markets without previously obtaining business permits from the local government. Though this approach initially results in massive increases in sales, it also fosters resentment by local governments, which eventually band together to force the company to shut down its operations within their borders.

Sometimes, the negative impact of a corporate culture cannot be discerned without noting multiple effects. For example, senior management harbors a basic mistrust of employees, and so implements a combination of security cameras in the office supplies cabinet, office badges for employees, biometric timeclocks, and locks on office doors. Taken together, employees gain the distinct impression that they are not trusted, which fosters an "us versus them" environment in the office that could easily become more poisonous. Consequently, managers need to be sensitive to how their actions are viewed by employees.

Another problem can arise when the existing culture conflicts with a change in strategy. Culture is difficult to change, so a rapid switch to a new strategy that conflicts with the existing culture may quite possibly result in the failure of the initiative.

EXAMPLE

A high-end car company has a culture of endlessly testing its products to ensure that they operate perfectly before launching them in the marketplace. Management decides that a new approach is needed to keep up with changing styles in the marketplace, where a new product version is launched every six months. The new strategy fails, because the more rapid launches conflict with the employee perception that due dates are secondary to producing precision automobiles.

A potential culture problem can arise when a business is acquired. The acquirer may attempt to impose its culture on the employees of the acquiree, who may not appreciate the change. This issue can be dealt with by analyzing the acquiree's culture as part of the due diligence process, to notify management of possible problem areas. Sometimes, the acquirer realizes that the success of its new acquisition is closely tied to various quirky cultural traits, and so chooses to leave the business alone, rather than tampering with the culture.

Summary

Culture can be a driving force behind the success of a business. However, it is not sufficient to just have a motivated workforce. Instead, culture must be coupled with relentless attention to profitability and cash flow, so that the business can continue to succeed against all forms of competition for an extended period of time. To do this, managers need to attend to all aspects of culture management on a daily basis, constantly communicating with employees and embodying the corporate vision. Further, they need to search for the right job candidates that are a great fit for the corporate culture, integrate them into the business, and promote them into positions from which they can also espouse the ideals of the company.

Chapter 8
Change Management

Introduction

The typical organization has a stable set of products and services, which it provides to customers in an established way. There are long-settled policies and procedures, training programs, and traditions that are all designed to operate the organization as it has been operated in the past. The longer an organization is in existence, the more likely it is that these systems and behaviors have become baked into the firm, with a level of rigidity that makes them hard to alter.

Such an organization will confront a number of situations in which it must change its ways or be faced with reduced performance or even the failure of the business. Examples of these changes are replacing an existing computer system, switching to a new product line, shifting decision making power down to production-line workers, and outsourcing a major department.

Despite the crucial need to make these alterations, the bulk of all change initiatives fail, because they are unable to cut through the molasses-link equilibrium of the business – it is just too difficult to carry through a revolution, upsetting existing practices and replacing them with new ones. The result is upset employees and wasted resources. In this chapter, we address the key elements of change management, showing how this difficult process can be achieved.

When Change Initiatives are Most Necessary

The amount and extent of change needed by a business is primarily based on its operating environment. If there is a brisk amount of competition, changes in the legal requirements for doing business, or continual technological disruptions, then a business will find that its internal systems must be constantly realigned to coincide with its operating environment. Examples of situations in which change initiatives will be needed are:

- An industry is deregulated by the government, letting in a hoard of new competitors
- A new trade agreement allows overseas competitors to flood the market with cheaper goods
- The market for a major software platform is disrupted when the same functionality is made available on a smartphone app
- The number of licenses available for operating a casino within a state is abruptly expanded

The pace of change in the operating environments of businesses is increasing, which means that many organizations will find that they need to engage in change initiatives on a more frequent basis. Change initiatives may also be required to correct issues that have developed within a business, irrespective of any changes in the operating environment. Sample situations are:

- An entrepreneur is managing every aspect of a business, and needs to alter the organizational structure to shift some responsibilities to others.
- An excessive level of bureaucracy is interfering with the efficiency of the business and its ability to create new products and services.
- Decision making has been pushed down into the organization to such an extent that it is difficult for managers to have employees follow the strategic direction of the business.
- The business is organized into rigid silos, where the functional areas do not interact. More teaming is needed to foster a higher level of interaction.
- There is a strongly hierarchical structure that is interfering with the responsiveness of the business, so management wants to push decision making down into the organization.

In short, change is usually imposed by forces outside of a business, but it may also be necessary from a structural adjustment perspective to make changes.

Tipping Point Leadership

One of the key elements in change management is to win over a critical mass of employees. Once this group is fully engaged in the project, a tipping point is reached that makes it much easier to successfully complete the project. If a tipping point can be reached, it is likely that the project can be completed within a reduced time frame and possibly even using fewer funds than had originally been anticipated.

Conversely, *not* achieving a critical mass of supporters greatly lowers the odds of success. Those few true believers will spend an inordinate amount of time fighting against the inertia of other employees, likely achieving reduced or minimal results over a long period of time.

Given how critical the tipping point is, what actions can a manager take to make it more likely that the tipping point can be achieved? Here are several options:

- *Require direct experience*. Require employees to experience the problems themselves. This amplifies the severity of the problem and weakens resistance to change. For example, if customers are complaining about lengthy wait times on the company's customer service phone line, make employees call the line and see for themselves the extent of the problem. It is not sufficient to simply make note of a numerical decline in performance, which is excessively abstract – employees need to experience the issues personally.
- *Concentrate resources*. Shift the bulk of all manpower and funding to focus on those few highly specific areas that are causing the most trouble. Doing so causes immediate improvements that give this approach instant credibility.

For example, if there are 20 identified problems causing long customer service wait times, concentrate attention on just that one issue causing 80% of the trouble – incorrect call center staffing during peak periods.

- *Focus on key personnel.* Key personnel are well connected within the organization and/or have the ability to block or obtain resources. Convince these key personnel of the need for change, and they in turn will bring along their networks of employees within the company, as well as their access to resources. Doing so is far more efficient than spending time trying to win over every employee. For example, if a senior person in the call center staff is considered the de facto leader of the staff, fully involve this one person in the effort, and let her convince her compatriots to help.
- *Shut down blockers.* Bring an experienced and respected political insider onto the team who can identify likely change blockers. This person can assist in determining the messaging or other actions to be employed against each targeted blocker. The actions taken can range from quantifying the targeted problem to firing the individuals causing trouble. Also, develop a broad coalition of people who are willing to support the change, thereby isolating those who are resisting it.

We recommend enacting *all* of the preceding activities as part of a focused change management effort. By doing so, the odds of successful project completion will increase dramatically.

Development Laboratories

One way for an organization to reach a tipping point in gaining acceptance for change is to enact change intensively in just one or two locations, such as a store, factory, or production line. At these locations, make it known that no one will suffer if a change initiative fails. Instead, allow project teams to "go wild" with ideas. Also, support these locations with the best employees, as well as significant funding and consulting assistance as needed.

> **Tip:** Testing laboratories should be located in healthy markets, so that their natural operating results are already positive. Otherwise, even great improvements in a bad market can yield results that do not appear overly inspiring to the rest of the business.

Over time, a few improvements will bubble up from the general pool of average enhancements or outright failures. These improvements represent how the company's other operations *could* perform. With demonstrable successes readily available for viewing in these testing laboratories, it is much easier to convince a significant number of visitors that change will work. Once enough people have been rotated through these locations to experience the changes, resistance to change elsewhere in the business should crumble, making it much easier to spread these improvements throughout the organization.

To realize the maximum leverage from ideas generated at a development laboratory, the management group needs to organize an ongoing series of tours to rotate people from other parts of the company through the facility. In addition, once workable ideas begin to be generated at the laboratory, organize intra-company conferences to go over how these ideas are implemented and what types of outcomes can be expected from them.

Bottom-Up and Top-Down Change

When considering the issues that can arise for leaders in a change initiative, it is useful to ponder the effects of bottom-up and top-down change. In a bottom-up effort, employees are strongly encouraged to assist in creating the ideas that drive change. Senior management presents the general area in which change is needed and provides support, but employees are expected to provide the bulk of the change activities. The focus of these changes tends to be on the culture of the organization and the behavior of its employees – activities that cannot be mandated by executive action. For example, a bottom-up effort can be used to improve product quality or increase employee productivity. In this environment, managers act as coaches, helping employees to work together to arrive at the best decisions. This process results in considerable employee support, but change will occur relatively slowly, perhaps over a number of years.

A possible problem with bottom-up change is that the systems and processes of an organization will indeed be transformed – but not the corporate hierarchy that was already in place to manage the organization. For a widespread bottom-up effort to truly succeed, the senior management team must be willing to recognize that a more appropriate management structure should be used. This usually means switching from a strongly hierarchical structure with many levels to a flatter organization where much of the decision making responsibility is shifted deep into the organization.

In a top-down environment, senior management makes all key decisions and forces them upon the organization. Input from the employee base is not expected or encouraged. The focus of these changes tends to be on the structure of the organization, such as outsourcing departments or spinning off subsidiaries – items that can be addressed with a few quick decisions, usually within a relatively short period of time. Clearly, decisions made in this environment are much less likely to be supported by employees, since they are not involved in the process. However, it can result in exceedingly rapid change, which can be important when a business is facing serious problems and needs solutions at once.

Neither one of these approaches is perfect. In a top-down change environment, a business is more likely to be aggressively downsized, which causes major fractures between the management team causing the pain and the work force upon which the changes are being inflicted. In a bottom-up environment, managers may become so attached to the workforce it is supporting that they are unable to cut back on staffing levels to any significant degree. One way to reconcile these problems is to first pare away those parts of the organization that are clearly not working, using a top-down approach to mandate the changes. Once the business has been shrunk down to a more manageable size, consider switching to a bottom-up decision process in order to build the capabilities of the remaining organization over the long term. However, the bloodshed from the first phase of the transaction may so badly color the actions of the management team that employees are not willing to work with them in the second phase of the operation.

Change Management Process Steps

Anyone involved in a change initiative must understand that there is a specific process flow that has been proven to work, and that each step in this process must be thoroughly addressed before a change can be considered to have been successfully completed. To greatly improve the odds that a change initiative will be accepted within an organization, follow these steps:

1. *Create a sense of urgency.* This involves the discussion of existing or looming crises facing the business, as well as major opportunities. If there is no sense of urgency, it is nearly impossible to budge people from their zones of complacency. This is a particular problem in businesses that have had a history of success, where employees have no experience with problems that could obliterate sales and profits.
2. *Assemble a guiding coalition.* Locate those key people within the business who are willing to lead a change effort, and assemble them into a functioning team. This group must have sufficiently powerful titles, budgets, expertise, and networks within the business to drive through change.
3. *Develop a vision.* Devise a vision for the change effort, as well as an overarching strategy for how that vision will be achieved. This should be an easily understandable and compelling vision, not a complicated laundry list of improvement efforts. An organization can rally around a clear vision, but will be put off by an excessively detailed or unfocused one.
4. *Communicate constantly.* Use multiple communication channels and a high degree of repetition to communicate the vision and supporting strategy throughout the business. These communication channels may include not just the usual e-mails and newsletters, but every possible form of communication, such as during performance reviews, training classes, and quarterly financial reports. Further, the coalition leading the change effort should present an example of the best possible behavior needed to support the change. Only comprehensive messaging will shape the opinions of employees.
5. *Eliminate obstacles.* Any obstacle interfering with the change effort must be eliminated. This may include the replacement of existing processes, structures, and personnel. In essence, any bottleneck interfering with a project should be anticipated and dealt with as expeditiously as possible. When a serious obstacle remains in place for any period of time, the probability of success declines precipitously.

6. *Create wins.* Plan for a series of short-term and highly-visible wins, and reward employees for achieving them. These wins should be measurable and therefore unambiguous, so that naysayers cannot claim that the wins are really just a matter of opinion. Examples of short-term wins to be celebrated are:

   - Increase in inventory record accuracy
   - Increase in on-time shipping percentage
   - Increase in market share
   - New products are rolled out

7. *Roll forward.* With the initial wins just noted, the project earns an increased amount of respectability, allowing the guiding coalition to establish more goals, implement more changes, and eliminate more barriers to success.

8. *Lock in changes.* Once change initiatives have succeeded, integrate them into the fabric of the business, so that there will be no backsliding. This can involve integration into policies and procedures, employee training, and compensation plans.

All of the preceding steps must be followed, or else a project will experience a high risk of failure. However, if just one of the preceding steps must be targeted as being absolutely essential, it is the creation of a guiding coalition. More specifically, the group responsible for pushing change must not simply be a slight variation on the existing corporate hierarchy. If the existing hierarchy were managing the business effectively, there would be no crisis that requires change. Consequently, the coalition needs to operate outside of the normal operating structure of the business, working as an independent entity.

Creating a Sense of Urgency

The first step in the process of change management is to make very clear to the organization the extent and severity of the problems that it faces. This can be done in multiple ways. For example, the president could assemble information about declining sales, profits, on-time deliveries, quality levels, and so forth, and disseminate it throughout the organization. The distribution of this information could be accompanied by ongoing presentations to employees, informal chats, e-mails, and any other communications method that will force the organization to confront the issue.

The statement of the problem may be accompanied by information about how management plans to deal with the problem. It may take time to uncover the best possible ways to do this, but it is useful to present to employees an ongoing statement of the most likely path. The steps taken will likely involve a certain amount of pain, perhaps in the form of layoffs or shifting employees into new positions. If so, the information sharing may appear to be all bad – there is a problem, and the road to success will be difficult. Consequently, senior management must also strike a note in the discussion that there is a realistic way to succeed that will result in a better organization.

The discussion must be extensively applied throughout the area requiring change, for a large proportion of the affected employees must be willing to strongly support a change initiative. For example, out of an accounting department of 50 employees, one might need 20 of them (40% of the total) to be willing to devote a significant amount of time to a project. If only a few employees are reacting to the sense of urgency and the vision being promulgated, then the initiative will likely fail.

Perhaps the key issue interfering with a sense of urgency is the presence of its reverse – a sense of complacency. The entire management team in an organization may be complacent for any number of reasons, including the following:

- Criteria for what constitutes good performance have been set too low
- Managers do not go out into the field to view conditions for themselves
- The presence of functional silos, where performance is judged just on each silo rather than the company as a whole
- There is a history of success
- There is lots of busy work that interferes with strategic analysis
- There is no system for collecting or reviewing information from customers
- There is not a culture of confronting each other
- There is not an obvious crisis

When there are many factors contributing to a sense of complacency, it can be exceedingly difficult, if not impossible, to impart any sense of urgency to the organization. Actions that could be taken to deliver a strong jolt to an organization include the following:

- Selling a palatial corporate headquarters and moving into second-rate office space
- Selling off excessive assets, such as the company jet
- Replacing those managers who are most wedded to the existing situation
- Selling off the worst-performing subsidiaries
- Requiring that bonuses only be paid if tough goals are met
- Measuring company performance solely on its cash flows
- Forcing managers into the field to talk to customers and suppliers

Members of the Guiding Coalition

No one person has the power to drive through a change initiative, unless the business is quite a small one. In all other organizations, there are just too many people to work through, which calls for a substantial coalition to provide guidance. This is especially the case when many changes must be made, since just one person would be completely unable to oversee the process.

The nature of the membership in the coalition guiding a project is critical to its success. Of most importance is to have multiple members of operational senior management supporting the project. This group has the greatest ability to influence the direction of budgeted funds, as well as the power to force others to accede to its wishes. In addition, there must be leaders in this group, people who can drive the change process forward. When there are too few leaders on a project and too many managers (a common occurrence), the likely outcome is too much attention to planning and too little attention to communicating the change to employees. An additional concern is to keep anyone with a large ego out of the guiding coalition. These people tend to take over teams, are not accepting of the opinions of others, and generally overwhelm everyone else.

Tip: The process of building a guiding coalition may uncover individuals who are too powerful to be left out of the group, but who will either be passive contributors or active opposers of the change initiative. This may be a good time to remove these people from the organization.

It makes little sense to put a manager in charge of a change initiative who does not have the sheer managerial heft that a person in an operational capacity can bring. For example, the chief operations officer runs most of an organization, and so can drive through changes that the chief planning officer does not have a prayer of achieving.

To a lesser extent, it is also useful to gain supporters among the technical specialists in an organization. This group may have a considerable amount of respect within the organization, due to their knowledge, and so can be more powerful supporters than might initially be indicated by their titles.

An additional group to consider adding to the guiding coalition is customers and/or suppliers. This group may have a direct interest in certain changes that impact them, and may even be drivers of the change. As such, they can work to bring about the cooperation of other customers and suppliers.

Yet another possibility for membership in the coalition is the company union. This group more commonly acts as a block to changes, if those changes will impact jobs. However, there are many situations in which a prospective change will increase the survivability of the business; if the union can be made to see that a project will protect jobs, then the union can become a powerful supporter.

Developing a Vision

A vision for the outcome of a change initiative is a major requirement for the success of the project. A vision statement can be used as the basis for directing the actions of employees, as well as for inspiring their actions. Without a core vision, the actions taken as part of a project will likely devolve into a variety of activities that are not compatible with each other and chew up a large amount of time and cash. Further, plotting the direction of a change initiative without a guiding vision means that each decision point will require an inordinate amount of time to resolve, which can destroy morale.

The ideal vision statement can be expressed in one or two sentences, and clearly states where a business realistically wants to go in the future. If the statement is too detailed, it probably just contains a laundry list of action items that management wants to engage in, without tying the items together into an overarching direction.

A prospective vision statement should be tested to see if it is realistic. This means working through the details to see if the organization has the funding, capacity, personnel, competitive environment, and other factors to actually achieve the vision. For example, a vision for a hamburger stand to become the biggest hamburger chain in the world might seem a trifle excessive, whereas downsizing the vision to be the largest chain in the county might be entirely possible. If a vision is clearly outrageous, then employees will not believe it to be credible, and so will ignore it.

EXAMPLE

Davis McMurty has been promoted to the position of president of Nova Corporation, which produces and operates deep field telescopes for several international astronomical organizations. The company has barely been making any money for the past few years, so Mr. McMurty assembles a list of cost-saving and revenue-generating initiatives to pull the company out of its rut. The changes are presented to employees, who roundly ignore every one of them.

On the advice of a consultant, Mr. McMurty tries again, but this time starts with the following vision statement:

> Nova Corporation seeks to protect the planet by building and operating the best scanning telescopes, with the intent of spotting meteors that could impact the Earth.

Employees react strongly to this vision statement, which results in a major drive to obtain every possible contract to provide meteor detection services. Based on the vision statement, employees also have an interest in improving the reliability and quality of the company's telescopes, which gives it a further advantage in the marketplace.

A vision may result in significant personal pain for some employees, but if the vision is sufficiently well-crafted, they will see that following the vision is the only way to proceed. For example, it is obvious that a company will be liquidated if it continues selling into the same market. The vision is to switch entirely to a different market, which will require the retraining of the entire salesforce and perhaps some layoffs, as well. Because the alternative is to have no jobs at all, the vision will likely be accepted by employees.

Once a reasonable vision has been developed, management must push the vision out to employees repetitively and through every possible means of communication. For example, the vision statement can be expounded upon in employee meetings, voice mails, e-mails, newsletters, and slogans. Despite this effort, there is a great risk that the message will be lost amidst the vast amount of information that passes through an organization each day. To improve the odds that employees will receive and understand the message, consider the following enhancements:

- Simplify the vision statement to the greatest extent possible, avoiding jargon. The result is a message that is easy to deliver and comprehend.
- Convey the message through multiple forums. When the same information is presented from every possible angle, people are more likely to remember it.

- Repeat the message as much as possible. A vision statement needs to be repeated thousands (not dozens) of times for it to sink in.
- Every member of management must tailor their actions to match the vision. If not, employees will assume that the message is a sham. For example, a cost-cutting vision is a sham when the entire senior management team flies first class.

Communicating Constantly

When issuing information about a change initiative to employees, the project manager must first consider what the change will do to them. This means exercising a high level of empathy, putting oneself in the shoes of every person being impacted. The crafting of messages to them must incorporate how a number of personnel factors will be impacted, including the items noted in the following exhibit.

Subjects of Ongoing Communication

Ability to work from home	Flexible working hours	Power and influence
Challenge level of the work	Level of autonomy	Teaming arrangements
Compensation	Opportunities for creativity	Working conditions

Once the manager has a general idea of how employees will feel about the change initiative, it is now time to craft the message and determine how it will be communicated.

EXAMPLE

New Centurion Corporation transcribes Latin texts, using the services of a number of Latin scholars who work from their homes. The company is planning to switch to a new corporate headquarters that is located ten miles away from the previous headquarters building. The move manager knows that the key consideration for this group is the number of miles they will have to drive for weekly meetings at the headquarters building. Accordingly, he creates a table that shows the altered driving miles for each employee, noting that the average drive will decline slightly.

A manager who is deeply concerned about the strategic ramifications of a change initiative may make the mistake of communicating with employees solely about strategy issues. Employees are likely to be more concerned with how a project will impact their specific working conditions and whether they will continue to be employed. Given these differences in information requirements, the manager might engage in a lengthy presentation to employees, and yet answer none of their questions or concerns.

EXAMPLE

Nova Corporation has been approached by a major competitor about joining forces as a combined entity. Nova's president calls a meeting with the staff to inform them of the discussions. He focuses on how the proposed merger will result in more market share for the combined entities, but not the main issue for employees, which is whether they will retain their jobs.

Prior to this announcement, employees generally felt that they were partners in a growing enterprise. After the announcement, their feelings changed in the direction of believing they were simply a cost of the business that would likely be disposed of in order to create efficiencies for the combined entity.

A key element of the communications plan for a project is to understand that communications go in two directions. The project team must be willing to discuss issues with employees on an ongoing basis. This means taking the time to listen to their concerns and suggestions, and to respond within a reasonable period of time. When employees realize that management is actually listening to them, it is quite likely that the employees will become more cooperative, while also making suggestions of their own for improving the outcome of the project.

When there is no communications plan for a project, the project manager may fall into a trap of continually communicating with only those people she is comfortable with. Doing so excludes a number of other people, who may think that they are not included in the "in" crowd, and so will tend to resist the project. To avoid this trap, develop a plan for methodically discussing issues with anyone who is even remotely impacted by the project. This approach may shrink the number of sceptics, and may also uncover information related to the project that the manager had not been aware of.

Another technique enhancing communications is for the project team to anticipate the types of objections that will be raised, and have answers prepared in advance. When a project is initially presented to employees, these objections and answers can be included in the initial presentation, thereby short-circuiting a number of complaints. This is especially important when affected employees may lose their jobs or be reassigned as a result of the change.

EXAMPLE

A project team has been assigned the task of automating an entire production line. The project team leader works through how this will impact each production employee, noting where they will be reassigned or when they can expect their employment to be terminated. He then calls a meeting with the production staff and presents exactly how the change will affect them, and apologizes for its negative impact on them. The meeting is open-ended, and he ends up spending an hour answering questions.

The result is an increased level of employee turnover in the weeks following the meeting, but at a rate one-third that of another production line, where the team leader only posted a notice about future terminations and reassignments, with no follow-up meeting. Further, the other production line experienced a much higher rate of absenteeism and a decline in the level of product quality before it was automated.

Another communications issue to deal with is the likely employee response that this is "just another turnaround plan" to save the company. In many cases, a company will have run through multiple initiatives (and perhaps multiple presidents), to the point where employees shrug off each new plan as a doomed effort. In this situation, it can help to note specifically why a former plan failed, and how the new plan differs from the old one.

In cases where employees appear to be reasonably loyal to the company, it can make sense to lay out all of the facts of the situation, along with a realistic analysis of what the company hopes to achieve through a change initiative. This approach assumes that the recipients are sensible people who can be trusted to evaluate the information by themselves and see the project team's point of view. In situations where employees are slanted more strongly away from the project, it may be necessary to not only provide this information, but also be more actively persuasive by stressing the benefits of change. This more active approach cannot be pushed too hard, or else it will be perceived as false advertising.

EXAMPLE

Franklin Drilling is abandoning one of its oil fields in North Dakota and is shifting all production work to a different field in Colorado. Franklin has offered relocation packages to everyone working in North Dakota. The project leader has issued the relocation package to the North Dakota employees, but it has been met with a certain amount of suspicion. He decides to repackage the offer, noting a number of "soft" benefits, including the increased amount of shopping, professional sports, and schools in Colorado. The repackaged deal meets with a higher approval rating from employees. The two communications were identical in terms of their "hard" content, but the repackaged offer paid more attention to persuading the recipients.

The communication challenge becomes more difficult as the project rolls forward. At various times, employees will be depressed by the lack of progress, have to deal with the departures of colleagues, and perhaps cuts in compensation. At these times, the manager must be able to balance the need to impart realistic information with a reasonably optimistic tone that shows the way to a brighter future. This can be quite difficult, since employees must be encouraged to move forward with their assigned tasks while still being allowed time to process the loss of co-workers and possibly significant job alterations.

As changes take root within the organization, a key focus must be on praising those employees whose efforts have resulted in the changes. The intent is to associate positive feedback with support of the project, so that employees will become more deeply involved in hopes of continuing to receive more praise (which may include more compensation).

Another communications factor to consider is how to most effectively respond to employee queries about the progress of tasks, and how a project will impact them. One of the best approaches is to engage in group question-and-answer sessions. These sessions allow the project manager to tailor status reports to the needs of the audience, as well as to respond to a large number of questions within a short period of time.

> **Tip:** During question-and-answer sessions, have someone record the questions asked by employees, and post responses to the most common questions on a company intranet site or in a newsletter. By doing so, the most frequently expressed concerns can be addressed with the entire population of employees.

A major concern when dealing with communication issues is balancing the efficiency of the method used against the effectiveness with which information is delivered. E-mail is undoubtedly the most efficient method, since news can be distributed instantly to locations around the world. However, it ranks quite low on effectiveness, for it is perceived to be impersonal and represents a relatively poor way to obtain feedback. Communications in person are the reverse – they are highly effective, but are extremely inefficient. There is no ideal communication method that works in all situations. Instead, the method must be tailored to the circumstances.

EXAMPLE

The president of Pianoforte International has made the difficult decision to shift the production of the company's upright piano to a foreign location in order to reduce costs. The change will not be made for six months, so he needs employees to remain committed to their jobs for a substantial period of time; temporary workers cannot fill in for people who have worked on this product for the last 20 years. The president could issue a notice to the workers or have a subordinate give the bad news. However, given the critical need for continuity on the job, and as a sign of respect for the workers, he meets with them in person and stays as long as anyone has questions.

Eliminating Obstacles

Any number of obstacles can get in the way of a change initiative, which will either stop it entirely, divert it down a different path, or delay its implementation. Consequently, one must be aware of the issues that can arise and how to deal with them.

The worst obstacles are people with sufficient power to either stop or hinder a change initiative. One way to deal with this group is to involve them in the project, so that they can have some degree of control over the outcome. This does not mean that they can twist the project entirely to their own ends. However, their concerns will be heard and incorporated into the project to a reasonable extent. If the level of change is sufficient, they may then be encouraged to support the project. The issue, of course, is altering the objectives of the project just enough to gain their support, without moving away from the long-term objectives that the project was originally designed to attain.

Incorporating the views of a sceptic brings up a key issue from which project managers tend to suffer, which is not listening. They may be so involved in the righteousness of their visions that they try to push through changes without listening to anyone. This can be a fatal flaw, for sceptics may be taking their positions for a very good reason – there could be issues with a change initiative that will make it unworkable in its current form. Consequently, the project leader should always block out enough time to discuss her efforts with sceptics, and genuinely probe their viewpoints. It is entirely possible that their opinions are crucial to the success of the project.

There are other cases in which a person blocking a project is doing so for less valid reasons, such as an attempt to retain his power base within the company. When this is the case, attempt to marginalize their influence over the project by keeping them or their representatives off the project team and the committee controlling the project. A more indirect approach is to stuff the project team and committee with supporters, thereby overwhelming the votes controlled by the blocker. If the person is still having a negative impact on the project, it may be necessary to replace him with someone who is more supportive of the change effort.

If there is a coalition of people blocking a project, model what the effect would be if one or two people could be removed from the group. If doing so would result in a substantial decline in the power of the blockers, bargain with a few targeted individuals to shift them into supporters. This might result in modest changes to the project, or the inclusion of these people on the project team or the supervising committee.

Another obstacle to change is the structure of the organization. When people from multiple functional areas must sign off on a proposed change, the work required to gain the approvals will dampen the enthusiasm of even the most ardent supporter. Further, requiring the collaboration of multiple functional areas slows down the change initiative. To avoid these issues, consider examining the organizational structure in advance, and adjusting it so that authority for changes is centralized under just one person.

Yet another obstacle is when the work force is not sufficiently trained in how to do the work that a change initiative requires of them. They may be willing to put in extra time to learn on their own, but in the end will probably not be able to perform at a peak level. The solution is to identify what types of training are needed, provide it, and then conduct periodic tests to see if additional training is needed. In particular, there will probably be training gaps related to specific on-the-job skills. More than likely, the company will have to invest in additional training to ensure that everyone involved in a project is completely capable of performing as asked.

A further consideration is whether the company's systems support the change initiative. Ideally, all systems should encourage employees to participate in changes. For example:

- The sales manager wants to open up a new sales region, but no one wants to sell there, since the commission structure will result in lower earnings. The structure should be altered to provide for a higher commission rate for the first few years.
- A product development initiative has solicited new ideas and received none. The compensation system can be altered to provide for higher pay rate increases when an employee has a history of providing ideas that are turned into viable products.
- The company is pushing a higher level of customer service, but the human resources department is still giving preference to those recruits willing to accept a low hourly pay rate. The hiring criteria should be overhauled to increase the hiring of people who are genuinely interested in assisting customers.

Creating Wins

One of the key elements in the process of implementing change is to plan for and achieve a series of short-term wins. By doing so, it becomes apparent that a project is succeeding in reaching its goal, thereby bringing in additional support. Further, these wins provide proof that the project manager is capable of delivering on the entire project. Without a series of short-term wins, the reverse situation occurs – people begin to doubt that the project can be completed, and turn into active doubters. Further, the project sponsors have a more difficult time obtaining additional funding as the months and years pass without any visible success. In addition, it is difficult to maintain an adequate sense of urgency when deliverables may be years away. In short, it is essential to plan for and achieve a series of ongoing targets as a project progresses.

It will be necessary to actively search through project plans and locate those milestones that can be celebrated at regular intervals. This may require the project team to even alter the plan somewhat, redirecting resources toward milestones that will be most helpful in pushing along the project. Thus, the need for short-term wins should be considered during the initial project planning, as well as at regular intervals thereafter.

The milestones that can be used as short-term wins must be carefully selected. The ideal milestone should be one that has the following characteristics:

- There are few or no identifiable technical hurdles
- There are no bottlenecks in terms of people or processes that could stop work

- The project segment can be implemented by a small group
- The project segment already has adequate funding

There are few downsides to the use of short-term wins. There can be complaints that the achievement of a series of milestones requires more resources than if a project team simply focuses on the end result, with no intermediate crises to achieve the various wins. However, without those wins it is quite possible that the project will lose its funding and any sense of urgency. Consequently, some diversion of resources can be considered reasonable compensation for keeping a project on track.

> **Tip:** Ensure that all short-terms wins are seen as group wins, where many take credit. Otherwise, a win may be seen as going entirely to the credit of the project manager, which can cause resentment within the team.

Rolling the Project Forward

One of the change management process steps was to use initial wins to build momentum, moving from one milestone to another. After a long series of these wins, management might be tempted to declare victory, pull back any further funding as being unnecessary, and move on to other activities. However, a basic rule of measuring progress is that there is either advancement or decline – there is no steady state. As soon as management begins to ignore a project, the results gained from it will begin to worsen – and it will be very hard to rebuild momentum. Consequently, it is almost never a good idea to declare victory and move on to other things.

A more appropriate way to deal with change management is to continue allocating a reasonable amount of funding to these projects, as well as providing them with senior management support for an extended period. By doing so, the changes become baked into the culture of the company. At this point some modest amount of support may still be needed, but the changes are then seen as being so essential to the success of the company that there will be little residual opposition to them.

The best way to roll forward projects is to continually target any existing systems that do not align with the principles established for the change effort. These systems must be reconfigured to seamlessly integrate with the new changes. Otherwise, the force of tradition within the company will tend to support these older systems over the newer ones, forcing the newer systems to be adapted toward their previous state.

Another roll forward issue is centered in the human resources department. When interviewing job candidates, the human resources staff should screen them to see if they will support existing change initiatives. In addition, the human resources group needs to alter its training programs to be fully supportive of all change projects. By doing so, employees are constantly reminded of the company's commitment to their projects and their roles in supporting the projects. Further, the human resources manager should provide input as part of any personnel advancement discussions, to point out those employees most supportive of change management. Taking these steps creates an environment in which change is more likely to be supported by employees.

> **Tip:** The board of directors must be solidly behind all change initiatives. They will then realize that any president they hire must support those initiatives. Otherwise, they may hire someone who has other priorities, and who will then ignore what may have been years of change efforts.

Locking in Changes

The last change management step is to fully integrate the new systems into the company, to the extent that the changes are considered to have been fully institutionalized. If changes are not locked in, they will instead be considered alien to the way things have traditionally been done, and so will be gradually dismantled. This is a critical issue, for beliefs about how a business "has always been run" can persist for decades, and may eventually shut down what initially appears to be a successful change initiative.

EXAMPLE

Mole Industries was built on a core belief that the company would concentrate on the highest-quality trench digging equipment, and that customers would then be attracted to the excellent products. This belief appeared to be true for many years, until sales began to flatten out. At that time, a new president was hired who wanted to change the focus of the organization toward partial customization of products to exactly meet the needs of Mole's largest customers. This change resulted in a burst of sales as customers flocked to the new business model.

Glowing with success, the president retired after his fourth year with the company. From that point on, the company's ingrained focus on high quality products gradually reduced the amount of customization allowed, on the grounds that quality levels would be lower on partially-customized products. After three years, no customization was offered at all, and the company was right back where it had started.

The problem was that the new initiative had not been given enough time to take root within the organization, so the older belief structure took over.

There are a number of ways to lock in changes, including the following:

- *Publicize results.* Inform employees fully about the results of the changes. This means continually publicizing results where they are easily available to employees. Simply posting results on a trend line is not sufficient. Also produce an ongoing series of articles that tie the changes made to the favorable results experienced by the company; these articles should be explicit about cause and effect. The outcome should be a situation in which any employee can discuss how a change management project had a beneficial impact on the company.
- *Promote change agents.* The senior management ranks should *only* be stocked with people who actively support change within the company. Otherwise, the

installation of even one relatively passive senior manager could undo years of work, resulting in new systems gradually being dismantled or ignored.

- *Attack disruptive behavior.* Whenever there is a case of disruptive behavior within the business, senior management publicly and vigorously criticizes the person causing the disruption. Doing so sends a strong signal to all parties involved regarding what will not be tolerated within the organization.
- *Localize decision making.* Employees are more likely to support change on a long-term basis when they made the decisions related to the change. This means that managers must coach employees in how to make decisions for themselves, rather than by imposing decisions from above.

Once changes have succeeded, integrate them into the fabric of the business, so that there will be no backsliding. This can involve integration into policies and procedures, employee training, and compensation plans. It can also be useful to wait a few months and then review how well change initiatives have taken hold within the organization. If there is significant backsliding, managers may need to alter their process for change implementations to make the outcomes "stickier," while also applying pressure to return completed projects to their original performance levels.

There are a number of reasons why the results of a completed project may backslide over time. Possible reasons, along with offsetting solutions, are noted in the following bullet points:

- *Employees leave.* Those responsible for the change decide to work for a different company. This effect can be mitigated by developing a succession plan for all positions, including ongoing training programs. Also, pay attention to career development planning and reward systems to reduce employee turnover rates.
- *Accountability not clear.* It is not clear who is accountable for maintaining performance levels, so that performance levels decline. This effect can be stymied by including responsibilities in job descriptions and measuring outcomes as part of employee performance reviews.
- *New hires alter systems.* New people brought into the company are not as invested in existing systems, and seek to replace them. Promote from within and use extensive training to mitigate this issue.
- *Funds run out.* A change effort may require a certain amount of ongoing funding, so if the funds are stopped, the project halts. Be sure to plan well in advance for the appropriate amount of budget allocations to ensure that this does not happen.
- *Employees are tired.* When a project runs for an extended period of time, employees become tired of the ongoing push for improvement, and are more likely to stop supporting the project. The effects of this common problem can be minimized by chopping up the project into smaller pieces and relaunching each successive piece with a new focus.

A possible issue for the change manager to be aware of is that it can take employees quite a long time to become accustomed to a new role. They need time to realize that their old tasks have changed to new ones, to get used to the new activities, and then to accept them as the new "norm." This transition period can mean that employees will unexpectedly push for a return to the old ways – perhaps months after the project was considered to have been completed – because they have not yet accepted the new system. Consequently, it may be necessary to maintain the pressure for change for much longer than might initially appear to be warranted.

The Ideal Change Management Leader

A person who can lead a change initiative is not necessarily the same as a person who does a good job of running a department. The latter person is managing a status quo situation where a high level of efficiency is rewarded. The former person needs a substantially different skill set, which is:

- *Problem solver*. The person must be able to effectively elicit solutions from her team, or find solutions directly.
- *Results focused*. The person has a definite goal, which is to achieve the next milestone in the project plan, and ultimately to complete the change initiative by the planned date.
- *Responsible*. The person is comfortable with the responsibility that goes with making the series of decisions needed to complete a project, without repeatedly running the decisions up to a higher authority for approval.
- *Politically aware*. The person understands the power structure of the business, and can effectively work with people throughout the organization and business partners to complete change initiatives.
- *Maintains momentum*. The person is aware that interest in a change project can flag over time, especially when there is a fair amount of ongoing resistance. A change leader must be seen to be actively involved in the project, thereby pushing along others involved in the same effort.

This skill set is so critical that it may be wiser to wait for a better person to become available than to launch a project with a less-qualified person in charge of it.

A corporate insider is the default position picked to be a change management leader, since this person has authority within the organization, is (hopefully) trusted by employees, and has a network of associates who can be tapped for assistance.

Summary

It is essential to follow every step in the change management process, since each one addresses a separate success factor. For example, a strong guiding coalition is needed to provide support for a project, while short-term wins are needed to prove that a project team will eventually succeed in rolling out an entire change initiative. When any of these steps are ignored or completed within an excessively short period of time, this will likely result in a less successful outcome or outright failure. Consequently, the management team must become accustomed to the concept that change initiatives require a lengthy effort before they can succeed.

Chapter 9
Management Control Activities

Introduction

The last of the key management responsibilities is controlling the activities of a business. The control function involves the use of ongoing monitoring activities, as well as measurements and variance analyses, to determine how well an organization's operational and financial results are meeting expectations. With a solid system of controls, managers can determine not only whether goals are being met, but also the causes of problems. This chapter covers the essential elements of a control system, with a particular emphasis on budgetary control and variance analysis.

The Control System

A system of control is comprised of the following four activities:

1. *Establish standards*. Managers need to decide which targets must be met in order to achieve the strategic plan, and to establish standards for these targets. For example, there may be a target of achieving $5 million of sales in the northwest region, which calls for a standard of $800,000 of sales per salesperson. These standards need to be clearly defined so that changes in performance can be measured.
2. *Measure performance*. There must be a performance measurement system in place that tracks the actual results against which standards can be compared. Measurements for financial results are relatively easily derived from the accounting system, but this is not necessarily the case for operational performance measurements. A business may need to install a relatively expensive tracking system for each of its operational measurements, which can limit the number of measurements being tracked.
3. *Compare to standards*. Once a measurement has been recorded, it is compared to the associated standard in order to calculate a variance. If there is a sufficiently large unfavorable variance, management takes action to investigate the underlying problem.
4. *Take corrective action*. Once management is aware of the problem and has investigated its causes, it can take remedial action. This can even involve a change in the standard on which the variance was based, if it is determined that the standard is too difficult to achieve.

From a financial perspective, the control system is embodied by the budget and any variances arising from a comparison of the budget to actual results. These topics are addressed later in the chapter.

Management by Exception

Management by exception is the practice of reviewing the financial and operational results of a firm, and only bringing up issues with management if results represent significant differences from the expected or budgeted amount. For example, a company controller may only notify management of a problem when expenses are the greater of $15,000 or 30% higher than expected.

The purpose of this concept is to only bother management with the most important variances from the planned direction or results of the business. Managers will likely spend more time investigating and correcting these larger variances. The concept can be fine-tuned, so that smaller variances are brought to the attention of middle- or lower-level managers, while a massive variance is reported straight to the senior management team.

The management by exception concept is quite effective, for the following reasons:

- It minimizes the amount of financial and operational information that management needs to review.
- Employees can devise their own approaches to achieving the results mandated in the company's strategic plan. Management will only step in if significant exception conditions exist.
- The company's auditors will likely inquire about these larger variances as well, so management should investigate them in advance in order to provide knowledgeable answers to the auditors.

Despite these advantages, there are a few problems with management by exception, which are:

- It is based on the existence of a budget, against which actual results are compared. If the information in the budget was not well formulated, there may be a large number of variances, many of which are irrelevant because the baseline for comparison is incorrect.
- It requires the use of financial analysts who prepare and present variance summaries to management. This means that an extra layer of corporate overhead is required to make the concept function correctly.
- It is based on the hierarchical command-and-control system, where decisions are made by a central group of senior managers. If the structure were decentralized instead, there would be less need for management by exception, since local managers can monitor conditions on a daily basis, and so would not need an exception reporting system.

Control Issues

Controls are typically based on a set of standards that are derived through an analysis of company operations, as well as its financial statements. For example, management may decide that it will closely monitor the number of customer orders that are shipped within 24 hours of order receipt, with a goal of 95% being shipped within that period. Or, it may decide to closely monitor the proportion of early payment discounts that are taken by the accounts payable staff, with a goal of 100% being taken. A large organization may adopt dozens or even hundreds of these standards as the basis upon which management controls the business.

A problem with the use of these standards is that management tends to become fixated on them, to the exclusion of other issues that are not being tracked in any way. For example, a business that focuses too much on shipping customer orders promptly might not track the investment in inventory, which tends to increase in order to keep enough stock on hand to ensure that customer orders are fulfilled quickly. The result can be a high fulfillment rate, but at the cost of a runaway investment in working capital. This example highlights another concern, which is that there can be unintended consequences to establishing a particular measurement as a control point. Thus, control standards need to be viewed from the perspective of the entire organization, to ensure that the outcome is overall improvement for the whole business.

Another concern with the use of standards is that they will eventually be met, and then remain as the focus of management attention. When managers fixate on these old standards, the company is no longer improving, since the organization has reached its natural maximum abilities in the targeted areas. When this happens, it makes sense to continue monitoring how well the standards are being met, but to also formulate new standards in other areas that can be used as the basis for further improvements to the organization. For example, when the focus has been on achieving a high order fulfillment rate, management can set additional standards for minimizing the amount of time it takes for orders to reach customers, perhaps through the use of regional warehouses or overnight delivery services.

Budgetary Controls

A budget is a document that forecasts the financial results and financial position of a business for one or more future periods. At a minimum, a budget contains an estimated income statement that describes anticipated financial results. A more complex budget also contains an estimated balance sheet, which includes the entity's anticipated assets, liabilities, and equity positions at various points in time in the future. A prime use of the budget is to serve as a performance baseline for the measurement of actual results. Budgets may also be linked to bonus plans in order to direct the activities of various company employees.

The key driver of any budget is the amount of revenue that is expected during the budget period. Revenue is usually compiled in a separate revenue budget. The information in this budget is derived from estimates of which products or services will sell, and the prices at which they can be sold. Forecasted revenue for this budget cannot be derived just from the sales staff, since this would limit the information to the extrapolation of historical sales figures into the future. The chief executive officer provides additional strategic information, while the marketing manager addresses new-product introductions and the purchasing staff provides input on the availability of raw materials that may restrict sales. Thus, a group effort from many parts of a company is needed to create the revenue budget.

Once the revenue budget is in place, a number of additional budgets are derived from it that relate to the production capabilities of the company. The following components are included in this cluster of budgets:

- *Ending inventory budget.* As its name implies, this budget sets the inventory level as of the end of each accounting period listed in the budget. Management uses this budget to force changes in the inventory level, which is usually driven by a policy to have more or less finished goods inventory on hand. Having more inventory presumably improves the speed with which a company can ship goods to customers, at the cost of an increased investment in working capital. A forced reduction in inventory may delay some shipments to customers due to stockout conditions, but requires less working capital to maintain. The ending inventory budget is used as an input to the production budget.

- *Production budget.* This budget shows expected production at an aggregated level. The production budget is based primarily on the sales estimates in the revenue budget, but it must also take into consideration existing inventory levels and the desired amount of ending inventory, as stated in the ending inventory budget. If management wants to increase inventory levels in order to provide more rapid shipments to customers, the required increase in production may trigger a need for more production equipment and direct labor staff. The production budget is needed in order to derive the direct labor budget, manufacturing overhead budget, and direct materials budget.

- *Direct labor budget.* This budget calculates the amount of direct labor staffing expected during the budget period, based on the production levels itemized in the production budget. This information can only be generally estimated, given the vagaries of short-term changes in actual production scheduling. However, direct labor usually involves specific staffing levels to crew production lines, so the estimated amount of direct labor should not vary excessively over time, within certain production volume parameters. This budget should incorporate any planned changes in the cost of labor, which may be easy to do if there is a union contract that specifies pay increases as of specific dates. This budget provides rough estimates of the number of employees needed, and is of particular interest to the human resources staff in developing hiring plans. It is a key source document for the cost of goods sold budget.

- *Manufacturing overhead budget.* This budget includes all of the overhead costs expected to be incurred in the manufacturing area during the budget period. It is usually based on historical cost information, but can be adjusted for step cost situations, where a change in the structure or capacity level of a production facility strips away or adds large amounts of expenses at one time. Even if there are no changes in structure or capacity, the manufacturing overhead budget may change somewhat in the maintenance cost area if management plans to alter these expenditures as machines age or are replaced. It is particularly important to adjust this budget if management contemplates running a production facility at close to 100% utilization, since doing so requires a significant incremental increase in many types of expenditures. This budget is a source document for the cost of goods sold budget.

- *Direct materials budget.* This budget is derived from a combination of the manufacturing unit totals in the production budget and the bills of material for those units, and is used in the cost of goods sold budget. The bills of material must be accurate if this budget is to be remotely accurate. If a company produces a large variety of products, this can become an excessively detailed and burdensome budget to create and maintain. Consequently, it is customary to estimate material costs in aggregate, such as at the product line level. It may also be necessary to state expected scrap and spoilage levels in this budget, especially if management plans to improve its production practices to reduce scrap and spoilage below their historical levels.

- *Cost of goods sold budget.* This budget contains a summarization of the expenses detailed in the direct material budget, manufacturing overhead budget, and direct materials budget. This budget usually contains such additional information as line items for revenue, the gross margin, and key production statistics. It is heavily used during budget iterations, since management can consult it to view the impact of various assumptions on gross margins and other aspects of the production process.

Once the revenue and production-related budgets have been completed, there are still several other budgets to assemble that relate to other functions of the company. They are:

- *Sales and marketing budget.* This budget is comprised of the compensation of the sales and marketing staff, sales travel costs, and expenditures related to various marketing programs. It is closely linked to the revenue budget, since the number of sales staff (in some industries) is the prime determinant of additional sales. Further, marketing campaigns can impact the timing of the sales shown in the revenue budget.

- *Administration budget.* This budget includes the expenses of the executive, accounting, treasury, human resources, and other administrative staff. These expenses are primarily comprised of compensation, followed by office expenses. A large proportion of these expenses are fixed, with some headcount changes driven by total revenues or other types of activity elsewhere in the company.

A budget that is not directly impacted by the revenue budget is the research and development budget. This budget is authorized by senior management, and is set at an amount that is deemed appropriate, given the projected level of new product introductions that management wants to achieve, and the company's competitive posture within the industry. The size of this budget is also influenced by the amount of available funding and an estimate of how many potentially profitable projects can be pursued.

Once these budgets have been completed, it is possible to determine the capital budgeting requirements of the company, as well as its financing needs. These two topics are addressed in the capital budget and the financing budget:

- *Capital budget.* This budget shows the cash flows associated with the acquisition of fixed assets during the budget period. Larger fixed assets are noted individually, while smaller purchases are noted in aggregate. The information in this budget is used to develop the budgeted balance sheet, depreciation expense, and the cash requirements needed for the financing budget.
- *Financing budget.* This budget is the last of the component budgets developed, because it needs the cash inflow and outflow information from the other budgets. With this information in hand, the financing budget addresses how funds will be invested (if there are excess cash inflows) or obtained through debt or equity financing (if there is a need for additional cash). This budget also incorporates any additional cash usage information that is typically addressed by the board of directors, including dividends, stock repurchases, and repositioning of the company's debt to equity ratio. The interest expense or interest income resulting from this budget is incorporated into the budgeted income statement.

Once the capital budget and financing budget have been created, the information in all of the budgets is summarized into a master budget. This master budget is essentially an income statement. A more complex budget also includes a balance sheet that itemizes the major categories of assets, liabilities, and equity. There may be a statement of cash flows that itemizes the sources and uses of funds.

The complete system of budgets is shown in the following exhibit.

The System of Budgets

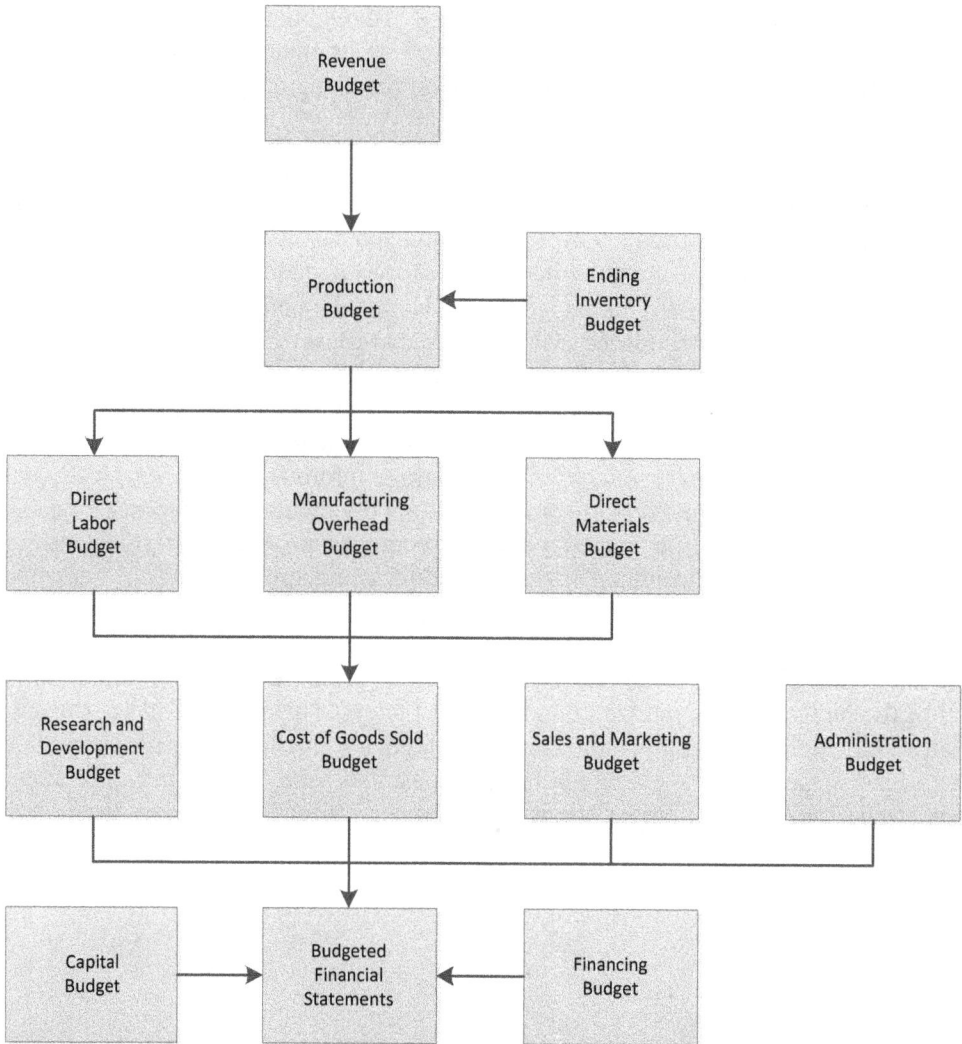

Employee staffing levels are usually included in each of the various budgets, so that employee compensation is fully integrated into the expenses in each budget. However, since compensation comprises a major proportion of all company expenses, it may be useful to also create a staffing budget that summarizes headcount and compensation for all areas of the business. This information is useful for determining whether there will be a sufficient number of employees to support planned revenue levels, as well as to provide guidance for the recruiting and layoff plans of the human resources department.

The system of budgets frequently includes another activity that is not officially a part of the budget – compensation plans. These plans are prepared by the human resources department for selected individuals within the company, and define exactly which budgeted targets a person must attain in exchange for a bonus payment. There is a separate compensation plan for each person, so they are not mentioned in the system of budgets, other than as a budgeted amount of additional compensation.

In summary, the system of budgets ultimately depends upon the revenue budget and the amount of planned ending inventory. These two budgets directly or indirectly influence the amounts budgeted in many other parts of the corporate budget.

After creating a budget, compare it to actual results so that management can see how well the business is performing in comparison to their expectations. This can be done at a general level, merely reporting differences between budget and actual revenues and expenses. However, this does not show the reasons why variances have arisen. In the following sections, we address the various reporting formats that give management the actionable information they need to address unfavorable budget variances.

General Reporting Format

If a completed budget is loaded into the accounting software, there will almost always be a budget versus actual reporting format for the income statement and the various departmental income statements. This report reveals any variances between the budgeted and actual amounts. A budget variance is the difference between the budgeted amount of expense or revenue and the actual amount. The budget variance is favorable when the actual revenue is higher than the budget or when the actual expense is less than the budget. The format of such a report is similar to the one in the following sample.

Sample Budget versus Actual Income Statement

	Actual Results	Budget Results	Variance ($)	Variance (%)
Revenue	$1,000,000	$1,100,000	-$100,000	-9%
Cost of goods sold:				
Direct materials	300,000	330,000	30,000	9%
Direct labor	100,000	90,000	-10,000	-11%
Manufacturing overhead	150,000	155,000	5,000	3%
Total cost of goods sold	550,000	575,000	25,000	4%
Gross margin	$450,000	$525,000	-$75,000	-14%
Administration expenses	175,000	160,000	-15,000	-9%
Sales and marketing expenses	225,000	205,000	-20,000	-10%
Net profit or loss	$50,000	$160,000	-$110,000	-69%

This report format does not reveal a great deal of information by itself, since it only notifies management of the presence *of* a variance, not the reason *for* the variance. Further, the budget upon which the variance is calculated may be so far out of line with actual results that the variance is essentially meaningless.

A subtle variation on this report format is to position the largest-dollar items at the top of the report, so that the areas in which variances are likely to be largest are where management can more easily see them. The following example illustrates the concept.

Sample Sales and Marketing Department Monthly Report

Expense Item	Actual	Budget	$ Variance	% Variance
Wages	$85,000	$82,000	-$3,000	-4%
Commissions	18,000	19,500	1,500	8%
Payroll taxes	8,000	7,500	-500	-7%
Trade shows	25,000	28,000	3,000	11%
Travel and entertainment	11,000	7,000	-4,000	-57%
Office expenses	6,500	3,500	-3,000	-86%
Promotional materials	5,000	5,000	0	0%
Other	1,200	500	-700	-58%
Totals	$159,700	$153,000	-$6,700	-4%

Note how the preceding report is structured to place wages and related expenses at the top of the report; this is because compensation costs are the largest expenditure for many departments, and so should be a center of attention.

An alternative format is one that presents a historical trend line of revenues and expenses for each line item in the income statement. Doing so eliminates the risk of comparing a completely inaccurate budget to actual results. A sample report format follows.

Sample Trend Line Report Format

	Jan.	Feb	Mar.	Apr.	May
Accounting fees	$1,000	$1,100	$1,050	$1,900	$1,150
Legal	0	0	5,000	0	250
Maintenance	550	575	400	600	3,250
Office expenses	925	2,800	890	790	850
Travel and entertainment	6,500	1,200	1,350	1,400	995
Utilities	500	310	420	1,600	375
Totals	$9,475	$5,985	$9,110	$6,290	$6,870

The key assumption behind a trend line report is that most expenses do not vary much from period to period. If that assumption is true, then the report is excellent for highlighting anomalies over time.

No matter which of the preceding report formats are used, it is rarely sufficient to simply issue financial information to managers without at least some explanation of the larger variances. Instead, investigate the larger variances and issue a separate report that delves into the reasons for them. The following sample report states the amount of each expense or revenue item that requires explanation, and then spends a fair amount of time describing the situation.

Sample Variance Discussion Report

Line Item	Discussion
Product Alpha revenue	Revenues were $100,000 lower than expected, due to a product recall and free replacement. The problem was a design flaw that is being investigated by Engineering. Recommend stopping sales until an engineering change order is released.
Direct materials expense	Freight expense was $40,000 higher than expected, due to air freight of late delivery from overseas supplier. Recommend sourcing the part locally.
Rent expense	Expense was $20,000 lower than expected, due to renegotiation of building lease. Note that the lease now runs an additional three years.
Travel and entertainment expense	Expense was $25,000 higher than expected, due to damage to rental party room during company Christmas party.
Utilities expense	Electricity cost was $15,000 higher than expected, due to unusually cold December temperatures. Recommend additional building insulation.

The best reports of this type very clearly quantify the issue and state the exact cause of the problem, possibly with an accompanying recommendation. The report needs to be sufficiently detailed that management can use it to resolve the underlying problem.

Revenue Reporting

To report on specific types of variance issues related to revenues, the key variance calculations are for the selling price variance and the selling volume variance. We describe the calculation and usage of both variances in this section.

Selling Price Variance

The selling price variance is the difference between the actual and expected revenue that is caused by a change in the price of a product or service. The formula is:

(Actual price - Budgeted price) × Actual unit sales = Selling price variance

An unfavorable variance means that the actual price was lower than the budgeted price.

The budgeted price for each unit of product or sales is developed by the sales and marketing managers, and is based on their estimation of future demand for these products and services, which in turn is affected by general economic conditions and the actions of competitors. If the actual price is lower than the budgeted price, the result may actually be favorable to the company, as long as the price decline spurs demand to such an extent that the company generates an incremental profit as a result of the price decline.

EXAMPLE

The marketing manager of Quest Adventure Gear estimates that the company can sell a green widget for $80 per unit during the upcoming year. This estimate is based on the historical demand for green widgets.

During the first half of the new year, the price of the green widget comes under extreme pressure as a new supplier in Ireland floods the market with a lower-priced green widget. Quest must drop its price to $70 in order to compete, and sells 20,000 units during that period. Its selling price variance during the first half of the year is:

($70 Actual price - $80 Budgeted price) × 20,000 units = $(200,000) Selling price variance

---

There are a number of possible causes of a selling price variance. For example:

- *Discounts*. The company has granted various discounts to customers to induce them to buy products.
- *Marketing allowances*. The company is allowing customers to deduct marketing allowances from their payments to reimburse them for marketing activities involving the company's products.
- *Price points*. The price points at which the company is selling are different from the price points stated in its budget.
- *Product options*. Customers are buying different product options than expected, resulting in an average price that differs from the price points stated in the company's budget.

Sales Volume Variance

The sales volume variance is the difference between the actual and expected number of units sold, multiplied by the budgeted price per unit. The formula is:

(Actual units sold - Budgeted units sold) × Budgeted price per unit

= Sales volume variance

An unfavorable variance means that the actual number of units sold was lower than the budgeted number sold.

The budgeted number of units sold is derived by the sales and marketing managers, and is based on their estimation of how the company's product market share, features, price points, expected marketing activities, distribution channels, and sales in new regions will impact future sales. If the product's selling price is lower than the budgeted amount, this may spur sales to such an extent that the sales volume variance is favorable, even though the selling price variance is unfavorable.

EXAMPLE

The marketing manager of Quest Adventure Gear estimates that the company can sell 25,000 blue widgets for $65 per unit during the upcoming year. This estimate is based on the historical demand for blue widgets, as supported by new advertising campaigns in the first and third quarters of the year.

During the new year, Quest does not have a first quarter advertising campaign, since it was changing advertising agencies at that time. This results in sales of just 21,000 blue widgets during the year. Its sales volume variance is:

(21,000 Units sold - 25,000 Budgeted units) × $65 Budgeted price per unit

= $260,000 Unfavorable sales volume variance

There are a number of possible causes of a sales volume variance. For example:

- *Cannibalization*. The company may have released another product that competes with the product in question. Thus, sales of one product cannibalize sales of the other product.
- *Competition*. Competitors may have released new products that are more attractive to customers.
- *Price*. The company may have altered the product price, which in turn drives a change in unit sales volume.
- *Trade restrictions*. A foreign country may have altered its barriers to competition.

Overview of Cost of Goods Sold Variance Reporting

A number of variances have been developed for expenses categorized within the cost of goods sold. When you create a budget, you are creating a standard cost against which actual costs and usage can be compared. There are two basic types of variances from a standard that can arise, which are the rate variance and the volume variance. They are:

- *Rate variance*. A rate variance is the difference between the actual price paid for something and the expected price, multiplied by the actual quantity purchased. The "rate" variance designation is most commonly applied to the labor rate variance, which involves the actual cost of direct labor in comparison to the standard cost of direct labor. The rate variance uses a different designation when applied to the purchase of materials, and may be called the purchase price variance or the material price variance.

- *Volume variance.* A volume variance is the difference between the actual quantity sold or consumed and the budgeted amount, multiplied by the standard price or cost per unit. If the variance relates to the sale of goods, it is called the sales volume variance. If it relates to the use of direct materials, it is called the material yield variance. If the variance relates to the use of direct labor, it is called the labor efficiency variance. Finally, if the variance relates to the application of overhead, it is called the overhead efficiency variance.

Thus, variances are based on either changes in cost from the expected amount, or changes in the quantity from the expected amount. The most common variances to report on are subdivided within the rate and volume variance categories for direct materials, direct labor, and overhead. The primary variances are noted in the following exhibit.

The Primary Variances

	Rate Variance	Volume Variance
Materials	Purchase price variance	Material yield variance
Direct labor	Labor rate variance	Labor efficiency variance
Fixed overhead	Fixed overhead spending variance	Not applicable
Variable overhead	Variable overhead spending variance	Variable overhead efficiency variance

All of the variances noted in the preceding table are explained in the following sections, including examples to demonstrate how the variances are applied.

Purchase Price Variance

The purchase price variance is the difference between the actual price paid to buy an item and its standard price, multiplied by the actual number of units purchased. The formula is:

(Actual price - Standard price) × Actual quantity = Purchase price variance

A positive variance means that actual costs have increased, and a negative variance means that actual costs have declined.

The standard price is the price that engineers believe the company should pay for an item, given a certain quality level, purchasing quantity, and speed of delivery. Thus, the variance is really based on a standard price that was the collective opinion of several employees based on a number of assumptions that may no longer match a company's current purchasing situation.

EXAMPLE

During the development of its annual budget, the engineers and purchasing staff of Quest Adventure Gear decide that the standard cost of a green widget should be set at $5.00, which is based on a purchasing volume of 10,000 units for the upcoming year. During the subsequent year, Quest only buys 8,000 units, and so cannot take advantage of purchasing discounts, and ends up paying $5.50 per widget. This creates a purchase price variance of $0.50 per widget, and a variance of $4,000 for all of the 8,000 widgets that Quest purchased.

There are a number of possible causes of a purchase price variance. For example:

- *Layering issue*. The actual cost may have been taken from an inventory layering system, such as a first-in first-out system, where the actual cost may vary from the current market price by a substantial margin.
- *Materials shortage*. There is an industry shortage of a commodity item, which is driving up the cost.
- *New supplier*. The company has changed suppliers for any number of reasons, resulting in a new cost structure that is not reflected in the budget.
- *Rush basis*. The company incurred excessive shipping charges to obtain materials on short notice from suppliers.
- *Volume assumption*. The budgeted cost of an item was derived based on a different purchasing volume than the amount at which the company now buys.

In what level of detail should one investigate a purchase price variance? The key issue is not to waste time on variances so small that managers are not going to take action. Instead, report on the 20 percent of issues that usually cause about 80 percent of the variance. The following sample report format should contain sufficient information for a manager to engage in corrective action.

Sample Purchase Price Variance Report

Item No.	Item Description	Purchase Price	Standard Price	Variance	Reason
123A	Widget trim	$8.00	$7.00	-$1.00	Ordered below standard quantity
234B	Widget blue color	4.25	3.00	-1.25	Ordered odd size lot
567Q	Widget arm	20.00	16.50	-3.50	Incorrect specifications
891D	Widget case	15.00	12.00	-3.00	Ordered on short notice
112R	Widget housing	130.00	115.00	-15.00	Ordered below standard quantity
150F	Widget lens port	82.15	78.00	-4.15	Supplier price increase
115G	Widget trigger	4.25	3.75	-0.50	Ordered on short notice
227V	Widget base	37.50	32.00	-5.50	Supplier price increase
772J	Widget packing crate	24.00	21.50	-2.50	Ordered odd lot size

Material Yield Variance

The material yield variance is the difference between the actual amount of material used and the standard amount expected to be used, multiplied by the standard cost of the materials. The formula is:

(Actual unit usage - Standard unit usage) × Standard cost per unit

= Material yield variance

An unfavorable variance means that the unit usage was greater than anticipated.

The standard unit usage is developed by the engineering staff, and is based on expected scrap rates in a production process, the quality of raw materials, losses during equipment setup, and related factors.

EXAMPLE

The engineering staff of Quest Adventure Gear estimates that eight ounces of rubber will be required to produce a green widget. During the most recent month, the production process used 315,000 ounces of rubber to create 35,000 green widgets, which is 9 ounces per product. Each ounce of rubber has a standard cost of $0.50. Its material yield variance for the month is:

(315,000 Actual unit usage - 280,000 Standard unit usage) × $0.50 Standard cost/unit

= $17,500 Material yield variance

There are a number of possible causes of a material yield variance. For example:

- *Scrap.* Unusual amounts of scrap may be generated by changes in machine setups, or because changes in acceptable tolerance levels are altering the amount of scrap produced. A change in the pattern of quality inspections can also alter the amount of scrap.
- *Material quality.* If the material quality level changes, this can alter the amount of quality rejections. If an entirely different material is substituted, this can also alter the amount of rejections.
- *Spoilage.* The amount of spoilage may change in concert with alterations in inventory handling and storage.

It can be extremely difficult to ascertain the reasons for a material yield variance, since it is caused by operational issues in the production area, rather than something easily searchable in the accounting database. Consequently, it rarely makes sense to investigate anything but the largest variances. If you choose to do so, the report format is similar to the purchase price variance report just described, except that it is in units, rather than dollars. A sample report follows.

Sample Material Yield Variance Report

Item No.	Item Description	Actual Usage	Standard Usage	Variance	Reason
123A	Widget trim	540	500	-40	Incorrect standard
234B	Widget blue color	200	150	-50	Materials too old; disposed of
567Q	Widget arm	1,500	1,100	-400	Supplier shipped short
891D	Widget case	800	-720	-80	Incorrect machine setup
112R	Widget housing	150	0	-150	Item declared obsolete
150F	Widget lens port	300	100	-200	Receipt counting error
115G	Widget trigger	280	225	-55	Scrap due to machinist error
227V	Widget base	460	300	-160	Item declared obsolete
772J	Widget packing crate	950	800	-150	Damaged in transit

Labor Rate Variance

The labor rate variance is the difference between the actual labor rate paid and the standard rate, multiplied by the number of actual hours worked. The formula is:

(Actual rate - Standard rate) × Actual hours worked = Labor rate variance

An unfavorable variance means that the cost of labor was more expensive than anticipated.

The standard labor rate is developed by the human resources and industrial engineering employees, and is based on such factors as the expected mix of pay levels among the production staff, the amount of overtime likely to be incurred, the amount of new hiring at different pay rates, the number of promotions into higher pay levels, and the outcome of contract negotiations with any unions representing the production staff.

EXAMPLE

The human resources manager of Quest Adventure Gear estimates that the average labor rate for the coming year for Quest's production staff will be $25/hour. This estimate is based on a standard mix of personnel at different pay rates, as well as a reasonable proportion of overtime hours worked.

During the first month of the new year, Quest has difficulty hiring a sufficient number of new employees, and so must have its higher-paid existing staff work overtime to complete a number of jobs. The result is an actual labor rate of $30/hour. Quest's production staff worked 10,000 hours during the month. Its labor rate variance for the month is:

($30/hour Actual rate - $25/hour Standard rate) × 10,000 hours = $50,000 Labor rate variance

There are a number of possible causes of a labor rate variance. For example:

- *Incorrect standards.* The labor standard may not reflect recent changes in the rates paid to employees (which tend to occur in bulk for all staff).
- *Pay premiums.* The actual amounts paid may include extra payments for shift differentials or overtime.
- *Staffing variances.* A labor standard may assume that a certain job classification will perform a designated task, when in fact a different position with a different pay rate may be performing the work.

Labor Efficiency Variance

The labor efficiency variance is the difference between the actual labor hours used to produce an item and the standard amount that should have been used, multiplied by the standard labor rate. The formula is:

(Actual hours - Standard hours) × Standard rate = Labor efficiency variance

An unfavorable variance means that labor efficiency has worsened, and a favorable variance means that labor efficiency has increased.

The standard number of hours represents the best estimate of the industrial engineers regarding the optimal speed at which the production staff can manufacture goods. This figure can vary considerably, based on assumptions regarding the setup time of a production run, the availability of materials and machine capacity, employee skill levels, the duration of a production run, and other factors. Thus, the multitude of variables involved makes it especially difficult to create a budget that you can meaningfully compare to actual results.

EXAMPLE

During the development of its annual budget, the industrial engineers of Quest Adventure Gear decide that the standard amount of time required to produce a green widget should be 30 minutes, which is based on certain assumptions about the efficiency of Quest's production staff, the availability of materials, capacity availability, and so forth. During the month, widget materials were in short supply, so Quest had to pay production staff even when there was no material to work on, resulting in an average production time per unit of 45 minutes. The company produced 1,000 widgets during the month. The standard cost per labor hour is $20, so the calculation of its labor efficiency variance is:

(750 Actual hours - 500 Standard hours) × $20 Standard rate

= $5,000 Labor efficiency variance

There are a number of possible causes of a labor efficiency variance. For example:

- *Instructions.* The employees may not have received written work instructions.
- *Mix.* The standard assumes a certain mix of employees involving different skill levels, which does not match the actual staffing.
- *Training.* The standard may be based on an assumption of a minimum amount of training that employees have not received.
- *Work station configuration.* A work center may have been reconfigured since the standard was created, so the budget is now incorrect.

Variable Overhead Spending Variance

The variable overhead spending variance is the difference between the actual and budgeted rates of spending on variable overhead. The formula is:

Actual hours worked × (Actual overhead rate - Standard overhead rate)

= Variable overhead spending variance

A favorable variance means that the actual variable overhead expenses incurred per labor hour were less than expected.

The variable overhead spending variance is a compilation of production expense information submitted by the production department, and the projected labor hours to be worked, as estimated by the industrial engineering and production scheduling staffs, based on historical and projected efficiency and equipment capacity levels.

EXAMPLE

The cost accounting staff of Quest Adventure Gear calculates, based on historical and projected cost patterns, that the company should experience a variable overhead rate of $20 per labor hour worked, and builds this figure into the budget. In April, the actual variable overhead rate turns out to be $22 per labor hour. During that month, production employees work 18,000 hours. The variable overhead spending variance is:

18,000 Actual hours worked × ($22 Actual variable overhead rate - $20 Standard overhead rate)

= $36,000 Variable overhead spending variance

There are a number of possible causes of a variable overhead spending variance. For example:

- *Account misclassification.* The variable overhead category includes a number of accounts, some of which may have been incorrectly classified and so do not appear as part of variable overhead (or vice versa).
- *Outsourcing.* Some activities that had been sourced in-house have now been shifted to a supplier, or vice versa.
- *Supplier pricing.* Suppliers have changed their prices, which have not been reflected in the budget.

Variable Overhead Efficiency Variance

The variable overhead efficiency variance is the difference between the actual and budgeted hours worked, which are then applied to the standard variable overhead rate per hour. The formula is:

$$\text{Standard overhead rate} \times (\text{Actual hours - Standard hours})$$

$$= \text{Variable overhead efficiency variance}$$

A favorable variance means that the actual hours worked were less than the budgeted hours, resulting in the application of the standard overhead rate across fewer hours, resulting in less expense incurred.

The variable overhead efficiency variance is a compilation of production expense information submitted by the production department, and the projected labor hours to be worked, as estimated by the industrial engineering and production scheduling staffs, based on historical and projected efficiency and equipment capacity levels.

EXAMPLE

The cost accounting staff of Quest Adventure Gear calculates, based on historical and projected labor patterns, that the company's production staff should work 20,000 hours per month and incur $400,000 of variable overhead costs per month, so it establishes a variable overhead rate of $20 per hour. In May, Quest installs a new materials handling system that significantly improves production efficiency and drops the hours worked during the month to 19,000. The variable overhead efficiency variance is:

$$\$20 \text{ Standard overhead rate/hour} \times (19,000 \text{ Hours worked - 20,000 Standard hours})$$

$$= \$20,000 \text{ Variable overhead efficiency variance}$$

Fixed Overhead Spending Variance

The fixed overhead spending variance is the difference between the actual fixed overhead expense incurred and the budgeted fixed overhead expense. An unfavorable variance means that actual overhead expenditures were greater than planned. The formula is:

Actual fixed overhead - Budgeted fixed overhead = Fixed overhead spending variance

The amount of expense related to fixed overhead should (as the name implies) be relatively fixed, and so the fixed overhead spending variance should not theoretically vary much from the budget. However, if the manufacturing process reaches a step cost trigger point, where a whole new expense must be incurred, then this can cause a significant unfavorable variance. Also, there may be some seasonality in fixed overhead expenditures, which may cause both favorable and unfavorable variances in individual months of a year, but which cancel each other out over the full year.

EXAMPLE

The production manager of Quest Adventure Gear estimates that the fixed overhead should be $700,000 during the upcoming year. However, since a production manager left the company and was not replaced for several months, actual expenses were lower than expected, at $672,000. This created the following favorable fixed overhead spending variance:

($672,000 Actual fixed overhead - $700,000 Budgeted fixed overhead)

= $(28,000) Fixed overhead spending variance

There are a number of possible causes of a fixed overhead spending variance. For example:

- *Account misclassification.* The fixed overhead category includes a number of accounts, some of which may have been incorrectly classified and so do not appear as part of fixed overhead (or vice versa).
- *Outsourcing.* Some activities that had been sourced in-house have now been shifted to a supplier, or vice versa.
- *Supplier pricing.* Suppliers have changed their prices, which have not been reflected in the budget.

Problems with Variance Analysis

There are several problems with the variances described in this chapter, which are:

- *The use of standards.* A central issue is the use of standards (i.e., the budget) as the basis for calculating variances. What is the motivation for creating a standard? Standard creation can be a political process where the amount agreed upon is designed to make a department look good, rather than setting a target that will improve the company. If standards are politically created, variance analysis becomes useless from the perspective of controlling the company.
- *Feedback loop.* The accounting department does not calculate variances between actual and budgeted results until after it has closed the books and created financial statements, so there is a gap of potentially an entire month from when a variance arises and when it is reported to management. A faster feedback loop would be to eliminate variance reporting and instead create a reporting process that provides for feedback within moments of the occurrence of a triggering event.
- *Information drill down.* Many of the issues that cause variances are not stored within the accounting database. For example, the reason for excessive material usage may be a machine setup error, while excessive labor usage may be caused by the use of an excessive amount of employee overtime. In neither case will the accounting staff discover these issues by examining their transactional data. Thus, a variance report only highlights the general areas within which problems occurred, but does not necessarily tell anyone the nature of the underlying problems.

The preceding issues do not always keep accounting managers from calculating complete sets of variances for management consumption, but they bring up the question of whether the work required to calculate variances is a good use of staff time.

Which Variances to Report

A lot of variances have been described in this chapter. Should they all be reported to management? Not necessarily. If management agrees with a reduced reporting structure, one can report on just those variances over which management has some ability to reduce costs, and which contain sufficiently large variances to be worth reporting on. The following table provides commentary on the characteristics of the variances.

Characteristics of Variances

Name of Variance	Commentary
Materials	
Purchase price variance	Material costs are controllable to some extent, and comprise a large part of the cost of goods sold; possibly the most important variance
Material yield variance	Can contain large potential cost reductions driven by quality issues, production layouts, and process flow; a good opportunity for cost reductions
Labor	
Labor rate variance	Labor rates are difficult to change; do not track unless you can shift work into lower pay grades
Labor efficiency variance	Can drive contrary behavior in favor of long production runs, when less labor efficiency in a just-in-time environment results in greater overall cost reductions; not recommended
Overhead	
Variable overhead spending variance	Caused by changes in the actual costs in the overhead cost pool, and so should be reviewed
Variable overhead efficiency variance	Caused by a change in the basis of allocation, which has no real impact on underlying costs; not recommended
Fixed overhead spending variance	Since fixed overhead costs should not vary much, a variance here is worth careful review; however, most components of fixed overhead are long-term costs that cannot be easily changed in the short term
Revenue	
Selling price variance	Caused by a change in the product price, which is under management control, and therefore should be brought to their attention
Sales volume variance	Caused by a change in the unit volume sold, which is not under direct management control, though this can be impacted by altering the product price

The preceding table shows that the variances most worthy of management's attention are the purchase price variance, variable overhead spending variance, fixed overhead spending variance, and selling price variance. Reducing the number of reported variances is well worth one's time, since reporting the entire suite of variances calls for a great deal of investigative time to track down variance causes and then configure the information into a report suitable for management consumption.

How to Report Variances

A variance is a simple number, such as an unfavorable purchase price variance of $15,000. It tells management very little, since there is not enough information on which to base any corrective action. Consequently, one should dig down into the underlying data to determine the actual causes of each variance, and then report the causes. The following table is an example of the level of variance detail to report to management.

Sample Variance Report

Variance Item	Amount*	Variance Cause
Purchase Price		
Order quantity	$500	Bought wrappers at half usual volume, and lost purchase discount
Substitute material	1,500	Used more expensive PVC piping; out of stock on regular item
Variable Overhead		
Rush order	300	Overnight charge to bring in grease for bearings
Utility surcharge	2,400	Charged extra for power usage during peak hours
Fixed Overhead		
Property taxes	3,000	Tax levy increased by 8%
Rent override	8,000	Landlord charge for proportional share of full-year expenses
Selling Price		
Marketing discounts	4,000	Customers took discounts for advertising pass-through
Sales returns	11,000	450 units returned with broken spring assembly

* Note: All amounts are unfavorable variances

The preceding table can be expanded to include the names of the managers responsible for correcting each item noted.

Ratio Analysis

Ratio analysis is an excellent tool for evaluating a number of issues with a business, such as its liquidity, efficiency of operations, and profitability. This analysis requires the comparison of various line items in a firm's financial statements, and is especially useful when used in the following two ways:

- *Trend line*. Calculate each ratio over many consecutive periods, to see if there is a trend in the calculated information. The trend can indicate financial difficulties that would not otherwise be apparent if ratios were being examined for just a single period.

- *Industry comparison*. Calculate the same ratios from the financial statements of competitors, and compare the results across all of the companies reviewed. Since these businesses probably operate with similar investments in fixed assets and have similar capital structures, the outcome of this analysis should be roughly similar ratios. When this is not the case, it can indicate a potential issue or an opportunity to generate outsized profits.

There are dozens of ratios that could be used for analysis purposes, but only a small core group is needed to gain a reasonable understanding of a business. These ratios are:

- *Current ratio*. Compares current assets to current liabilities, to see if an entity has sufficient cash available to pay for its immediate obligations.
- *Days sales outstanding*. Compares receivables to annual revenue, to see if a business is able to effectively issue credit to its customers and be paid back within a reasonable period of time.
- *Debt to equity ratio*. Compares debt to equity, to see if a firm has an excessive debt load that it may not be able to pay back.
- *Dividend payout ratio*. Compares dividends paid to net earnings, to determine the proportion of earnings that is paid to investors. If the percentage is low, there may be room for dividend payments to increase, depending on the need for cash within the business.
- *Gross profit ratio*. Compares the proportion of earnings from the sale of goods or services to net sales. A decline in this percentage may indicate pricing pressure on the core operations of a business.
- *Inventory turnover*. Compares the cost of goods sold to ending inventory, to estimate how frequently inventory is sold off and replaced over the course of a year. A low turnover figure indicates that a business has an excessive investment in inventory, and so is at risk of having obsolete inventory.
- *Net profit ratio*. Compares net profits to sales. A low proportion can indicate the existence of pricing pressure from competitors or a bloated cost structure.
- *Return on assets*. Compares net profits to total assets. A low return on assets indicates that too many assets are needed to generate a return.

For more information about ratios, see the author's *Business Ratios Guidebook*.

Open Book Management

Open book management is the practice of giving all employees access to an organization's financial and operational information. Doing so gives employees a greater sense of involvement in the business, so that they are more inclined to support the entity's performance targets. This approach only works if there is a significant amount of employee training, so that they fully understand the information they are being given.

Open book training is especially effective when it is combined with a gain-sharing program, so that employees benefit from their participation in the operations of the firm.

Open book management is an excellent way to involve employees in the ongoing monitoring of a business, since they can see where there are failings, as well as opportunities for improvement. Their feedback can then be used to improve the business, for which the results appear in the reports that are then shared with the employees.

This approach works best when employees are given training in how to interpret financial information, which can spark discussions about how to improve company operations, as well as how to avert layoffs during periods of economic decline.

The Tension between Employee Freedom and Operational Control

Employees tend to work best when they have a significant amount of freedom to pursue a variety of options and make their own decisions on behalf of the organization. However, this can present a problem for managers who are trying to manage to a deadline and a budget, which requires them to regulate employee behavior to some extent. This regulation typically involves the ongoing review and approval of employee activities.

A good way to balance the two is to set up clearly-defined guidelines for employees to follow, and then let them roam at will, as long as they align their decisions with the guidelines. Those guidelines should cover the following:

- The purpose of the business – its reason for existence.
- The priorities of the business – the key goals that it wants to achieve.
- The principles of the business – the most essential guidelines for action, as well as limits on behavior.

Knowing the purpose of a business motivates employees, while a detailed understanding of priorities and principles gives employees the detailed knowledge upon which to base their decisions.

These guidelines should give employees a full understanding of the manner in which they are helping the business. This approach means that managers are still allowed to provide input into decisions, but employees can still proceed with their activities without any approval mechanism. This can involve the retraining of managers about ceding direct authority to their direct reports. Also, policies related to employees should focus on the development of their abilities, rather than monitoring their behavior.

This approach entails giving employees a significant amount of responsibility, so the recruitment process needs to be highly selective. Further, compensation levels should be high, to reflect the increased amount of responsibility that employees are taking on.

The guidelines that a company devises should be monitored and updated constantly, to reflect ongoing changes in the business. Also, the firm must continue to immerse employees in the details of its plans so that they are constantly considering whether their actions are compliant with them. This is a particular concern when a company is growing rapidly, so that a large proportion of the staff is new.

Summary

A great many variance calculations were discussed in this chapter. Just because they have been presented here does not mean that it is necessary to create an elaborate reporting structure that contains all of them. Consider instead that management usually does not have time to read such a report, much less act on it. A more effective variance report is one that states just a few major variances, but with their causes readily understandable and which can be acted upon at once. A really effective manager does not just rely on variance reports, but is instead constantly touring the workplace and making inquiries to see if there are any new issues requiring immediate resolution. This latter approach can be such an effective control that variances never have a chance to get big enough to appear on a variance report.

Chapter 10
Employee Recruiting and Appraisal

Introduction

A major organizational imperative for the manager is to recruit people who closely match the requirements of the firm, and to give them feedback in the form of constructive performance appraisals. Without strong skills in both areas, a manager is more likely to find herself working with a dysfunctional or underqualified group that never achieves its potential. In this chapter, we cover a number of concepts and techniques for spotting the right job candidates and discuss how to have a useful performance appraisal discussion with an employee.

Recruitment Principles

What are the underlying principles that form the basis of a successful recruitment program? The following bullet points note the need for an aggressive system designed to root out qualified prospects on an ongoing basis:

- *Precisely define the need.* Do not recruit based on a boilerplate job description, since this will attract a broad range of applicants who must be sorted through. Instead, revise the published job description to state not only the work involved, but also the work environment in which a candidate will be placed, and the type of personality that will work best in that environment. Doing so heightens the interest of those people most likely to mesh well with the company's culture; less-qualified candidates are less likely to apply when they can see that their applications will not be considered.
- *Develop a pipeline of prospects.* When there is no immediate need to hire an employee, there is a tendency to not maintain a network of prospective recruits. This can be a problem when a specific skill set is needed, and the company is then faced with reviewing a large number of potential candidates, about whom it knows nothing. By maintaining contact with a group of qualified individuals with whom the management team is familiar, it is possible to assemble and replenish a high-quality group of candidates in short order.
- *Require networking by all managers.* The networking task should not be limited to the top management team. Instead, force the entire management group to maintain a list of potential candidates, which are regularly discussed amongst the team.
- *Offer recruitment bonuses to staff.* Spread the recruitment networking mission throughout the company by offering recruitment bonuses to employees. These bonuses are paid if an employee presents the company with a qualified candidate who is then hired and stays with the company beyond a minimum

review period, such as 90 days. This approach works well, since employees have their own networks, and so can spread the company's number of total contacts among a large population of potential candidates.

- *Manage the exit process.* When qualified employees leave the company, be sure to manage the exit process carefully, to maintain lines of communication with these employees, as well as to make it clear that there may be positions available for them if they choose to return. If there are a large number of former employees who can be drawn upon as job candidates, consider setting up an alumni network; doing so yields a regularly-scheduled series of events and communications designed to maintain strong ties to the company.
- *Maintain a corporate presence.* If potential candidates appear to cluster around certain events or activities, have the company maintain a presence in these areas. This may involve event sponsorships, making employees available as speakers, and so forth.
- *Target top performers.* The best potential recruits are those that are already considered top-notch by their current employers. One can locate these employees by examining employee awards publicized by competitors. In more research-oriented fields, review published works and the citations of other research to determine who is being referenced the most.

Most of the preceding points focus on a proactive approach – the company is actively looking for specific individuals. This is different from the more common passive approach, where a business advertises a job opening and waits to see who applies for the position. The first approach requires more up-front effort but yields better candidates, while the latter approach requires more back-end effort to examine a multitude of resumes, and may not yield *any* outstanding candidates.

Key recruiting principles can also include what *not* to do. For example, plastering the company's needs across every job posting site on the Internet is likely to yield a deluge of applications, nearly all of which are from candidates whose qualifications are not a good match for the posted jobs. It is better to be as specific as possible in spreading the company's recruiting activities to just those markets in which the best candidates are located.

Internal Hiring

It is always worthwhile to promote from within the company, because the organization already has experience with applicants, and so has an excellent idea of whether they can fit into a new position. In addition, giving priority to internal candidates gives employees a discernible career path, and so gives them fewer reasons to leave the company in search of promotions elsewhere.

A further reason for giving preferential treatment to insiders is that moving employees into presumably more senior positions opens up the lower-level positions in which they were previously working. Lower level positions are generally easier to fill, since their job requirements are not so specific and require less experience. Also, the lower-level positions can be opened up to internal candidates, thereby allowing for a number of internal promotions.

An additional consideration is that the internal recruiting process does not involve advertising or the use of recruiters. Consequently, internal recruiting is far less expensive than external recruiting.

In some organizations, the culture is considered a key element in the strategic positioning of a business. For example, a bank may require rigorous initial training in how to deal with customers. When this is the case, hiring internally ensures that job applicants are already fully conversant in the company culture, and so require much less training than would otherwise be the case.

When corporate insiders are promoted into more senior positions, this ensures that the existing corporate culture will be enforced by them. A likely result is that key elements of the corporate culture will be passed along to the next generation of employees. Conversely, hiring outsiders into senior positions makes it more likely that the existing culture will be modified or replaced, which may interfere with the work environment.

When internal recruiting is used, the human resources staff generally delays going outside the company until all possible internal applicants have been considered. Doing so eliminates the cost of outside advertising and recruiting fees. However, if it is decided that no internal candidates have the requisite skills for an open position, the result is a lengthy delay before external candidates are considered.

Another downside to the use of internal hiring is that outsiders are rarely brought into the more senior positions in a company. This can be a problem when the corporate culture is insular, with little consideration of new ideas originating from outside the company. This problem is magnified in situations where the company is in financial straits, and needs a radical restructuring in order to stay in business.

If a company chooses to create a formal system of internal hiring, it should incorporate the following elements; doing so results in a more effective internal hiring process:

- *Career path discussions*. Formulate a range of possible career paths for each employee, and go over these options with the staff. The discussion should include the sequence of jobs that a person could follow to arrive at a senior-level position, the requirements of each successive job, and the expected time required before the next-level job should be pursued. Employees will then know which job postings to pursue, and may request that they be notified when specific jobs are made available for internal fulfillment.
- *Detailed job posting*. Employees must know as much about an open position as possible. Otherwise, they risk entering a new position for which they are poorly qualified, and in which they may fail. Also, since the company is presumably also filling the job they just left, it is not possible for someone failing in a new position to return to their old position.
- *Clear job bidding process*. Clearly define how an employee can apply for a posted job (known as *job bidding*). This means creating a standard application form, clarifying the time period during which applications are accepted, and

sending notifications to employees to inform them of the progress of their applications.

- *Universal postings.* The general policy should be that all open positions are first made available to current employees. Doing so supports the understanding that employees can take advantage of a career path within the company. Otherwise, blocking some jobs from an internal posting can result in the opposite impression, and a higher likelihood that employees will seek advancement elsewhere.
- *Time period.* Always keep an internal job posting open internally long enough for all employees to become aware of and apply for the position. If there is an immediate need to fill a position, it may be possible to compress this time period by proactively making the position known to anyone possessing the correct qualifications.

A potential concern is how employees are handled if the decision is made not to promote them into an available position. If handled in an insensitive manner, employees may leave the company entirely, taking their institutional knowledge with them.

External Hiring

The management team may conclude that there are no qualified candidates within the company for a position, and decide to recruit outside. This reaction usually comes from several favorable views of external hiring, which include:

- *New concepts.* A hidebound organization can profit from fresh viewpoints on how to manage the business, which can be provided by outsiders.
- *Competitor knowledge.* A person may be hired from a competitor, thereby bringing information about the competitor's processes, strategies, and products into the company.

These viewpoints have merit, especially when a company is in financial difficulty and needs a radical new approach that cannot be provided by the in-house staff. However, there are also a number of issues with external hiring, which include the following:

- *Failure rate.* The failure rate for employees hired from the outside is usually much higher than for internal hiring candidates. This is because companies have a more difficult time discerning the ability of an outsider to fit into a specific position, given the short duration of the hiring process.
- *Cost.* The company must pay for advertising and recruiter fees to obtain access to outside candidates.
- *Time.* It can take a substantial amount of time to locate a qualified outside candidate for a position. Since there is also a higher failure rate for this type of hire, the result can be multiple recruiting rounds that can take a long time to result in a long-term hire. In addition, it takes longer for an outsider to fully assimilate the corporate culture, so that they do not become effective until a number of months have passed.

- *Morale.* If internal employees feel that they have been passed over in favor of an outsider, their morale may decline, they may leave the company, or they may work against the newly-hired person.

If the stated issues with external hiring do not overcome management's wishes to search outside of the company, the discussions in the following sections can provide some direction regarding different areas in which recruiting can be conducted.

General Hiring Principles

Before delving into the many aspects of hiring, it is useful to discuss several principles that should guide the management team during the hiring process, which are noted in the following sub-sections.

The Hiring Priority

The hiring process should have a high priority with the management team. It is all too common for the multitude of daily decisions to sidetrack hiring activities, delaying key hires for weeks or even months. An average candidate for a position may not have other job offers, and so is willing to tolerate these delays. However, the best candidates are available for only a short period of time, after which they can be expected to take the best offer they have been given. In effect, hiring delays automatically remove the best candidates from consideration.

This means that the entire management team *must* give top priority to the hiring process. No matter how essential all other activities may appear to be, the organization must bring in the best possible candidates to ensure its long-term prosperity. If a particular manager is continually delaying hiring decisions, it may be necessary to replace this person with someone who has a clearer understanding of workplace priorities.

Respect for Candidates

The best candidates will only accept job offers if they feel that they have been dealt with in an appropriate manner during the hiring process. For example, the hiring manager has thoroughly read each candidate's resume prior to an interview, and knows the exact requirements of the applicable position; this gives candidates a clear impression that interviews are important to the manager. Also, the manager keeps a recruit fully informed about where he or she is in the hiring process, so there is never any concern about being stuck in limbo. Further, the manager evinces interest in the candidate during interviews, asking penetrating questions that are relevant to the position in question, while fully answering any questions posed by the candidate. The net effect of this behavior is that candidates feel that they have been treated fairly, and so are more likely to accept a job offer.

If a manager does *not* engage in this type of behavior, the best candidates will likely be driven away, leaving the company with a reduced pool of lesser candidates who are willing to tolerate less-than-optimal behavior from hiring managers.

Resume Analysis

At a smaller business, there is nothing wrong with a manual review of each incoming person's resume to see if it might meet the criteria for a job. But what about in a larger organization where thousands of resumes may be received each day? These organizations scan incoming resumes into resume management software. The software searches the scanned text for key words, work history, education, and years of experience. The system then ranks resumes based on the job criteria, and presents to users a list of the most likely candidates. Those resumes that are clearly unsuitable may never be seen by a human resources person.

Once the automated analysis (if any) is complete, the next step is to examine the remaining resumes by hand. Since some resumes are professionally prepared, it can be difficult to ascertain from the information presented whether someone is the genuine article, or has stitched together a sketchy background into a polished presentation. Here are some techniques used to pluck the better resumes from the pile:

- *Cover letter*. If an applicant spends the time to craft a cover letter that is specifically targeted at the requirements posted for a job, this indicates considerable interest in the company. The absence of a cover letter shows that someone is simply bulk e-mailing information to every possible employer.
- *Employment gaps*. An unexplained gap in the chronology of jobs is a major indicator of a problem. Applicants may try to hide these gaps by extending the work periods listed for jobs before and after these gaps, or by only reporting employment by year, not by month and year. However, if someone was unemployed for a period of time, there may be a good reason for it.
- *Flat growth*. If there is no trend line of continuing career advancement, there is probably a good reason for it. A better resume indicates continuing advancements in responsibility and job title. However, this may not be a valid indicator of poor performance for technical or creative positions, where someone may be quite happy in a particular role and wants to remain in it.
- *Formatting and typos*. If a resume is poorly formatted, it reveals either inadequate knowledge of the word processing software or a lack of professionalism. Even a small number of typographical errors leave the impression that someone does not care enough to proofread their resume.
- *Job bouncing*. If a candidate has continually bounced from job to job after short stays at each one, look out. This can indicate that the person is unable to fit in, or that multiple employers have encouraged them to move on for some reason.
- *Job titles*. Read the description for a job to see if it matches the associated job title. For example, someone with a company controller title might actually have the responsibilities of a bookkeeper. Also, delve into the details of a vaguely-worded, non-standard job title to see if the title is overblown.
- *Passive associations*. When applicants are not actually responsible for an activity or an outcome, they may insert words that imply a passive association with these items. For example, a low-level clerical type may have

"participated in" a major project, but only to the extent of buying coffee for the rest of the project team.

- *Word count.* Someone fabricating portions of their background is more likely to provide a relatively skimpy amount of information. Conversely, if an applicant has overloaded a resume with lots of detail, it is more likely that the content is correct.
- *Letters of recommendation.* If a letter of recommendation comes from an employer that is no longer in business, or if the writer of the letter cannot be reached, discount the letter entirely; the recommending person and the related organization may be a fabrication.

Thus far, we have discussed issues to look for that will result in resumes being eliminated from consideration. What about issues that allow the reviewing person to locate top-quality candidates? The following sequence of activities might help:

1. *Match to key requirements.* Decide in advance which aspects of a job description *must* be fulfilled by an applicant, and screen specifically for these items. It is best to keep the list of these gateway requirements as refined and well-considered as possible. For example, an audit firm may decide that the only "hard" requirement for a job applicant is a degree in accounting. This should result in a modest number of resumes that have cleared the first hurdle.
2. *Match to broader requirements.* Compare the remaining resumes to the other requirements of the position that are considered important, but not critical. There may be no resume that meets every requirement, but several are likely to meet a mix of the requirements. If no resumes are left after completing this step, the position requirements may be too harsh.
3. *Enumerate holes.* The initial resume review may reveal that the information supplied appears to approximately match the job requirements, but there are some gaps in the supplied information for which additional information should be obtained. Document these resume holes.
4. *Screen by phone or video.* Contact applicants by phone or videoconference in order to answer the questions documented in the last step. This step can be expanded into a full-blown interview. An alternative is a two-step process; if the answers supplied to questions documented in the last step are answered in a satisfactory manner, continue with a more comprehensive interview during the same contact. For the first step, a five-minute call may be sufficient. For a full phone interview, the duration may be closer to 30 minutes.
5. *Invite to interview.* The preceding steps should have refined the list of possible candidates to a manageable number. Invite this group to come in for interviews. If these steps result in an excessively small number of interview candidates, consider inviting a few of the people whose resumes did not quite measure up to the job requirements; sometimes, a valid candidate will stand out from this group.

A concern when using videoconferencing for interviews is that the interviewer cannot see the body language of the candidate, so a reduced amount of information is collected.

Conducting the Interview

The most important part of the hiring process is the interview. When conducted properly, it can provide deep insights into the motivations of a candidate, while also presenting an opportunity to sell the company to the best candidates. In the following sub-sections, we explore ways to improve a candidate's initial impressions of the organization, which interview questions are the most effective, how much the interviewer should say, and several related topics.

Initial Interview Impressions

A candidate is evaluating a company from the moment he walks through the door. To convey the best impression, make sure the receptionist knows the person's name and ensures that the person is comfortably seated with an offer of a drink. Consider installing a welcome board in the reception area, and post the person's name on it. Also, do not make the person wait; come out immediately and personally escort the candidate to an interviewing area. If there will be a delay, then introduce yourself at once and explain the reason for the delay.

A good way to begin an interview is to thank the candidate for coming, and see that he is comfortable. If possible, both parties should sit near a side table or in a conference room; avoid sitting around the standard office desk, since it builds a barrier between the two parties and thereby introduces an excessive level of formality. Also, engage in non-intrusive small talk for a few minutes. Once the candidate appears to be settled and comfortable, the main part of the interviewing process can begin, which is a series of questions posed by the interviewer.

Interview Questions

A good way to structure an interview is to work through each of the prior jobs listed on a candidate's resume, with most of the attention concentrated on the last decade of work. Address the following topics:

- *Work dates*. All time periods should be accounted for. If there is a date range on a resume that is not linked to a specific period of employment, inquire into the details. If date ranges are only given in years (not in month/year format), a candidate may be attempting to mask periods of non-employment.
- *Reasons for job changes*. Understand why the person switched employers at each point in her career. A consistent pattern may emerge, such as conflicts with supervisors, being unable to tolerate adversity, or being bored with the current position. A "deep dive" into these reasons can uncover the underlying career motivations that drive a candidate. If a person claims to have been part of a large layoff, inquire into the size of the layoff; if it was quite small, the reason for the layoff may have been performance-based. If there were

multiple rounds of layoffs, ask how many rounds the person survived before being let go; a late-round lay off indicates that the former employer considered the person to be quite valuable.

- *Responsibilities.* Understand the types and number of positions that reported to the candidate, and to whom she reported. It may be necessary to dig deep in this area, since some job titles are much more grandiose than a person's actual responsibilities.
- *Situation.* Have the person describe the situation at each company, including the challenges to which it was subjected and how she made changes to alleviate each concern. A crisp answer can reveal that a candidate is comfortable with spotting issues and their solutions.
- *Metrics.* A candidate should be able to describe how well she performed against performance targets. For example, a salesperson should know how well she performed against a sales target, while a department manager should remember how well expenses tracked against the annual budget.

There may also be a number of questions that do not pertain to specific jobs, but which can be used to gain a better understanding of a candidate. The questions asked should not be random. Instead, the interviewer should have constructed a standard set of questions in advance that tie back to the criteria for the job. The main point of these questions is to see if the candidate can be a good performer in the designated position.

What should be the structure of a question? The ideal question is open ended, requiring a candidate to respond with an "essay," rather than a yes/no answer. The open ended approach allows the interviewer to see how a person structures a response, reveals the person's level of knowledge, and also provides the largest amount of detailed information. In addition, this type of question may result in information being provided that the interviewer would not have thought to ask for. Here are several examples of open ended questions:

Introductory Questions:

Tell me about how your job search has been going so far.

What criteria are you using to select your next company?

Tell me how you've progressed through the ranks to reach your current position.

How have you added value to your current job?

Job Knowledge Questions

Accounting position: You state in your resume that you have consistently closed the books in one day. Please describe how you compress the closing activities.

Customer service position: When an irate customer calls in, how do you handle the situation?

Engineering position: Walk me through how you develop a new product.

Purchasing position: If you were the purchasing manager, how would you go about organizing the department to minimize the cost of purchasing?

Sales position: If you were the sales manager, what type of commission system would you use to increase sales?

Critical Incident Questions:

Accounting position: We are having a problem issuing financial statements within a few days of month-end. How would you handle that?

Customer service position: We sometimes receive calls from customers who are irate about slow delivery times. How would you handle such a call?

Engineering position: We have been experiencing some product failures on our new baby carriage product line. How would you go about investigating the reason for the failures?

Purchasing position: We are trying to shift more low-dollar purchasing over to employees with procurement cards. How would you handle the transition?

Sales position: We are thinking about opening a new sales region. How would you go about setting the commission structure for it?

Situational Questions:

You state in your resume that you increased productivity in your department by twenty percent. How did you go about doing that?

Why did you leave your last job?

What interests you about this job? How do you think you can improve it?

In what sort of work environment do you operate best? How much structure do you need in order to work at your best level?

Tell me about a situation where you had a disagreement with someone at work – how did you handle it?

Tell me about the most difficult project you have ever been assigned – how did you handle it?

What did you do in your last job to increase revenues? Reduce expenses?

Tell me about your most creative achievement in the work place.

Tell me about a time when you took action without first getting the approval of your boss?

How do you deal with mediocre or poor performers?

When you have to let someone go, how do you deal with it?

If you were to be given the job of running this department, how would you organize it?

Hypothetical Questions:

Suppose an employee comes to you with a claim of sexual harassment. How would you handle it?

Your company has decided to shut down your department. How would you inform the employees of the department?

General Questions:

Tell me about your organizational style.

How do you build consensus?

What kind of mentoring style do you have?

How do you deal with stress?

Describe your communication style with your co-workers.

How do you like to handle business meetings?

Under what circumstances would you consider relocating to a different city?

What skills do you think you should improve upon next year?

When I contact your references, I will ask them about your strengths and weaknesses. What do you expect they will say?

When I contact your references, which person do you think will give the weakest reference? Why?

To dredge up the maximum amount of information from an interview, it is useful to employ probing questions, which are questions that attempt to discover additional information after a primary question has been asked. For example:

- *Nudging probe.* A simple statement such as "And?" or "So?" is used to nudge a candidate to continue with a response.
- *Clearinghouse probe.* A follow-up question such as "Is there anything more you can tell me about what you did at that job?" is designed to uncover any residual information on a topic that has not already been revealed.

- *Informational probe*. This question is designed to extract more information when the initial answer to a question is too brief. For example, "And why do you think he responded in that way?"
- *Reflective probe*. This question is used to clarify what a candidate has just said. For example, "So you're saying that you would leave that position even if your boss were to retire?"
- *Restatement probes*. When a candidate does not initially provide an answer to a question, try again with a restated version. For example, "Let me rephrase the question. What were your views on the fraud investigation into your department?"

While conducting an interview, look for non-verbal cues from a candidate. If someone is unable to look you in the eyes or crosses his arms in a defensive gesture, it is possible that the answer they are providing is not entirely correct or false in some respect. If so, use these cues as indicators that additional questions should be inserted to probe whatever the issue may be.

A likely result of these questions is that the answers given will not yield complete information. If so, by all means ask additional questions to round out the needed response. However, do not spend a large amount of time traveling down a path of inquiry on an unrelated subject. All that does is reduce the amount of time available to complete the primary set of questions.

Interviewer Comments

Asking questions means that the interviewer should talk as little as possible – after all, the main point of the interview is to obtain information from the candidate, not the other way around. This can be difficult for a chatty interviewer, especially when aided by a candidate who realizes that the more time spent talking by the interviewer means less time responding to pointed questions. Many interviewers have a more favorable opinion of candidates who cajole them into talking; while this may be based on a deep-seated appreciation for a good listener, it is not a valid way to judge the overall worthiness of a candidate.

This does not mean that the interviewer should be tight-lipped about the company. On the contrary, an interview can be a good time to market the high points of why a person would want to work for the organization. However, it is better to shift this commentary to a point later in the interview, after the interviewer's key questions have been addressed.

A further issue when answering questions is to avoid telling the applicant exactly what the company is looking for. If this is done, the applicant merely has to construct answers that exactly match the qualifications that have just been revealed. Instead, give the applicant only the general aspects of the open position.

Towards the end of the interview, the interviewer might engage in some marketing of the company. This means highlighting the benefits of working there, the possibilities of job advancement, and so forth. However, it would be erroneous to engage in excessive flights of imagination when extolling the virtues of the company. Doing so only creates expectations in an employee that will not be met. Instead, be realistic. If the typical pace at which employees are promoted is three years, then say so. If a person is likely to be engaged in data entry work for ninety percent of the working day, then say so. If a job involves travel more than half of the time, make sure that a candidate knows about this issue. This more factual approach results in employees arriving for their first day of work with a clear idea of what to expect. Also, it means that some candidates will turn down a job offer because they realize they will not enjoy the type of work that a position requires; this is acceptable, since the company can then find candidates more willing to engage in the necessary activities.

By the end of an interview, the interviewer should have a reasonable idea of what a candidate considers to be a good work environment, what she is looking for in a new position, and how she will relate to co-workers. Also, there is a good chance that a few negative items will have been uncovered, such as a tendency to blame co-workers or hold grudges, a lack of energy, passivity (as indicated by a lack of achievements), or unrealistic expectations.

A key consideration is whether a candidate would be a good fit for the company's culture. The interviewer will need to piece together from the interview discussion whether a candidate's values, work ethic, and personal circumstances will result in a close culture fit. For example, a person who believes in the 40-hour work week will not fit in well with a hard-driving startup company. Similarly, a hard-core introvert might not fit into a company where working in teams is considered a key element of the organization's success.

Interviewing Red Flags

Certain statements made by candidates during interviews can serve as red flags that a person would not be a good employee. Look out for the following items:

- *Boss was at fault.* The person places all of the blame for her departure from the last company on her boss. The boss could indeed be awful, but it is more likely that the candidate shared the blame to some extent, and is not willing to own up to it. Expect the same behavior to be repeated if the person is hired.
- *More compensation.* The person is strictly looking for more money. This person should be considered a mercenary, who will only stay as long as it takes to obtain even more pay from another company.
- *Overwork complaints.* The person considers the work load in her previous job to have been excessive. Expect the same complaints if overtime at the company is needed on a regular basis.
- *Passiveness.* If there is no indication of substantive accomplishments, this may be someone who simply shows up for work, without displaying any aggressive behavior to improve the business.
- *Victim posture.* If the person claims to have constantly been a victim of others, she probably has a low capacity for dealing with adversity.

- *No weaknesses*. If a person admits to having no weaknesses at all, there is likely to be an issue with a lack of openness, or a denial of the need for self-improvement.
- *Multiple job switches*. If a candidate switches employers on a frequent basis, this pattern is likely to occur again, with the company being the victim the next time around.

Applicant Evaluation

All interviews have been completed. What process should be used to organize the evaluation process? Consider using the following steps:

1. *Collect interview summaries*. Contact everyone involved in the interview process, and request a copy of their notes from the interviews.
2. *Conduct review meeting*. Many managers prefer to make their own hiring decisions. We counsel against this, since it is useful to obtain alternative opinions. At a minimum, meet with the human resources person most closely associated with a specific position search to discuss findings. Better yet, meet with everyone else who interviewed the candidates.
3. *Investigate differing opinions*. If there are differing opinions about a certain aspect of any candidate, investigate further. This may mean conducting additional reference checks or even having a candidate return for additional interviews. These extra steps are mandatory when the difference of opinion is in regard to a major issue, such as the exact role of a candidate in his previous job.

What logic should be applied to the selection of the best candidate? Here are several issues to consider before delving into the selection process:

- *Objective analysis*. Focus tightly on the stated requirements of the job. Match the attributes of each candidate to those stated requirements. The finalists for a position should represent a close fit. In addition, understand in advance which of the stated requirements are the most important, and do so *before* recruiting for a position; otherwise, it is not uncommon to decide that the strongest attributes of a favored candidate are the most important requirements for a position.
- *Awareness of biases*. Each interviewer has a personal bias toward (or away from) certain characteristics. A person might favor younger, older, more athletic, or more outgoing people. Or, they tend to believe that a specific characteristic is paramount, such as having a CPA designation. It is useful to be aware of these biases, if only to understand why a certain candidate is being favored. Here are several types of biases that can intrude on a hiring decision:
  - *Halo effect*. A common problem in the evaluation of applicants is the overwhelmingly favorable reaction to just one aspect of an applicant that overshadows everything else. Perhaps an applicant is an Olympic athlete or a retired professional baseball player, or someone who is

locally or even nationally famous. If so, there is a common tendency to focus on that one dominant characteristic and downplay all other considerations. It can be difficult to step away from this situation and give a more balanced opinion of someone. Sometimes, waiting a day or two before rendering an opinion can provide more perspective on the situation.

o *Cloning effect.* A manager tends to hire those candidates who are most like him, even though the characteristics of the job for which an interview is being conducted may require someone entirely unlike the manager. For example, if the manager is an outgoing sales manager, he is more likely to hire a similarly outgoing person, even though the position for which a person is applying is a proposals clerk, which requires an introverted and detail-oriented personality.

o *Latest person interviewed.* There is a tendency to hire from among the last people interviewed, since the interviewers' memories of these people are the most current. This issue can be alleviated by keeping notes about each of the candidates.

o *First impression.* An interviewer may render a snap decision about a candidate within the first few moments of meeting the person, perhaps based on the way in which he or she shook hands, or is dressed, or based on some other characteristic that has little to do with future performance.

o *Negative emphasis.* An interviewer may more heavily weight a negative aspect of a candidate than the person's positive aspects.

o *Nonverbal bias.* An interviewer may overemphasize the impact of body language. For example, an interviewer may view negatively a person who slouches or frowns during an interview, despite being a fully-qualified candidate.

We now arrive at the actual decision process. How do we determine which candidate will be the best fit for a position? The following factors can all contribute to the decision:

- *Past performance.* If a person has been a top performer in the past, there is a good chance that this behavior will continue into the future. However, this concept should only be applied if there has been consistently excellent performance over a long period of time. Any drop off in the past few years can also be assumed to carry forward. Also, a person might have been a star performer in her last position specifically because of a unique business environment, such as having a large budget or a large support team. In order for this success to be duplicated, it may be necessary to approximate the same business environment. This issue can be explored during the interviewing process by asking how the environment in the last position contributed to his or her success.

- *Test results.* The only test that is a sure indicator of something is the drug test. All others have varying degrees of reliability. Even a simple skills test for typing accuracy may not be entirely accurate if the person taking the test was nervous when doing so. Consequently, most tests can be considered as indicators of possible outcomes, but are not necessarily to be relied upon as the overriding factor in a hiring decision.
- *Rating scale.* Consider creating a matrix in which each finalist is given a score based on the weighted key criteria for the position. The scoring scale should be sufficiently broad that some differentiation can be established between the perceived abilities of the candidates. Thus, a scoring system of zero to 10 is to be preferred over a rating that only spans one through three. The success of this method depends upon the objectivity of the people providing the scores; if one person is heavily favored, they are likely to twist the rating scale to ensure that this candidate scores the highest. A sample weighted rating scale is shown next.

Sample Candidate Rating Scale

Candidate name: Mr. Jones

Position: Collections clerk

Key Job Criteria	Weighting	Score	Extended Score
Prior experience	5	8	40
Communication skills	5	6	30
Call database skills	3	2	6
Teamwork skills	2	1	2
Total			78

Complete reliance upon a rating scale system is not always a good idea. For example, the preceding rating scale might drive someone to hire Mr. Jones, because his overall scores in the key categories are quite high. However, the scoring system also reveals an extremely low score in teamwork skills, which indicates that the candidate could be a crotchety person who might not fit in. In this case, the low weighting for teamwork skills might be worth re-evaluating.

- *Internal referrals.* Have the company's star performers interview a candidate. If these interviewers recommend that a person be hired, give these recommendations extra weight. The reason is that top-level performers are more likely to recognize kindred spirits, and so are best at identifying people with high potential.
- *Intangible factors.* Some aspects of a candidate are not easily quantified, and yet can be decisive factors in the hiring decision. If a person gives the appearance of being unusually energetic, well-rounded, level-headed, or creative, these factors might outweigh the more quantitative aspects of a job's

requirements. Intangibles can be particularly important in positions where a person has a considerable amount of latitude in how a job is performed. Conversely, intangibles are less likely to sway the hiring decision for a highly regimented position.

A final thought on candidate evaluation is how deep to drill down into the candidate pool. It is possible that the first few candidates offered a position will turn down the offer. If so, a company may find that the best remaining candidate does not have as much experience as the prior candidates, or perhaps there are concerns about character or skills. If so, offering this person a job increases the risk of failure, as well as organizational disruption. Instead, it may be better to not hire at all or to extend the job search to locate a new pool of candidates, than to hire a non-optimal candidate.

The Onboarding Concept

Onboarding is the process of helping new employees understand a firm, including how it functions, the people working within it, and their interactions. Onboarding also involves assisting new hires in gaining the confidence of the people around them and in assisting to establish their authority within the organization. More specifically, onboarding involves the following areas:

- *Learning the business.* A new hire needs to understand the business model of the organization – what it does, the nature of its customers and suppliers, and the other players in the industry. Also, a new employee should understand the company's products and services, as well as how they are delivered to customers.
- *Learning the department.* A new hire needs to fully understand the requirements of his or her job. This involves more than examining a job description. In addition, the person should understand where there are problems within the function, what initiatives are currently underway, and the direction in which management wants to see this function go.
- *Learning the people.* Each new hire needs to interact with a different set of people within (and outside of) the organization. This requires the person to recognize each individual, where they fit in the corporate hierarchy, what they do, and what sort of interaction is needed with each one.
- *Learning the politics.* The dynamics of how employees work together varies from one organization to the next. The new hire needs to understand who to approach to get work done.
- *Learning the culture.* Each organization has its own culture, which is a shared set of assumptions and values. If a new person does not understand the culture, she may soon find that she is not fitting in with her fellow employees.

The Need for Onboarding

When an organization only engages in a perfunctory level of onboarding activity, it suffers in two ways. One is that new employees take much longer to become fully effective in their jobs. The second issue is that employees are more likely to quit – and quite soon – if they do not feel as though they are fitting into their new work environment. It is difficult to quantify the delayed effectiveness of new employees, except to point out that they will be less efficient and effective for a number of months.

It is much easier to lay out a number of issues that arise from having a high rate of employee turnover. Consider the following:

- *Reduced skill level.* When a person is hired, she was presumably the best candidate for the position. Therefore, when she quits, the company must now hire the second-best candidate – which could represent a significant downgrade in talent. This issue is more pronounced, because the best performers will not tolerate a poor onboarding environment and so are more likely to leave. Less talented individuals will feel that they are lucky to have a job at all, and so are less likely to leave. In short, a business with a low-grade onboarding process will have few "A" level employees.

- *Loss of knowledge.* When there is a high level of turnover, institutional knowledge gradually leaks out of the business because it is passing through so many employees within a short period of time. Only by retaining employees for a number of years can they accumulate a full set of institutional knowledge from more senior employees.

- *Altered agendas.* Every new hire arrives on the job with a different agenda. Some want to aggressively make changes, while others are more settled and prefer the current environment. This difference in agendas is especially pronounced at the management level, where managers can impose their agendas on others. When the first choice for a senior management position quits, the second-choice person who is brought in as a replacement may have a completely different agenda and so could take the company down an entirely different path from what had been the case before.

- *Social media impact.* People who quit due to the onboarding incompetence of an employer may talk about the issue on social media. If so, the company now faces fallout from the adverse publicity, since other potential job candidates will be turned away by these comments. It is entirely possible that a number of otherwise highly qualified candidates will never apply for open positions, so the company never sees some of the choicest candidates.

- *Recruiting cost.* When an employee leaves, the employer must pay for the costs associated with the recruitment of a replacement person. This can include the cost of advertisements, commissions paid to recruiters, travel for interviews, and so forth – the total can represent a substantial part of a person's first-year compensation.

The social media impact reverses when new hires have an excellent onboarding experience. In this case, the employment brand of the business is bolstered when employees begin to post positive comments on social media about how well the onboarding process functions. This news gets out to potential job candidates, who are now more willing to apply for jobs at the company and accept its job offers.

A business that has a high-grade onboarding process gains from the experience when its employees eventually leave the firm. They will likely have experienced a high degree of career development with the company, and so will be more likely to view the organization favorably. Given this orientation, they may return to the firm at some point in the future or direct business to it. They may also send promising job candidates to the company. Thus, a quality onboarding process can generate returns even after employees have moved on in their careers.

See the author's *Employee Onboarding* course for more information about how to create a world-class onboarding process.

The Performance Appraisal

A performance appraisal is the process used to evaluate an employee's on-the-job performance, which tells an employee how well he is performing against expectations. This is a process, not just a meeting. The process leading up to the meeting involves collecting information about how the employee has performed against a set of predetermined goals and determining how to structure the meeting. During the meeting, the manager and employee discuss this prior performance against goals, and then address future plans. Future plans involve setting new goals for the employee, which may address current performance issues, as well as strengthening the employee's skills in order to enhance his or her career. The appraisal meeting concludes with documentation of the agreements reached during the meeting, which is signed off on by both parties.

Benefits of the Performance Appraisal

There are several good reasons for engaging in performance appraisals. In general, the appraisal process is used to form a structure for the relationship with one's employees. When managers know they must deliver a performance appraisal, they will spend more time observing what is happening in their departments and distilling these observations down into a succinct document. The result is the following benefits:

- *Concentrated focus.* When written properly, a performance appraisal concentrates the attention of an employee on a relatively small number of negative issues that need to be corrected, as well as a small number of behaviors and actions taken that are positive. By narrowing the focus of the discussion, the employee's attention is directed toward key items and away from minor issues that are of little consequence. For example, if a collections person has a remarkable ability to see the viewpoint of late-paying customers, this should be highlighted as being a valuable contribution to the company, while a few minor violations of the company dress code can be downplayed or ignored entirely. In short, a good performance appraisal allows an employee to prioritize actions in the direction of those issues that will really make a difference.

- *Goals discussion.* A formal meeting is a good place in which to discuss future goals, because goals need to be addressed in a lengthy conversation that touches upon available resources, the employee's existing skill set, and how the goals interact (or interfere) with each other. This type of conversation is not possible in the brief daily interactions that a manager has with his staff.
- *Legal protection.* A well-documented performance appraisal can protect a company from a legal action brought by a disgruntled or terminated employee, since it provides evidence for any actions taken. Further, an employee who has been through the performance appraisal process and is then terminated is less likely to be surprised by the termination, since he was thoroughly advised about performance issues during the appraisal meeting.
- *Personal development.* A performance appraisal is a good place in which to discuss exactly which types of training and experiences will result in a more qualified employee, which can then be used to advance in his or her career.
- *Basis for promotion.* When deciding whether to promote someone, the manager needs to assemble information about the person's skills and behavior patterns, as well as the opinions of other people who have worked with the individual. All of this information can be found in the documentation used to create a performance appraisal.
- *Workforce assessment.* When performance appraisals are completed for all employees, the management team can assess the overall strength of the organization's workforce, noting those on both sides of the performance bell curve. This information can be used for targeted training and the selection of new hires.

A final comment about the benefits of a performance appraisal is that employees are more likely to believe what their manager is saying, because she has been observing and analyzing their performance over the past year, and so is in the best position to make cogent statements about their performance.

Issues with Performance Appraisals

Despite the positive issues just noted, performance appraisals have been castigated in the business press for a number of years. There are several reasons for the negative publicity, which are:

- *Data dump.* A full year of feedback is delivered to the employee in massive load, which can be quite a lot to take in. Also, because managers are called upon to collate and summarize information for an entire year, and on a task that most of them find distasteful, the result may be review documents that are hurriedly written and which are based less on well-researched facts than on hearsay or general impressions.

- *Categories of feedback.* The typical performance appraisal uses a standardized form, in which the manager must write comments pertaining to specific categories, such as attention to detail or leadership capability. These categories may have little to do with how a person is performing in his current position, and so provides no meaningful feedback. This is a particular concern in a small startup company, where each employee may be responsible for many areas, which cannot be easily reviewed within a standardized form.

- *Numerical scoring.* Managers routinely score employees on a numerical scale, perhaps ranging from 1 to 5 or from 1 to 10. Whatever the range may be, it can be quite difficult for a manager to clarify why (for example) he scored an employee as a six on communication skills, versus seven or eight. Also, some managers are tough graders, while others are easy graders, which lead to disparities in scoring across departments.

- *Forced ranking.* Some organizations rank their employees based on their performance appraisals, so that a few people come out on top and are considered high achievers, while others are classified within the bottom category, and so receive reduced compensation increases (if any) and less choice career opportunities. A problem with this approach is that the separation between the two ends of the continuum (or just between the medium and low-performing classifications) may be quite minimal, so that a small change in a person's performance appraisal could result in a major change in his rating within the company. Also, several years of eliminating people in the low-performing category will result in a bottom group that is actually quite talented, but which is still being let go.

- *Ignores teams.* The work environment has changed in the direction of having small teams be responsible for work, with those teams being regularly altered. It is quite difficult to discern the performance of just one person from the performance of his or her teammates.

- *Dated information.* Some issues noted in the discussion may be related to events from months before, which the person may hardly remember, and concerning events for which the person may no longer be responsible.

- *Based on manager biases.* A review is written from the perspective of a manager who may have any number of biases, such as being in favor of introverts who work long hours. Also, managers tend to give higher rankings to employees who are the most like them. These biases can result in skewed reviews that completely ignore some aspects of an employee's performance.

- *Basis for termination.* Some organizations routinely fire their lowest-rated employees, as measured on the performance appraisal. This introduces a huge amount of stress for employees, who know they may be fired immediately after a performance review has been issued.

- *Delayed recognition of poor performance.* Some managers prefer to wait until a year has passed before using the performance appraisal process to flag poor performance. Doing so means that a poor performer will continue to flail for an unconscionably long time before any action is taken. When criticism is withheld until the annual evaluation, employees may feel blindsided by what looks like an overwhelmingly negative attack.

- *Stress level.* The annual review has a reputation for being a stressful event, so the employee likely comes into the meeting feeling stressed, and so is less able to respond to the comments being made.
- *Managers spread thin.* When a business has a flat organizational structure, a manager may be responsible for quite a large number of employees – perhaps several dozen. When this happens, it is difficult for a manager to spend an adequate amount of time reviewing employee performance and translating this review into an appraisal form.
- *Paperwork.* A final issue is that the performance appraisal process can create a massive amount of paperwork. Creating performance reviews also uses up a significant amount of the time of managers, which could be put to use on other tasks.

When these factors are combined, it should be no surprise that performance appraisals tend to have a large proportion of negative outcomes, where the recipient feels so beaten down that his performance may suffer for days or weeks thereafter. This is because the structure of a traditional appraisal is that the manager is judging the employee, which is hardly perceived as a friendly discussion between peers.

A key underlying concept of the *traditional* performance appraisal is that an organization gets a fixed amount of talent when it hires someone, so the process is oriented toward motivating the best employees with money and promotions, while the weak employees are weeded out. This approach used to work when there was an abundant supply of labor, where weak employees could be easily replaced. This is no longer the case. In addition, this approach ignores the idea that all employees *are* capable of change; that they can be coached and trained to be better performers. By placing an emphasis on the latter mindset, the appraisal process can be transformed into something entirely different.

The preceding list of concerns is *so* long that one can reasonably expect both managers and their subordinates to view the process as being at least flawed, if not deeply dissatisfying. In an economy where it is difficult to locate qualified staff, managers should be looking at ways to reduce these points of dissatisfaction, so that employee retention levels will increase.

The Ideal Performance Appraisal Environment

Before getting into specific improvement opportunities, it can be useful to address what the ideal performance appraisal environment might look like. Rather than the cat-and-mouse relationship too often found in a traditional appraisal session, a better approach is to create a supportive climate in which there is a free exchange of ideas between the parties and a mutual discussion of where to go from here. In this enhanced environment, it is far less likely for the employee to react negatively to the manager, or not react at all, sitting in stubborn silence.

Ideally, the employee should contribute to each aspect of the discussion, put forward ideas, and get credit for them. Further, the person should already have a good idea of what will be discussed in the meeting, so there are no significant surprises. The manager should provide substantial feedback, noting specific instances in which performance was lower or higher than expectations. The commentary about performance should be based on standards that were mutually agreed upon during prior meetings, so there should be no surprises for the employee.

The outcome of a meeting in the ideal appraisal environment is that the employee continues to view the manager as a resource who can help to solve performance problems.

The Performance Discussion

There are multiple aspects to the actual performance discussion between a manager and an employee, so we have split up the commentary on the meeting into several subsections.

Conveying the Message

A performance appraisal can be a tense discussion, so the manager should be aware of how the message is being conveyed. This involves both verbal and nonverbal cues. It can be useful for the manager to engage in role playing before the actual meeting to see if he is displaying any conflicting or adverse verbal or nonverbal cues.

The Core Discussion

The manager's approach to dealing with an employee can vary markedly during a meeting. When an employee has been dealing with difficult times, the manager will need to exhibit empathy in sympathizing with the employee's situation. In other cases, the manager will need to revert to active listening mode in order to comprehend the employee's situation. And in other cases, the manager may need to be more forthright in describing a failing and what must be done to rectify the situation.

Generally, the discussion works best when the manager stops frequently to solicit input from the employee. Otherwise, there is a danger that the manager will run on at some length about an issue that may not reflect favorably on the employee, to the point where the employee is so depressed that he no longer wants to participate in the conversation. Examples of what the manager could ask are:

How do you perceive the situation?

What do you think worked in our favor?

What could have been done better?

It can help to begin with a discussion of the employee's strong points and how they relate to his having done a good job in specific areas. Doing so emphasizes the person's strengths. Encourage the employee to add any areas which he believes to be strengths. Doing so provides a broader base for positive discussion. For example:

> Your goal had been to increase sales in the Midwest region by $500,000, and you achieved a sales increase of $620,000.

> Your goal was to halt the unauthorized return of goods from our retail customers. You instituted a return authorization system, which dropped those returns to zero. This was critical for the company, since we were losing $50,000 per month on these unauthorized returns. Thank you!

Some managers have a hard time praising their employees during the normal course of the working day, perhaps because they are swamped with a number of other activities. If so, this is a good time to remedy the deficiency. In the second of the preceding examples, the manager specifies exactly why the person's performance was so important, and then thanks him for it.

This does not mean that the manager should overwhelm the employee with nothing but good news. Casting everything in a positive light leaves the employee wondering what needs to be improved. Instead, provide specific examples of areas in which improvement is needed, and address what the person *should* be doing. These examples can include the gap between the goal and the employee's actual performance, while also noting why this is an issue. For example:

> We wanted to complete the design work for the Antigravity Forklift last year, but your designs were not completed for an additional four months. This meant that three competitors were able to launch competing products before our product hit the market. We estimate that delaying the release date cost the company $15 million.

When telling an employee about problem areas, do not "sugar coat" the message. The employee must understand that there is a problem, and that there will be consequences if the problem is not rectified. When this message is watered down in order to avoid a stressful meeting or to avoid hurting the employee's feelings, the outcome is an employee who does not believe there is much of a problem, and so will be less likely to correct it.

Again, encourage the employee to participate in this discussion and listen carefully to the reasons given for any problems. If the employee is not responsive, then pose a series of questions to extract more information about the situation. For example:

> Are there any work tasks that are interfering with your core responsibilities?

> Are there any distractions in the office that we can eliminate for you?

> What sorts of training can you take that might make your job easier?

> Are there any other types of support that we can give you?

Keep asking questions until enough information has been accumulated to make decisions about how to proceed.

It is essential to provide a balance of praise and criticism. When there is an excessive amount of criticism (especially all at once), the employee is more likely to become defensive and anxious, and will refuse to contribute to the discussion. One way to avoid a preponderance of criticism is to focus on just those areas most in need of improvement. Lesser issues can be dealt with at a later date.

Employee Reactions

Employee reactions to a performance discussion can span the entire spectrum of possible outcomes. The author once had an employee slam her forehead down on a conference room table and refused to raise her head for the rest of the discussion. A more common response is a complete shutdown, with the employee refusing to say anything. Others can become loud and abrasive, though the majority will still carry on a reasonable discussion. Since there are many possible reactions, it is essential for the manager to listen carefully to anything said by the employee, and also to watch for visual cues.

Future Planning

The preceding discussion should only comprise a small part of the total conversation, ideally not more than 25%. It is better to focus on the future, coaching the employee to set a small number of specific, achievable goals. These goals should be set based on how well the employee dealt with the goals from the prior year. Also, note how specific types of performance that are embodied in the goals matters in terms of the employee's career goals. For example:

> Learning about the cost structure of the company's new product line will position you to be eligible for a promotion to senior estimator, along with a pay increase. Learning about the cost structure is an essential requirement for someone in this job.

The manager should not impose goals on the employee, since the employee has not bought into these goals, and so is less likely to accomplish them. Instead, use an open-ended question to encourage the employee to create solutions, such as:

> How would you go about resolving the situation?

> What goals would you set to eliminate last year's performance gap?

> What goals will help with your career plans?

> Which goals would increase your role within the company?

> Which goals would yield the biggest return for the company?

As the employee puts forward possible goals, it can be useful to frame them within the context of the company. Some proposed goals may directly align with the corporate strategy, while others may greatly enhance the employee's skills or reputation, while doing little for the firm. At least some of the goals ultimately chosen by the employee should be of the former variety, while some may fall within the latter category – which may be needed in order to maintain employee interest in continuing to work for the company.

The employee should be encouraged to devise goals that are challenging, but not impossible. It will soon be apparent when a goal is simply not achievable, at which point the employee will likely lose interest in its pursuit. Conversely, an easy goal does not stretch a person, and may just allow him to park within the current job for an additional year without too much effort.

The manager should insist on goals that can be measured, such increasing sales by 7% or reducing the customer wait time by 12%. Doing so eliminates the risk of having an argument at the end of the year about whether a goal has been reached. Conversely, it is difficult to measure more amorphous skills, such whether a person has learned Spanish – does it involve memorizing a certain number of words, or perhaps learning a number of key phrases? And does the person need to just speak Spanish or write it too?

A final task for the manager is to keep the employee from formulating a large number of goals. When there are too many goals, the person's efforts will be scattered among them, leaving too few resources for each one. Instead, encourage the person to set just three or four quality goals that will have a notable impact on the person and/or the company.

At the end of the discussion, summarize what was discussed. This includes the following:

- The feedback given
- New performance goals
- The development plan to achieve the goals

Ask the employee to verify that the summary items are correct, and ask if there are any topics that have not been discussed. Be sure to give a copy of the completed form to the employee. There should be no unsettled issues before closing down the meeting.

Raises

Thus far, we have avoided any discussion of raises during a performance review. This is because there is some debate about whether compensation changes should even be included in these reviews. One view is that employees tend to focus on nothing but the pay raise, and so will ignore anything else that is said during the meeting. Instead, raises can be discussed separately, at a later meeting. This approach is recommended, in order to place a greater emphasis on performance issues. If raises must be included in the discussion, it is customary to discuss compensation near the end of the meeting, so that employees can see the relationship between their performance (which is discussed first) and any pay raises.

The Performance Appraisal Review Form

The performance appraisal review form does not have to be an overly intricate document. In essence, it only needs a text block in which the manager states the employee's performance expectations and accomplishments. There should be a header block in which the employee's name and appraisal date are listed, and a footer block for the signatures of the manager and employee. If a business wants to have a more elaborate document, the usual reason is to require managers to address specific areas that the company believes to be important. A sample performance appraisal review form appears next.

A more elaborate review form is useful when managers have a difficult time structuring their thoughts into coherent and cogent reviews. Instead, their reviews may wander off into areas that are of less importance to the long-term performance of an employee. When this is the case, add more line items to the review form that require specific areas to be covered (as noted in the following sample review form).

Sample Performance Appraisal Review Form

Employee name: David Matthews	**Position:** Treasury Assistant
Review date: December 20, 20X4	**Time period being reviewed:** 20X4

Job description: Maintains the corporate cash forecast, notifies the treasurer when to acquire more debt financing, and suggests amounts and durations for the short-term investment of excess cash amounts. Recommends hedging strategies to the treasurer.
Performance expectations: Will maintain the cash forecast with a sufficient level of detail and frequency to minimize situations in which the company will have unexpected borrowing requirements. Will recommend investment vehicles that maximize liquidity and safety. Will recommend hedging strategies in a timely manner, so that the company minimizes losses on exchange rates and interest rates.
Achievement of core performance expectations: ___3___
Comments: Needs to display much more initiative in owning treasury processes and making suggestions for how to improve processes and prevent the company from incurring additional risks.
Communication skills: The ability to listen to others and clearly describe issues   ___7___
Comments: Has a strong ability to listen to instructions being given, write them down, and unfailingly complete them as intended. However, tends to confine improvement suggestions to e-mails; is not aggressive in pursuing these suggestions. For example, he did not pursue a suggestion to automate the inclusion of payroll expenditures into the cash forecast.

Focus: The ability to set priorities and concentrate efforts on the most critical items	___2___
Comments: Always completes the oldest task first, putting newer tasks at the bottom of his priority list, even when the newer tasks are more critical. For example, he did not address a hedging request for the offsetting of the London loan until two weeks after it was needed.	
Initiative: The ability to drive change	___2___
Comments: Has a strong tendency to complete tasks as directed and then take no further action, even when there are issues that clearly need to be addressed. For example, he suggested that $1,000,000 be shifted into Treasuries in March, but then did not pursue the issue, resulting in the funds not earning interest for two months.	
Productivity: The ability to work in an effective manner	___4___
Comments: His work style is to thoroughly address every task given to him. This is not always good, since it results in too much time being spent on some lesser issues, leaving less time for major projects. For example, he set up a comprehensive control system for petty cash, but never had time to address a control system for wire transfers.	
Strengths: Strong clerical skills and takes direction well.	
Opportunities for improvement: Needs to assign priorities to tasks and take action when it is clear that key issues are not being addressed.	
Employee signature: *David Matthews* **Date:** *December 21, 20X4*	**Supervisor signature:** *Alan Darwin* **Date:** *December 21, 20X4*

In the preceding appraisal review form, the company chooses to emphasize communication skills, focus, initiative, and productivity for all employees, since all employees must be scored on these traits in the form. Other firms may choose to emphasize different areas, such as reliability or teamwork, as being more important to the organization, and will adjust the form accordingly.

Phrasing Suggestions

Many managers have difficulty writing performance appraisals, especially in regard to the specific phrases that most accurately describe an employee's performance. In the following table, we list phrases that could be used for different levels of performance, focusing on specific performance attributes. These phrases could be inserted into a performance review.

Sample Performance Phrases

Attribute	Well Below Expectations	Needs Improvement	Meets Expectations	Exceeds Expectations	Greatly Exceeds Expectations
Accuracy	Requires constant monitoring	Sometimes produces unreliable output	Maintains accurate records	Always checks for accuracy	Always produces error-free work
Attention to detail	Omits essential details	Can be careless with details	Always provides the expected level of detail	Understands when additional detail is needed	Meticulously attends to every detail
Conflict management	Tends to trigger conflicts in many situations	Does not actively address conflict situations	Remains steady and fair-minded in conflict situations	Routinely mediates interpersonal issues	Has a flair for resolving conflicts
Expertise	Lacks expertise in key areas needed for her job	Has not updated her knowledge, which is now out of date	Communicates effectively with non-technical staff	Has used her expertise to resolve several problems	Has applied her expertise to resolve major technical issues
Goal orientation	Is unable to deal with the most basic goals	Does not allocate enough attention to goals	Is committed to meeting goals	Has a strong goal orientation	Sets and meets challenging goals
Initiative	Needs to be continually badgered to complete work	Waits to be assigned new tasks	Works autonomously and without supervision	Looks for new assignments	Actively finds and resolves problems
Integrity	Has violated the company's standards for integrity	Rationalizes less ethical behavior	Has a strong sense of what is right	Demonstrates high levels of integrity	Embodies the company's values
Listening	Talks more than listens	Does not pay attention	Listens patiently	Encourages others to speak	Listens actively to what others say
Management skills	Treats employees as expendable resources	Routinely micro manages tasks	Listens to her employees	Encourages employee development	Displays superior coaching skills
Performance	Shows little interest in improving performance	Tolerates mediocre performance	Shows a steady improvement in performance	Prioritizes efforts to maximize results	Maintains the highest performance standards
Persuasiveness	Forces her ideas on others	Assumes that her ideas are the correct ones	Can persuade without applying excessive pressure	Takes the time to understand the needs of others	Excellent ability to build trust
Priority setting	Does not assign priorities to tasks	Can be sidetracked into lower-priority tasks	Alters priorities as needed	Ensures that top priorities are addressed first	Has excellent judgment in setting priorities

Attribute	Well Below Expectations	Needs Improvement	Meets Expectations	Exceeds Expectations	Greatly Exceeds Expectations
Profit orientation	Routinely spends more than budgeted amounts	Shows minimal interest in the firm's financial condition	Discusses cost management needs with staff	Focuses her staff on profit issues	Actively improves profits
Teamwork	Routinely clashes with other team members	Cooperates only when asked	Works well within the team	Creates a teamwork environment	Is critical to the success of the team
Timeliness	Routinely falls behind	Rarely completes tasks on time	Keeps projects on schedule	Creates realistic work schedules	Always completes work on time

When writing a performance appraisal, certain phrases can trigger charges of discrimination, and so should be avoided. For example, an obvious case of gender discrimination would be "she is not willing to be one of the guys," and could be replaced with "she needs to improve her ability to work with the team." Or, "if she wore makeup, customers would be more willing to work with her" is a clear case of gender discrimination, and could be replaced with "she needs to project a more professional image when dealing with customers." The same issue can arise with age discrimination. For example, "he doesn't seem to understand young people" could be replaced with "his suggestions do not resonate with our target audience."

Another area of concern is including phrases in a performance appraisal that appear to promise an employee continuing employment. For example, "he has a bright future at this company" or "he could be a vice president within three years" could cause trouble if the person's employment is suddenly terminated. Consequently, no statements should be made about future employment, the likelihood of a promotion, or reassurances regarding job security.

Summary

The proper management of employees begins with the recruitment process and continues through the ongoing appraisal of their performance. We cannot emphasize enough the need to spend as much time as necessary to locate the best possible job candidates, since the hiring of suboptimal people will downgrade company performance for years. The performance appraisal process needs to address those areas that are most essential to company performance. The manager needs to be very clear with employees about exactly which issues are impeding the progress of the firm toward its goals, so that they are focused on improvements in the correct areas. Recruiting and performance appraisals are among the most important manager skills, since they have a direct impact on the quality of the workforce.

Chapter 11
Employee Coaching

Introduction

An organization needs to provide coaching to its employees in order to improve their overall productivity and creativity. Without such attention, the management team will find that junior employees are more likely to be dependent on the more senior or experienced employees, which makes it difficult to improve and grow the business. In this chapter, we cover how a manager can decide when to initiate coaching sessions with employees, and how to conduct them.

The Reason for Coaching

Coaching is a set of training methods that focus on the needs of specific individuals, coupled with close observation of their performance and learning activities, leading to feedback regarding how they can further enhance their performance. Coaching can also be used as a management technique, where a manager gives guidance regarding the general direction needed, and the individual is allowed to figure out the best way to get there. Under both definitions, coaching cannot be considered exclusively a top-down, directive activity. Instead, managers work with employees in a collaborative environment to improve skills. The improvement of skills generally covers the following areas:

- *Deal with performance problems*. A manager deals with the shortcomings of her staff. For example, an employee has difficulty writing status reports, or is continually working late to address his standard daily work load. The manager can provide coaching to rectify these issues.
- *Enhance skills*. A manager can provide coaching regarding how to enhance existing skills, or to work on skills in entirely new areas. For example, someone with management potential has a difficult time confronting argumentative people. A manager can discuss this issue, focusing on the alternative confrontation methods available and perhaps engaging in role playing.
- *Improve productivity*. A manager can show employees how to increase their efficiency and effectiveness in conducting their daily tasks. For example, an employee does not understand how to investigate processing errors to determine the underlying causes. Proper coaching can involve discussions of different analysis methods that may apply to the situation.
- *Enhance the work environment*. When a manager is constantly working to improve the capabilities of her staff, this tends to result in a more positive work environment, which in turn tends to reduce employee turnover, since they have a better connection with the organization.

Forward-Looking Coaching

Coaching can be used to assess any issues that an employee may have with a future change to his job. For example, a manager could show an employee a job description for a position into which the person is about to be promoted, and ask for feedback regarding whether he can do the job. If he expresses any discomfort with certain aspects of the job, the manager can initiate a coaching process to enhance his skills in the indicated areas. By engaging in this level of forward-looking coaching, employees are much more likely to succeed when they transition into new positions.

The Coaching Difference

What is the difference between telling someone how to improve and coaching them in how to do so? Coaching involves letting them work their issues, using directive questions. The following example illustrates the concept:

EXAMPLE

An employee has a terrible time writing training documents. In particular, the materials are not well-focused. The department manager could simply mark up the materials in red ink, hand them to the employee, and tell him to make the indicated revisions. In this case, the employee is not being asked to think, only to revise, so there is a strong likelihood that he will continue to make the same mistakes.

Or, the department manager could instead meet with the employee and ask a number of questions pertaining to the offending documents, such as:

- Who will be the primary users of the training materials?
- What information does this audience probably already know?
- What information does this audience need? In what form should this information be presented to improve their learning experience?
- If you were a trainee, would the information in these materials be of assistance?

After thinking about the questions posed by the manager, the employee goes back to the training materials, prunes out the less relevant items, adds other materials, and clarifies some existing information. The manager finds that several additional rounds of meetings are needed, during which he poses other questions to further refine the employee's writing. At the end of the process, the manager has spent far more of her time than would have been the case if she had revised the materials herself. However, the employee now has a much better understanding of what high-quality training materials should look like. The result will be much better training materials going forward, which will radically reduce the manager's subsequent attention to this issue.

The amount of coaching work noted in the preceding example is substantial. Highly proactive managers who want to see immediate results can be uncomfortable with the several rounds of coaching sessions that may be required in order to obtain a particular result.

Investigating the Need for Coaching

Before setting up a coaching program, it can be helpful for management to evaluate whether the organization as a whole will be receptive toward the use of coaching. In many organizations that use "old school" management styles, employees are expected to deal with their own problems – to the extent that coaching is considered a newfangled thing that will only be tolerated at the behest of senior management. Indicators of situations in which coaching may not be accepted are:

- The presence of a risk-averse culture, where the emphasis is to keep doing everything the way it has been done in the past
- Profits are high, so there is little need for change
- There is a minimal human resources presence in the company, with an attendant reduced level of attention to personnel needs
- The funding for coaching must be extracted from existing department budgets, so managers will likely lobby to have their funding restored as soon as possible

The reverse of the points just noted might present an opportunity for a long-term coaching initiative.

When initially considering the use of coaching for employees, a manager should first make inquiries of employees regarding where their interests lie. Setting up any type of coaching program makes little sense if an individual has no motivation in the targeted area. Questions that could be asked to ascertain employee interest levels could include the following:

- What do you enjoy doing the most on the job?
- What do you enjoy the least on the job?
- What is your ideal job? Have you had a previous job similar to it?
- How would you restructure your current job to increase your value to the business?
- Which skills are you the most proud of?
- What work have you done in the past that you are proud of?
- Are there any areas in which you want to improve yourself?
- Are there any areas that you would prefer to avoid?
- Is there a skill you don't have that would result in an improvement in your job?
- Are there certain types of people that you prefer to work with?

Many employees will not answer these questions if they feel that management has not earned their trust. Instead, they will prevaricate or say nothing in order to protect their positions within the company. If this is the case, a manager may face a lengthy task of winning the trust of her employees, which may involve spending lots of time working with and listening to them, as well as spending time explaining the reasoning behind any decisions made that affect them.

Goal Setting for Coaching Sessions

When it appears that the environment within a business is ripe for coaching and employees are interested in the concept, it is time to set up goals for employees. Goals must come from the employee. If a coach were to impose goals, the employee would not have any buy-in, and so would be far less likely to work toward achieving the goals. Instead, an employee must take ownership of a goal and be strongly motivated to achieve it, and preferably within a short period of time. Under these circumstances, there is a driving need that a good coach can channel in the right direction.

A coach may find that the initial goal being presented by an employee is not the right one to be addressed. Instead, subsequent actions by the employee may reveal that the person is not really interested in the goal, or that he will abandon it under certain circumstances. To guard against these problems, the coach may elect to probe the circumstances surrounding the goal with a number of questions, such as:

- Is this goal a one-time issue for you, or does it keep coming up? [establishes whether there is a long-term performance problem]
- You keep saying that this problem will go away if you can just clear out your current work backlog and devote more time to it. Have you been able to clear your backlog in the past? [establishes whether work habits may be the real issue]
- How much of this situation can you alter? [establishes whether the person really has an attitude problem regarding a situation]
- What would the world look like if you never had to deal with this situation again? [probes for the core problem that must be dealt with]

The ideal goal that an employee derives should have the characteristics outlined in the following set of bullet points. If a goal has them, it is much more likely that a coaching engagement will have a meaningful outcome. The characteristics are:

- *Specific.* The goal is highly specific, so there is no question about exactly what needs to be achieved.
- *Measurable.* The goal can be clearly quantified with a measurement. For example, achieving a goal should result in an increase in sales of 20% within one year.
- *Attainable.* Attaining the goal is within the capabilities of the employee, and depends solely on his actions.
- *Relevant.* The goal is really important to the employee.
- *Time-specific.* There is a deadline for attaining the goal.

There are three general types of goals that can be pursued in a coaching arrangement, which are:

- *Debriefing.* The employee wants to discuss how a recent event went, usually in regard to a negative event and how to correct it. For example, a meeting has just ended, with a co-worker shouting at the rest of the team. The employee wants to discuss various ways to deal with the co-worker. Sample questions to ask (to continue with the same example) might include:

  o Tell me what happened.
  o Is there anything that triggered this outburst? Has it happened in the past?
  o How did you react to him?
  o Have you tried a different approach in the past that worked better?

- *Problem solving.* There are specific ongoing issues that an employee wants to discuss. For example, the sales manager may be continually overriding the efforts of the credit manager to impose tight credit controls, and the credit manager wants to discuss how to deal with the situation. These problems will continue unless a coaching session is used to formulate possible responses. Sample questions to ask (to continue with the same example) might include:

  o What is your perception of the sales manager's authority in this area?
  o Do you think he might have a different perception of the situation?

- *Long-term development.* This is a large goal that requires a substantial amount of work, and possibly a number of follow-up discussions to ensure that the employee has fully absorbed the work. For example, an employee wants to become more comfortable leading strategic planning meetings with senior management. Sample questions to ask (to continue with the same example) might include:

  o What would you say is your current comfort level with running a meeting?
  o When you have run a meeting in the past, how would you describe the success of the meeting?
  o Are there any particular issues that have worked well for you in the past?

Coaching Sessions

Coaching sessions are held at reasonable intervals; once a week or month is typical. If the department manager takes on the role of coach, then the manager needs to differentiate these sessions from any other meetings that might be held with the same employee. For example, a coaching session is not the same as the annual performance review (which tends to be retrospective), nor is it the same as ongoing meetings to discuss projects (which tend to address the future in the short-term).

What is the structure of a typical coaching session? There are a number of possible formats, but the following sequence of events is typical:

1. *Opening chat.* The coach wants to learn whether anything significant has happened since the last session, and so may open with "what's the most significant thing that has happened since our last meeting?"
2. *Status report.* The employee discusses the steps taken since the last meeting to address action items. A possible question to begin this event is "tell me about what you've been doing with your action steps" or "please tell me the status of your action items."
3. *Main discussion.* The coach walks through any previous action items that require further work, and then proceeds to a discussion of any additional issues that should be addressed in order to meet the goal of the coaching relationship. This may involve the creation of an additional set of action items. To address the first of these items, the coach could ask, "Which action items from last time do we need to talk about?" The second item could be addressed with "What is on the agenda that relates to achieving your goals?"
4. *Review decisions.* Go over the action items that the employee has agreed to. The intent is to clarify what the employee will do next. A possible question that the coach can use at this point is "tell me about your action items for the next week."

A key element of the last item is ensuring that the employee commits to take action. This could mean a commitment to a meeting, attending a training session, and so forth. Otherwise, it is quite possible that the individual will ignore the action items, and so will have no progress to report at the next meeting.

An employee might discover that additional resources are needed in order to complete an action item. If so, this can be addressed during a coaching session, or as a follow-up to a session, where the parties discuss how the resources can be obtained. This could involve funding, or perhaps an introduction to someone else who can provide the necessary resources.

An additional step that can be added to a coaching session is to spend a few minutes at the end of the session, discussing how the session went. The coach may have used a method that did not resonate well with the employee, or which the employee might have found to be unusually helpful. By addressing these topics, the coach can improve her technique or tailor her standard approach to the needs of a specific employee.

The time taken by a coaching session does not have to be long, assuming that the person running the meeting keeps it focused on the key issues. A half-hour may be sufficient for the discussion of status and future plans.

Coaching Models

There are several conversational models that a coach may use. For example, a coaching arrangement might begin with a goal, which the coach uses to identify a starting point for the change, followed by discussions to arrive at several potential courses of action to pursue, and ending with the selection of one path to follow. This approach works well when concrete action is needed. Questions that might be used by a coach under this type of coaching are:

1. What do you want to accomplish? [establishes the goal]
2. What have you accomplished in this area already? [establishes the starting point]
3. Let's come up with at least four possible solutions. [establishes courses of action]
4. Which of these options are you most interested in pursuing? [establishes commitment]

When this approach is followed, the coach may place a particular emphasis on discussing barriers that can interfere with achieving the goal. This may involve the exploration of how interested the employee is in following a specific path, and discussing what changes must be made in order to increase the employee's level of commitment. For example, if an employee is only moderately interested in a particular course of action, the reason may be a perception that a certain manager will resist the activity. If so, the coach digs into the reasons for this presumed level of resistance, and which other actions will be needed to eliminate it. By doing so, a path is found that results in much greater interest by the employee, since the perceived odds of success are so much higher.

A different approach is to spend more time exploring a broad range of potential courses of action, where the emphasis is more on self-discovery than on achieving a specific goal. The coach spends much more time exploring possible alternatives with quite broad questions, such as:

- Tell me about what has led up to the current situation.
- Explain why this is so important to you.
- Tell me more.

Once there are many alternatives to choose from, the coach then narrows the focus back down to a decision by the employee regarding which path to pursue, followed by the development of an action plan.

Coaching Inquiries

The coaching process does not necessarily involve having a coach provide specific advice to an employee about a highly-specific topic. Instead, a coach may adopt the role of exploring a particular issue in great detail, which requires an ongoing series of questions. The questioning approach works well in the following circumstances:

- *Problem resolution*. An employee is dealing with a specific problem. The employee is likely the expert in his area, and so is the best able to arrive at a solution. The manager asks questions to clarify the problem and see if the employee has considered the full range of possible solutions.

- *Option evaluation.* An employee may have to take action where there are several possible ways to proceed. The manager can ask questions to assist him in evaluating the various aspects of each option. This approach shows employees how to examine their alternatives and make choices.
- *Process improvements.* When there is a need to improve a process, the manager can use questions to explore issues with the current process, and how these issues can be rectified. Using questions shows employees how to think about the analysis of prospective process improvements.
- *Planning.* An inherent part of the planning process is the analysis of alternatives. Questioning can be used to focus attention on the most critical aspects of each alternative, and shows employees how to engage in planning analysis.

When coaching someone, the coach must be able to ask probing questions that force an individual to think – not just to respond with a simple "yes" or "no" answer. The latter type of question is called a *closed question*, while a question that cannot be answered with a "yes" or "no" is called an *open question*. Examples of open questions that a coach might use are:

- What will happen to your other obligations if you take on this additional work?
- How will this new job impact your family relations?
- What other options do you have for addressing the staffing shortage?
- What channels do you have to go through to gain approval for that?

Sometimes it is not necessary to ask a question to dig for more information. Instead, consider asking for more information. For example:

- You mentioned that you started getting nervous when speaking before groups of at least ten people. Tell me more about that.
- You mentioned that there were issues with your fellow managers after the Smith contract was signed. Please expand on that.

A further refinement of the coach's questions is to avoid any question beginning with "why," since this type of question tends to put employees on the defensive. For example, "why did you yell at him?" will likely raise an employee's defensive barriers. Instead, begin questions with "what" to defuse the situation, such as "What types of responses would you expect him to have?"

Probing Questions

No matter what the context of a coaching engagement may be, a coach will need to ask probing questions to better understand the background of an employee's situation. Without this in-depth background information, a coach may find after a number of sessions that he has been coaching an employee toward the wrong goal, or getting there via the wrong path. Here are examples of several probing questions that a coach could ask to collect background information:

- Give me some background on how this situation arose.
- Where do you see this situation going if you don't change anything?
- What's the best possible outcome?
- How have you responded to this type of situation in the past?
- When this situation comes up, how do you feel about it?
- How do you think the other party perceives the situation?
- Why is this important to you?
- What do you gain from this? What do you lose from this?
- What is your worst-case scenario?
- The last time this happened, how did you respond?
- What else is important?

Employees tend to focus on just a few solutions for how to achieve a goal, which may not leave them with a sufficient number of alternatives. Here are several probing questions that can be used by a coach to extract more alternatives from an employee:

- What is a more radical solution?
- What other options could you try?
- What have other people tried in similar circumstances?
- What other alternatives might be available if you had more funding or outside assistance?

Coaching Observations

A coach does not have to be someone who simply speaks in questions. That could be quite tiresome for the person being coached, who is constantly having all of his comments reframed as questions and cast back at him. Some of the most valuable comments that a coach can make are not questions, but rather observations that can offer a different perspective to the employee. Here are several examples:

Based on what you are saying, it appears that you are unwilling to speak up to offer suggestions when he makes a statement that you disagree with. Also, I've noticed the same behavior when you have described your interactions with other members of the management team. It may be that you are being unusually deferential because they have more senior positions. How do you feel about that?

During our last few staff meetings, I've noticed that you keep interrupting Joan and David when they are talking. It also appears as though you like to summarize issues and bring them to a conclusion quite rapidly. Both issues are cutting down on the amount of discussion within the department. Any thoughts about this?

The Transition to Action Steps

The questioning process needs to cover more than one possible course of action, so that an employee is forced to explore alternatives. For example, when soliciting more options from an employee, questions may be structured as "what could you do," with the emphasis on the word *could*. This emphasis is designed to explore possible alternatives, without asking for a commitment. When the focus of the coaching changes to locking down specific action items, questions may instead be structured as "what will you do," with the emphasis on the word *will*. The intent is to gain a commitment from the employee.

An employee may be stuck between several possible courses of action, and is not willing to commit to one of them. If so, the coach can select from several statements to drive the employee into making a commitment, such as:

- You don't seem ready to make a decision. What is standing in the way?
- You're saying that you could potentially go down that road. What is standing in the way?
- Is there anything more we should discuss before you can make a decision?

Breaking Out of the Box

The solutions that an employee proposes to a coach may fall within a tightly constrained box. For example, a person might only consider solutions that he can accomplish himself, or with essentially no budget. The coach needs to break through these preconceptions by getting an employee to think about alternatives that are outside of the person's self-imposed box. For example:

- Let's just say that you have an unlimited budget. What could you do then?
- Envision someone else being able to take over your job for the next three months. What would all of that spare time allow you to do?
- What would it take to double the size of your budget?
- Under what circumstances could you hand off this entire situation to someone else?
- You've stated that Manager Smith will disapprove a request in that area. What would it take to change his mind?

When Responses are Questionable

What should a coach do when the answers to his questions do not appear to be reasonable? The coach may believe that a response is completely unworkable. Issuing a highly negative remark at this point could squash any further input from the employee. Instead, consider another round of questions that can be used to clarify matters for the employee, so that they can see the full ramifications of the approach. For example:

- I'm not sure I understand; can you explain that again?
- Tell me about your thinking for that idea.
- What are the advantages and disadvantages of going down that path?
- I have a concern in regard to ___. How would you address that issue?

The outcome of these additional questions might be a greater understanding by either or both parties. It is possible that the manager may gain a greater understanding of the situation, and then becomes supportive of the idea.

Role Playing

Another way for a coach to offer value to an employee is to engage in role playing. The two re-create a situation that has already occurred (or which is expected to occur), and they work through various alternatives that the employee could have used (or will use) to deal with the situation. After each role playing variation, they talk through how effective it was, and how it can be improved.

A variation on role playing is for the employee to make a presentation to the coach, so that the coach can offer observations regarding how different aspects of the presentation can be improved upon.

Dealing with Silence

An employee may sometimes lapse into silence. It is entirely acceptable to let a period of silence extend for some time, since he may need the interval to ponder a question and formulate a detailed response. At other times, silence may simply indicate that an employee is bored, defiant, or uncomfortable. If one of the latter reasons is the case, the coach could (eventually) make a comment to encourage an answer, such as:

- I notice that you don't answer when we start to talk about ___. What is going on with that?
- I notice that you've been taking a long time to respond. Are there any reasons for that?

Another way to deal with the situation is to simplify the question, on the assumption that the original question was too difficult for the employee to sort through.

Coaching Session Preparation

A coach's advice does not provide much value to an employee if the advice is devised *during* a coaching session. Instead, set aside a small block of time prior to a session to contemplate what advice would be most effective. This thought process can also encompass any positive feedback to mix in with the advice. Then write down these thoughts in a reasonably orderly manner, so that they are readily accessible during a coaching session. This type of preparation can be performed days in advance of a session, if the coach wants additional time to consider her initial comments and perhaps make revisions to them.

Coaching Session Prep Form

To make a coaching session more valuable, the employee should fill out a form prior to the meeting that summarizes the actions he has taken since the last session.

Discussing the information on the form reduces the time spent on the opening stages of a session, leaving more room for other topics. In addition, if the form is sent to the coach prior to the session, the coach has more time to think about topics to address during the next session. Finally, the employee will then have time to review the report and consider the actions he has taken thus far.

The session prep form is intended to be quite simple, with just a few questions and lots of space for writing. The key questions are:

- *Achievements*. What have I accomplished since the last session?
- *Difficulties*. What problems am I facing right now?
- *Accountability*. Which action items did I not complete? What further steps must be taken to complete them?
- *Asset usage*. How do I want to use the coach in the next session?

On-the-Spot Coaching

In the preceding sections, the focus has been on a relatively formalized coaching process, where the assumption is that a coaching relationship will span a moderate period of time, perhaps several months. However, there are numerous cases in which effective coaching can be conducted on the-spot. These situations arise when there is a minor issue that can be dealt with at once, without any of the administrative overhead normally associated with coaching. For example:

- A manager notices that a spreadsheet submitted by a staff person does not contain a comparative column for information from the prior year. She points out why having this additional information makes the resulting report more useful for managers, since trends can now be discerned.
- A manager sees that when an employee makes presentations, she tends to focus her attention on the left side of the room, ignoring questions from those on the right side. She points out this issue, which the employee had not even noticed.
- A manager notices that an employee is issuing the daily sales report about one hour later than planned. She informs the employee that the report is needed earlier in the day, so that it can be used at the daily management meeting. The employee had not been aware of this requirement, and immediately alters his work schedule to make sure that the report is available by the required time.

The Ideal Coach

The ideal coach truly believes that an individual can improve. With this mindset, a coach is much more likely to push an employee to excel. If this were not the case, a coach might instead give up after one or two tries, saying, "ah, it is as I expected – he cannot learn."

The ideal coach is willing to intercede immediately when she sees a problem. By doing so, skills problems or incorrect behavior by a subordinate are not present long enough to become "locked in" and become irritants to co-workers. Instead, by addressing issues at once, the work environment operates much more smoothly.

The Poor Coach

Poor coaches have a strong tendency to focus on getting tasks done. This means that they focus on their own ability to complete tasks, rather than the abilities of their subordinates. When they have a choice of either completing a task or coaching a subordinate, task completion always comes first. This approach to management results in the following behaviors related to coaching:

- *Failed task management*. If a subordinate fails in a task, the poor coach's first reaction is to take away responsibility for the task, possibly doing it herself instead. Rather than taking corrective action, she is more likely to take punitive action, threatening dismissal if the employee does not improve.
- *Lack of delegation*. The poor coach finds it quite difficult to hand off tasks to subordinates, preferring to retain all but the simplest tasks.
- *Lack of planning*. The poor coach deals with those issues right in front of her, rather than attempting to plan ahead. The emphasis is on crisis management.
- *Minimal goal setting*. The poor coach sets few goals, and does not support her staff in completing those goals. Instead, the focus is on completing those tasks that require immediate attention.
- *Reduced feedback*. It rarely occurs to the poor coach to give feedback. When given, it is usually negative, involving those aspects of a task that were not done correctly. There is little recognition of a task well done.

It should be apparent that a poor coach is constitutionally incapable of handling employees. These people typically should not have been promoted into a manager position, since their skills clearly do not encompass the improvement of others.

Coaching Mistakes

There are a number of mistakes that a coach can make when engaging in coaching sessions. Here are examples of ways in which coaching can be misdirected:

- *Imposed solutions*. Some coaches try to find the ultimate solution for employees, based on what the person has told them. Such an approach may indeed result in a terrific solution that solves the employee's problems. However, it is more likely that the coach has thought of a sub-optimal solution, and then wastes time trying to impose it on the employee. A better approach is to explore all possible alternatives with the person, probing the benefits and issues associated with each one. Eventually, the employee will realize which option is best, and will automatically buy into the concept because he thought of it. This way of dealing with employee issues is effective, but requires the coach to subsume his ego in favor of finding the best outcome for the employee.

- *Impatience*. A spin-off of the preceding imposed solution mistake is to lose patience with employees. A coach may want to resolve an issue at once and impose a solution. However, doing so means that the employee never gets to learn from his mistakes, instead relying on the coach for answers. Though it may seem wildly unproductive, it is better to watch an employee work through situations and eventually arrive at the best outcome, building experience along the way. One way to deal with coaching impatience is to check in with an employee at various milestone points, to see how they are doing. Giving additional advice during these check-in points can keep an employee from going wildly astray, and can accelerate the learning process somewhat.

- *Molding advice*. A coach may be tempted to offer advice that essentially molds an employee into a junior version of the coach. Instead, be aware that all employees have their own unique skills, which should be maximized in accordance with their needs and desires. If a coach attempts to mold employees into her own image to an excessive extent, they will likely become disengaged from the process. Avoiding the molding trap requires an in-depth knowledge of the strengths and weaknesses of an employee, as well as what path he wants to pursue.

- *Excessive formality*. A coach may want to treat a coaching session as a major event. Doing so may require blocking out a large amount of time at long intervals, which does not provide an employee with any rapid feedback regarding immediate issues. Also, turning a coaching session into a major production can raise the emotional level of the meeting and therefore the defensive posture of the employee. Instead, consider treating feedback as a frequent event by distributing small snippets of advice as needed.

- *Going too long*. Some employees are simply not motivated in a particular position, and so are not interested in improving themselves, no matter how much coaching they receive. Or, bad habits may be so ingrained that these problems cannot be corrected. For example, a manager may be so concerned about transactional errors that she must handle everything herself – never delegating work to others. A coach could waste an inordinate amount of time with these individuals. If this appears to be the case, the solution could be that an employee is miscast in a particular role, and should be given a different job description.

In regard to the last point, an employee is less likely to be coachable when he denies that a problem even exists, or persists in blaming an issue on others. Conversely, if an individual only has issues at long intervals or in response to specific situations, a coach is more likely to be able to gain a reasonable improvement from the person in exchange for a modest investment of her time.

Lack of Time to Coach

What if a manager's working hours are completely filled, to the point where there is no time to provide any coaching to her staff? If so, search for transitional periods during the day, and provide coaching then. For example, if a manager is walking back from a meeting with an employee, take those few minutes to discuss the meeting and the employee's role in it. These travel-time coaching sessions can work well, because they can be used to provide immediate feedback to an employee regarding what they just did. Similarly, there may be plenty of time with employees while traveling, either in person or by calling them. The same approach can be used while commuting, for example by sending e-mails while on a train or bus.

Another way to deal with a lack of time is to apportion coaching time among employees, depending on their levels of ability. "A" players (who constantly exceed expectations) require the most coaching, since they have a tendency to burn out and to cause turmoil when they denigrate the efforts of lesser employees. Additional coaching in this area is worthwhile, since well-coached "A" players yield a higher return in their performance. Conversely, "C" players who routinely underperform may require vast amounts of coaching, and yet never reach even an average performance level. For "C" players, consider combining strict performance goals with a modest coaching investment; if their performance does not improve, they will need to leave the organization or be placed in other roles. By recognizing the types of employees being coached, one can better allocate a limited amount of coaching time.

The Efficient and Effective Coach

As noted earlier in this chapter, some forms of coaching can be completed in moments (see On-the-Spot Coaching), while other forms require a more formalized process that can, over a period of time, be quite time-consuming for a manager. In the latter case, there are some ways to improve the efficiency and effectiveness of a coach. For example:

- *Offer a coach-free period.* Some employees can turn around or enhance their performance on their own, without any coaching. In this case, they may simply not have known that there was an issue. A manager can point out an issue and then offer a coach-free period, thereby bypassing all coaching activities. The risk is that an employee will be unable to improve his performance during this period, perhaps hardening the attitudes of other employees against the person.
- *Ascertain motivation.* If an employee is unwilling to learn, there is no point in coaching him. The effective manager finds out right away if an employee is motivated to make changes. If not, coaching is not a viable option.
- *Delegate.* If an employee requires coaching in a specific skill or behavioral area, it may be more efficient to offload coaching duties to a specialist in the designated area. This can be an expensive solution if the coaching period is prolonged and the coach is a third party specialist.

The Role of Coaching in Employee Rankings

Managers tend to form immediate impressions about their employees that cannot be subsequently budged without a notable amount of effort. For example, if a manager hires a person and immediately decides that he is a star employee, any subsequent mistakes made by the person are tolerantly considered to be learning opportunities. Conversely, if the initial impression of a new hire is lower, then any mistakes made are considered to be reinforcement of the initial impression.

Coaching allows a manager to alter these initial impressions. Since coaching may be used continually over a long period of time, a manager gets to see many instances of the real capabilities of her employees to improve (or not). The outcome may result in a significant change in her initial impressions about employees, aligning the manager's opinions much more closely with the true state of affairs. Consequently, coaching can have a profound impact on the ability of a management team to sort through which employees are worthy of promotion.

Summary

Coaching is an essential management function. It improves the skills of employees, so that they become more productive and creative, allowing a business to grow more rapidly than its competitors. If managers are unable to engage in coaching as part of their daily activities or do a poor job of it, then they may not be suitable for their positions, and should be recast into other roles.

Chapter 12
Employee and Manager Training

Introduction

The point behind training employees is to improve the performance of the organization. This is especially critical when a company is constantly reinventing itself, either to increase its market share or simply to keep up with the competition. To this end, management pours money into training employees, hoping that doing so will make the organization more nimble, innovative, service oriented, and so forth. In many (if not most) cases, training does not result in such a performance boost – instead, employees soon revert to their old ways, ignoring what they have been taught. The underlying problem is that the organization must be properly designed to support training, so that employees are encouraged to implement what they have learned.

In this chapter, we discuss the issues related to training, how it can be better supported, and what types of training to give to managers.

Reasons for Training

There are multiple reasons why a business would want its employees to engage in training. Consider the following:

- *Skill gaps*. There are clear gaps between the current skill sets of employees and what they are expected to need in the future.
- *Consistency*. A key element in building a corporate culture is to ensure that all employees are taught the same company values and policies.
- *Competitive pressures*. When a competitor introduces a new process, product, distribution channel or other innovation, the company may need to react by quickly training up its own staff to match the actions of the competitor.
- *Position requirements*. When employees are being groomed for advancement or for lateral shifts across the organization, this frequently calls for additional training to fill the needs of the new positions being filled. For example, they may need to learn different work habits and social skills when they move into a management position.
- *Efficiency improvements*. When there is a need to improve the efficiency of a process, technical training in targeted areas may be needed. For example, employees could be trained in how to improve the efficiency of equipment changeovers for a new job.
- *Employee retention*. When employees are considered unusually valuable, training can be used as a targeted benefit to keep them from leaving the firm.
- *New product development*. Employee skills in the product development arena can be enhanced so that they have a better knowledge of how to create better

products, and to do so with a reduced cycle time. Training can be used to improve their knowledge of framing problems, choosing ideas, testing proto-types, and so forth.

Though there are many reasons to engage in training, the essential focus is on improving business performance. An organization is constantly improving as a result of its training initiatives. When performance improves, it is easy to justify a training program.

Reasons Why Training Fails

The many reasons just enumerated for having training should drive a business to have a highly effective training program – and yet this is rarely the case. Instead, businesses pour money into training endeavors and then experience minimal improvements in their performance. Why? The following issues all have an impact:

- *Lack of tailoring*. Many training programs are not designed to the specific needs of a business. Instead, they cover general topics that may be of modest interest to participants, but which do little to address the actual needs of the organization.
- *Lack of oversight*. Management may be signing off on training expenditures without paying attention to the types of training and how it is being supported within the organization. Instead, they simply treat the expenditure as another line item on the income statement to be approved.
- *Too much content*. A certain amount of time is required to effectively transmit information. If the trainer attempts to jam too much information into a training session, there is a risk that little or none of the information will be retained.
- *Entrenched methods*. When employees return from a training class, full of nifty new ideas, they find that the department's processes are entrenched in the old manner of doing things. Unless they are strongly supported by management, employees will find that they have little power to change the established system, and find it easier to return to their accustomed routines.
- *Lack of strategic clarity*. The management team may have set forth an uncoordinated set of goals and values. As a result, employees do not understand what is expected of them, and so do not take action to implement what they have learned.
- *Top-down style of management*. When decisions are being imposed from above, it is more likely that employees will follow the lead set by senior management, rather than trying out the new perspectives offered during training classes.
- *Cross-functional conflict*. Changes resulting from training frequently require the cooperation of multiple departments, so if one department manager refuses to cooperate, then an improvement project will not proceed.
- *Lack of upward knowledge transfer*. Employees may not be willing to inform management about the reasons for training failures.

When one or more of the preceding issues are causing training initiatives to fail, employees become increasingly cynical about the need for training, even though the managers imposing training are still enthusiastic about it. There are several reasons for this disparity. First, the human resources department has an interest in recommending training programs to support corporate strategies, since this department is responsible for training programs within the organization. And second, it can be difficult to measure the effectiveness of training programs, so that the employees spending so much of their time in training programs are aware of their lack of success, but this information never works its way back up to senior management through its standard set of reporting metrics. These issues mean that a company may keep spending money on training, even though the expenditures have little impact on company performance.

Training Strategy

The best return on investment occurs when training expenditures are closely aligned with an organization's strategy. When this is the case, training is a derivation of the direction in which a business wants to go, rather than being a standard set of training sessions that do not vary much over time. It also means that training is more likely to be custom-designed for the specific needs of the firm, rather than being the usual mix of outside training classes, seminars, and degree programs.

When training is used to directly support strategy, the training cost can vary markedly from year to year, depending on the need for it in the strategic planning documents. For example, if the business is re-orienting itself into a new market, this may call for a massive training effort to familiarize many employees with the requirements of that new market. Conversely, if a spin-off is planned in order to shrink the business, there may be only a minimal return on investment associated with training.

A fully-developed linkage between strategy and training mandates that training needs to be itemized at the level of the individual employee, where each individual is given a personalized development plan. Doing so ensures that each person sees the linkage between his or her training plan and the direction of the entire business, which contributes to a sense of involvement with and support for the business.

Motivations for Training

Employees should not feel that the time allocated to training activities is a burden. Instead, they should be focused forcefully on the need to engage in training. There are several ways to motivate employees. First, raise performance expectations, so that it is more difficult to attain the highest performance ratings. Employees will then realize that only by engaging in ongoing training activities can they hope to attain the highest ratings, which is linked to higher compensation. Second, minimize the linkage between seniority and compensation, emphasizing that compensation will instead be based on critical skills and exceptional performance. Doing so shifts a large part of the compensation budget into the hands of those employees who have engaged in training.

The Positive Impact of Management Support

Employees listen carefully to what their managers say, because managers have control over salary increases, promotions, and advancement. Consequently, employees will notice when managers do not actively support a training initiative. Perhaps a manager grouses about an employee being taken away from her tasks for the day to attend a training session, or maybe the manager says nothing at all about an upcoming class. In these situations, the employee assumes that the training is not important, and so shows up with the intention of simply attending the class and then returning to her job, with no intent to implement what she has learned.

The situation is entirely different when the manager is actively supportive. When a manager takes aside an employee and asks her to pay attention in class and bring back ideas to work on, then the employee is much more likely to attend the training with an attentive mindset. Thus, a strong signal from managers that training is important is a key driver of how well employees perform in training.

The proper positioning of an employee's mindset going into a training class is critical, since this attitude tends to be self-fulfilling. Thus, a person who greatly anticipates a training session is much more likely to use the resulting information than someone who has minimal expectations for a class.

Management support must continue after a training session has been completed. The manager should meet with everyone returning from a training class to discuss next steps to implement what they have learned, and follow up at regular intervals to check on progress. It is also quite useful for the manager *not* to dump a pile of work on a returning employee, so that there is no time for implementation work; instead, do the reverse and block out enough time for the employee to make the necessary changes. Finally, the manager should create the expectation of some kind of reward that is linked to a proper learning transfer into the workplace, thereby giving the employee an incentive to succeed.

Transferring Training to the Workplace

It can be quite difficult to transfer the knowledge gained in a training session back to the workplace. There are several reasons for this, including training that is not correctly targeted at company problems and the resistance of the organization to change. Another area of concern is that the training department does not take responsibility for the implementation of knowledge, and the departments in which trainees are located do not place a high priority on it. To minimize these issues, it is critical to have a discussion between the trainer and management *prior to* the development of training materials, to talk about the exact needs to be addressed by the training and how management plans to assist with any resulting implementations. For example:

- *Course development*. The group can talk about what employees have to do better for the department to be successful, and the goals to be achieved. The discussion may extend into the particular needs of specific individuals. The outcome is a training program that is specifically targeted at the needs of the business.

- *Management support.* The discussion could revolve around change management – how managers intend to support any new initiatives, break down resistance, and provide an adequate level of support, possibly including incentives. Since this discussion takes place *before* the training, managers are put on alert well in advance that their participation will be needed – and they now have time to plan accordingly.

Managers can also assist with the training effort by meeting with participants in advance to reinforce with them how important it is to fully understand the information being imparted to them during training. Also, if the training requires attendees to read training materials in advance, managers can assist by blocking out sufficient time for them to do so. Another option is for managers to encourage attendees to draw up a list of questions to bring to the training, regarding how they can apply the training to their jobs.

Near the end of a training session, the trainer can build in a discussion about how the employees plan to implement what they have learned. This can be a group discussion, where the participants work together to figure out a plan for how to proceed. By making it a group discussion, the trainer is trying to gain cohesion in the group, so that they will work together during the implementation phase. An essential part of this discussion is to come up with a list of the barriers that will likely be encountered, and how to work around them.

Once training has been completed, participants should meet with their managers at once, to discuss how they can implement what was learned. There should be a series of these meetings, initiated by the manager, to discuss progress and the level of support needed to ensure that the necessary changes are made. If an employee is not in a position where he can immediately make use of his new skills, a possible option is to include him on a cross-functional team or other special project where the skills *can* be used.

> **Tip:** Have training participants prepare periodic progress reports about what they are doing to implement what they have learned in the workplace.

When a manager finds that an employee has persistently *not* been able to implement what he has learned, a reasonable outcome is not to send that person to any additional training, since the company is not achieving any return on its training investment.

Training for New Managers

Employees are frequently promoted into management because of their excellent work in non-managerial areas, such as being a great customer service representative, a brilliant engineer, or a high-performing salesperson. The trouble is that these skills do not necessarily translate into the requirements for a management position, since being a great individual performer does not prepare a person for extracting high performance from others. Instead, they tend to behave the same as they did in their last successful positions, which does not translate into the behavior needed for a manager. To keep this damaging transition from occurring, one should discuss several key topics with new managers that will put them on the right track. These topics are:

- *Delegation.* A new manager will want to stay within her comfort zone, which means continuing to do her old job to the greatest extent possible, while also working as a manager. This is a recipe for overwork, so the first step is to ensure that all of the old tasks have been completely handed off to a replacement. Then discuss the concept of delegation, where the manager hands off tasks to others to complete, and then acts in a supporting role to assist when needed. This can begin with a few minor acts of delegation where the fallout from failure is low, so that the manager can experience how the process works.
- *Planning.* Have the new manager focus less on daily firefighting and more on long-term planning, so that her area of responsibility improves on a long-term basis.
- *Advice.* Point out that senior managers are available as a resource that she can access at any time for advice.
- *Feedback.* Discuss the need for feedback, so that the new manager understands why it is so important to discuss issues with employees as soon as they arise, rather than waiting for them to fester before taking action. She needs to understand that giving prompt and concise feedback is an essential requirement for the ongoing development of employees.
- *Comportment.* Irrespective of how a new manager actually feels (quite possibly nervous), it is essential to act calm in front of others. Doing so settles down one's direct reports, because they assume that everything is under control. Also, such comportment is considered desirable in mid-level and senior managers, so it is needed in order to be considered for further promotion.

The preceding topics can be discussed and reinforced over a period of time, since the training of a new manager should proceed for an extended period of time, perhaps initially on a daily basis, and then gradually shifting to a more delayed regimen, such as once a week. This approach means that the new manager has someone available for advice on a near-constant basis during the early days of her job, when advice is needed the most.

Experiences for High-Potential Managers

When a manager appears to have significant potential for advancement, it is critical to give the person a broad range of experiences, in order to be ready when a senior management position becomes available. The following are all possible options:

- Place them on a cross-functional team. One of the better ways to bring a new manager out of his departmental shell is to assign him to a team that requires interaction with representatives from other departments and business units. This is also a great way to develop contacts across the organization.

- Place them with an experienced team. A really junior manager who shows promise should be placed with a very experienced group of subordinates, preferably running a distinct business unit, so that he can soak up advice from the group about how to run a business.
- Give them an international assignment. Living in a different country and dealing with its culture can be an eye-opening experience for any aspiring manager, especially since it takes the person away from his comfort zone for a prolonged period of time.
- Place them on an acquisition integration team. When the organization is in the business of acquiring other companies, put them on an acquisition integration team. These are high-pressure situations that call for a significant amount of tact in merging operations and dealing with the acquiree's workforce.
- Assign them to a startup. If the company has just created a startup operation, this is a good place to assign promising managers. They get to deal with staffing, funding, and product rollout issues that people in a more established environment never see.
- Assign them to a turnaround. One of the most difficult assignments is to turn around a failing business, since it requires a thorough analysis of the strategic situation, employee layoffs, and structural changes.
- Assign them to dealing with external stakeholders. It can be useful for someone approaching a senior management position to first deal with outside stakeholders, to gain a view of their perspective of the company. For example, a person could be assigned to investor relations, or to dealing with regulators.

Larger organizations that can offer a mix of the preceding opportunities will set up a multi-year rotation plan for their best managers, so that they are constantly exposed to a variety of challenging environments that can polish them into deeply experienced managers.

Summary

An essential concept in training is that the training given must align with the needs of the organization. Thus, the type and quantity of training given is derived from the overall strategy and supporting tactics employed by a business. When the strategy or tactics change, then so too must the training plan.

A training program will be vastly more successful when it is integrated into a follow-up campaign that works to implement the information that has been learned. There should be a formal structure in place for working with trainees for an extended period of time to ensure that a solid business outcome is achieved. When employees know that they will be expected to perform after a training session has been completed, they will be much less likely to take on the role of a spectator, where they merely show up for a training class.

Chapter 13
Manager Decision Making

Introduction

One of the core skills of a manager is the ability to make decisions[4], which can trigger changes in strategy, tactics, processes, and resource allocations. Great managers are able to routinely sort through the available information, make assumptions that turn out to be correct, and then use this information to arrive at decisions that, in hindsight, represent reasonable choices. In this chapter, we cover the decision-making environment, the process used to make decisions, and several related topics.

The Decision-Making Environment

It is easy to look back on a bad decision and ask what on earth the responsible manager was thinking. Clearly, no one sets out to make a bad decision, so what contributes to their persistent recurrence? Consider the following issues:

- *Available information.* The amount of information on which a decision is based is rarely complete. For example, a decision to build a new production facility cannot realistically take into account the intentions of competitors, who might also decide to build similar facilities, resulting in an oversupply of product, which drives down prices and kills any prospect of earning a return on the initial investment.
- *Assumptions.* A decision may be based, at least in part, on one or more key assumptions that may prove to be incorrect. For example, the president of an airline decides to buy more passenger jets on the assumption that the price of jet fuel will not spike over the next ten years. When the price does indeed spike in the following year, the airline is forced to raise its ticket prices, lowering customer demand.
- *Biases.* The typical person operates under any number of biases. For example, one might assume that the historical trend will continue into the future, or give an unusually strong weighting to the first or last opinion heard about an issue. Another bias is to support decisions that have already been made; this can be quite a problem when the earlier decision relates to the funding of a project, since the manager now has a bias to continue funding it, even when it is clearly failing. Other biases are:

---

[4] Decision making is the process of selecting an alternative from a range of possible options.

o Confirmation bias, when the person tends to seek out information confirming past choices and discounting information that contradicts her past judgments.

o Framing bias, when the person distorts what he sees by focusing on certain aspects of a situation and downplaying others.

o Immediate gratification, when the person prefers decisions with short-term payoffs.

o Overconfidence, when the person has an unrealistically positive view of his capabilities.

o Randomness bias, when the person tries to create meaning out of random events.

o Representation bias, when the person assesses an event based on how closely it resembles other events, drawing analogies that don't exist.

o Self-serving bias, when the person takes credit for her successes and blames others for her failures.

- *Emotional impact.* The decision-making process can be clouded by excessive emotions, such as being unusually angry or happy. Simply being angry at the person bringing up an issue can result in an incorrect decision that would not have been made if the manager had viewed the situation in a more balanced manner.

- *Misplaced confidence.* A series of correct decisions can lead a manager to believe that he can keep making the right calls. This string of successes can lead to over confidence, especially when others heap praise upon the person. A possible outcome is that the person becomes less cautious and less detail-oriented in examining every aspect of decisions, eventually leading to a bad decision.

- *Risk propensity.* Some managers are quite comfortable with the idea of taking on a large amount of risk, while other managers will avoid any choice that carries a downside to it. This risk propensity tends to reduce the range of possible choices for the latter type of manager, while the former type of manager may not fully take into account the downside risk of a decision. The results in both cases can be suboptimal.

Decision Making Efficiency

An effective manager is constantly trying to systematize the decision-making process by developing rules for how to deal with certain recurring situations where there is a low risk of failure. For example, it may be necessary to reorder inventory items on a regular basis, or buy ad space on a website, or review candidates for a position that is needed on a recurring basis. Once these situations have arisen more than once, the manager can specify how the associated decision is to be made, document these rules, and then hand off the decision to a subordinate. By taking this approach, the manager is creating more time for major, one-time decisions that are poorly defined and which have major consequences for the business – in short, decisions that require the close attention of a manager.

EXAMPLE

The manager of Optimistic Winery is faced with two decisions – which supplier to use for the company's annual purchase of wine bottles, and how wide the row width should be for ten new acres of vine plantings in the south fields. Though the bottle purchase is a large one, it can be safely left in the hands of the purchasing manager, since it is a repetitive inventory purchase. The row width decision, however, is much more important, since it impacts the amount of grapes that can be produced and the types of tractors that can be used in the vineyard – and the decision cannot be reversed until the field is replanted in 30 years. Thus, the manager can hand off the bottle purchase decision, so that she can focus more of her time on the row width decision.

Essential Decisions for Management

We have just described a process for eliminating many day-to-day decisions from the purview of a manager. Doing so leaves time for a much smaller number of decisions that are vastly more critical to the well-being of the organization. These decisions usually involve a significant risk of loss for the business, coupled with a substantial amount of uncertainty. For example, a manufacturer of car ferries wants to develop an all-electric ferry, but does not know how well it will be received by customers. In this case, there is a massive risk of loss associated with developing a ferry that no one will buy, coupled with uncertainty about the degree of customer acceptance.

Examples of the types of decisions that are squarely targeted at managers are:

- A business is investing a significant amount of money in a new production facility, in expectation of an increase in customer demand when its new product launches in a few months. Then a recession hits, and demand begins to decline. Should the company complete the factory, put everything on hold, sell off the half-finished facility, or choose some other option?
- A business is situated in a cyclical industry, and has built up a reasonable reserve of cash. A recession hits, and customer demand for the firm's products plummets. Should it wait out the recession, or take a chance and use some of its horded cash to buy a failing competitor?
- A government has just eliminated a trade embargo against a country that had been abusing its citizens. A producer of low-priced agricultural equipment believes it could find a ready market for its products in that country, but there is a risk that the government will re-impose the trade embargo, which would result in the complete loss of any products or facilities that the company would situate in the new market. Competitors are rumored to be interested in the same market. Should the company hold back from this market or jump in?

183

Decision Making Tools

Are there any tools available for dealing with specific types of decisions that will impact their effectiveness? Here are several possibilities:

- *Investigate based on cost-benefit.* When the benefit to be gained from a decision is relatively minor, a manager is more likely to engage in only a minimal amount of investigatory work before selecting a decision option. There may be better alternatives available, but the manager does not have enough time to investigate them all, and the benefit linked to a better alternative is not such an incremental improvement that it is worth the extra time.
- *Build consensus.* Some decisions will impact many parts of a business, so the manager needs to build a consensus opinion among the impacted people. This will likely result in a modified decision outcome that balances the needs of everyone in the group. An added benefit is the substantial amount of debate that is usually needed to build a consensus. This type of decision tends to require a substantial amount of time.
- *Brainstorm.* Brainstorming is the process used to come up with creative new solutions by engaging in an open group discussion. Each attendee is encouraged to come up with as many ideas as possible, no matter how outlandish they may initially appear to be. A critique of the resulting ideas is only allowed after the initial idea generation phase has been completed. By barring any initial negative feedback, attendees feel less inclined to keep ideas to themselves.
- *Add diverse debaters.* The management team, or even the people at all levels within one department, tend to be a uniform group, with shared views of the world. This means that they can reach a group decision that seems right to them, but which is profoundly wrong. One way to avoid this uniform thinking is to debate an issue with a group that comes from all over the company, from the top and bottom of the corporate hierarchy, including a range of ages and experiences, in order to gain the broadest possible view of every aspect of a decision.
- *Add a devil's advocate.* Though few people like to play the role, it can be useful to assign someone the position of devil's advocate, always challenging the assumptions of everyone else in the group. It can be quite useful for the manager making the decision to take this role, so that no one else in the group knows which way she is leaning, thereby triggering a livelier debate.

It is also possible to improve decision making by conducting an after-the-fact investigation of each major decision. The point is to look at what worked, what did not, and how to make the decision process better the next time around. This investigation does not have to be overly formal; the intent is not to create a perfectly documented review, but rather to spot issues that can be improved upon in the workplace at once.

Steps in the Decision-Making Process

When dealing with a major decision, the manager should engage in a few steps that are designed to improve the outcome. These steps are:

1. Identify the problem or opportunity
2. Diagnose the problem or opportunity
3. Develop a set of alternatives
4. Select an alternative
5. Implement the chosen alternative
6. Obtain feedback

Each of these steps is discussed in the following sub-sections.

Identify the Problem or Opportunity

A manager needs to identify whether there is a problem (when current results are inadequate) or an opportunity (when current goals can be exceeded). This identification process is not easy, since most of them do not automatically present themselves to a manager. Instead, one must dig for them by regularly engaging with employees and business partners, reviewing both financial and operational reports, reading periodicals and attending industry functions. Many managers let problems and opportunities slide for years because they are incapable of identifying them.

Diagnose the Problem or Opportunity

Once a problem or opportunity has been identified, the manager has to understand what is causing it. It can be exceedingly difficult to locate a root cause, usually because it is obscured by some other issue. To find the underlying cause, one may need to make extended inquiries, exploring such issues as when, where, and how a problem is occurring.

It is possible that finding and correcting a single root cause will not completely eliminate a specific problem. If so, the analysis can be conducted on a recurring basis, in order to gradually locate and eliminate a series of issues. Eventually, the number of times the triggering problem arises may decline to such an extent that additional effort is considered unnecessary, though there may be additional issues still causing problems. The remaining issues are considered too immaterial to pursue, or their correction is not considered cost-effective.

The same approach applies to the identification of opportunities. The manager needs to define the opportunity, or else there is a risk of wasted resources. When formulating an opportunity description, the following concepts may apply:

- Is the issue important to the organization? Ideally, an opportunity should be linked to the mission of the firm. If it is not, then one may ask whether it is worth the resources of the business.

- Identify the gap to be closed. If there is a "nirvana" state to be reached, specify what it is. Doing so creates a quantifiable variance between the current state and future state at which solutions can be targeted.
- Narrow the scope. A broad project scope can scare away funding, and also may require a more substantial time commitment than the management team is willing to make. Narrowing the focus of an opportunity to a more manageable chunk can greatly increase its probability of success. Further, gaining experience with the correction of a small problem may result in efficiencies in regard to how to handle a broader, related issue.

To summarize the essential elements of a well-constructed problem or opportunity statement, it should focus on an acute and immediate issue. Here are several examples:

The printing press is experiencing a 20% downtime rate, which is caused by broadsheet tearing at the feed roller.

The candy is sticking in the hopper, which requires the staff to stop production and clean the hopper two additional times per day, resulting in an incremental increase in production downtime of 40 minutes per day.

The average wait time for a patient is 42 minutes before he or she meets with a doctor, which is 30 minutes more than the wait time advertised by the competing emergency room across the street.

Develop a Set of Alternatives

Decisions tend to have better outcomes when there are a number of alternatives available, rather than just two or three. To obtain a broad range of choices, it can be useful to ask for input from across the organization. By doing so, management is tapping into a pool of people with different knowledge and experience, and who may therefore have different insights on how to proceed. A side benefit of asking employees for help is that they are more likely to buy into the final decision.

When devising alternatives, consider the extent to which a solution might create new problems or exacerbate existing ones. In some cases, a proposed solution may worsen the current situation. When there is no alternative available that represents a clear improvement, it can make sense to park the issue for a period of time and revisit it at a later date.

Select an Alternative

When selecting an alternative, a manager seeks to strike a balance between a choice that minimizes the use of company resources, reduces downside risk, achieves the desired result, and most closely matches the organization's values. The alternative chosen will depend on many factors, such as the manager's tolerance for risk, the current financial situation, and the extent to which the manager believes in the company's stated values.

EXAMPLE

Derek Smith, a sales manager in the high-pressure container division for Armadillo Industries, is reviewing a request for proposals from a power company to construct a metal and concrete containment unit for a nuclear power generating facility. To submit a bid that will ensure a completely safe containment unit, Smith should propose a price of $90 million. However, to be assured of the win, the maximum bid should be in the vicinity of $80 million. To make any money at this lower price point, Smith will have to authorize a number of structural changes that could result in a containment breach if there is an earthquake. There is no history of earthquakes in the area where the power generating facility will be located, though nearby oil drilling activities could trigger a low-magnitude earthquake.

The high-pressure container division is generating profits well below its historical rate, and below the budget for the year. By approving an $80 million bid for a weakened containment structure, Mr. Smith can ensure that the division will meet its profit target for the year.

Another factor to consider is the Jones family, which owns Armadillo. They have consistently urged their managers to plan for the long term, and not put the company at risk of an epic failure. They have supported these statements by firing anyone who does not manage in such a manner.

Smith weighs the options and decides to pull out of the bidding, deciding that the correct decision is to abide by the company's values and not build a sub-standard containment vessel that presents some risk of massive fallout (!) for both the company and the area surrounding the nuclear plant. He immediately reorients the division's sales team toward a new search for projects in other parts of the world.

When a decision is an especially important one and there is some time available, it can make sense to discuss the issue with as many people as possible. It is quite likely that someone with unique experiences or knowledge can contribute a different viewpoint on the situation that results in an alternative decision being made.

Implement the Chosen Alternative

Once a decision has been made, the manager has to implement it. Many projects fail at this point, and for many reasons, such as:

- There is not sufficient funding available
- There are no personnel resources available
- Other managers will not support the decision
- The manager does not have enough time available to properly oversee the implementation
- The manager does not provide enough support for the decision
- The manager does not re-orient reward systems to support the decision

Conversely, engaging in the reverse of the preceding points tells the organization that a manager is deeply interested in and supportive of a decision, and will forcefully back up that decision whenever necessary. Employees consider a manager to be more supportive of a decision when he regularly measures the outcome of the related activity and follows up based on the results of that measurement.

Tip: There is a definite limit on the number of decisions that a manager can support, since each one requires a certain amount of follow-up time. Therefore, it can make sense to spread out key decisions, so that each one can be dealt with using an adequate amount of manager resources.

Obtain Feedback

Once a decision has been made and implemented, the manager should follow up to see if the desired outcome has been attained. This is a critical step, for it gives the manager feedback about one or more of the following:

- The outcome was less than expected, which may require another iteration of the decision process to take further action.
- The outcome was better than expected, in which case the manager should ponder what parts of the decision process may have contributed to this positive result, so that it can be built into the next decision process.
- The outcome worsened the existing situation, in which case the manager needs to conduct a more detailed review to determine what caused the poor decision or subsequent implementation. Otherwise, the same flaw may be built into the next decision process, thereby triggering further negative outcomes in the future.

When dealing with a deeply complex problem, it is almost inevitable that the first decision made to resolve the situation will not be sufficient – it is nearly always essential to engage in a decision review to see what went wrong, which then results in a corrective decision. A number of subsequent corrective decisions may be required before the problem has been adequately dealt with.

EXAMPLE

The Close Call Company is in the business of making rush deliveries within larger metropolitan areas. For years, it has relied on independent contractors to drive packages to their intended recipients. Recently, its managers have been pondering the possibility of using company-owned motor scooters instead, since they can weave through traffic that would stop an automobile. However, doing so presents the risk of injury to drivers on the company-owned scooters, which presents the possibility of a significant medical liability.

The initial decision is to test the motor scooter concept in Denver, accompanied by a 25% pricing premium if a package can be delivered within ten minutes, which can be used to offset the cost of liability insurance and the investment in scooters. This decision results in one-third of the customers being delighted with the rapid delivery, and two-thirds annoyed by the higher fee. This results in a further decision to only charge the premium if customers have first asked for the premium service, thereby eliminating customer annoyance. However, those asking for quicker delivery now want up-to-the-minute status reports on their packages, so management makes a further decision to roll out a mapping app that shows driver locations. Once the other customers hear about the new app, they want it too, so then management decides to roll it out with all customers.

In short, the initial decision to use motor scooters ended up calling for three additional management decisions. These additional decisions may eventually trigger more issues that call for even more decisions, thereby showing how a cascade of topics can be associated with an initial decision.

Approaches to Decision Making

Many managers will follow the rational, step-by-step methodology just outlined here. However, some have alternative approaches that appear to be ingrained – they are simply more comfortable using their own methods. Consider the following alternative techniques:

- *Analytical*. This manager likes to collect masses of data and then sift through it, searching for the best possible answer. This approach can work well for very complex and/or risky decisions, but also takes up an inordinate amount of time when used to deal with every decision.
- *Directive*. This manager makes rapid-fire decisions based on the available information, and preferably from a small number of decision choices. This approach is ideal for lesser day-to-day decisions as they relate to operations, but does not always result in the optimal choice, especially when dealing with more complex issues.
- *Social*. This manager likes to tap the opinions of others regarding the nature of a problem and how it may be solved. This can involve the consideration of many possible options, which can take an extended period of time. Given the amount of time involved, it is best applied to major decisions, and is not appropriate for day-to-day decisions that require rapid settlement.

The best managers may be more comfortable with a particular decision making technique, but can switch to alternative approaches, depending on the situation. For example, a manager may routinely use the directive approach for most decisions, and then switch to the analytical or social techniques for the most critical decisions.

It is possible that a manager will rely on intuition to make some decisions. Though intuition involves instinctive feeling rather than conscious reasoning, it should not be shortchanged. Intuition is derived from a person's experiences, training, ethical values, and accumulated judgment, and so is not just a "feeling" – it is actually the extrapolation of internalized judgment rules to new situations. Intuition can be quite useful for making rapid decisions in cases that are not critical to a business.

Summary

An essential element of the decision-making process is deciding which decisions require the most attention. One should be able to divide decisions into those that can be handed off or dealt with based on a few obvious alternatives, and those decisions for which the supporting information is incomplete and the outcomes are of more importance. Ideally, a manager should be spending the bulk of her decision-making time on the latter group of decisions, so that the greatest effort is associated with the most important decisions.

Chapter 14
Managing Teams

Introduction

A team is a group of people with complementary skills, which works together to attain a specific goal. This group is mutually responsible for its output. These are the essential components of a team – skills, togetherness, mutual responsibility, and a shared goal. Team members work closely to explore ideas, decide on future direction, deliver outputs, and measure the performance of the group. Participants may share work or rotate jobs among the group over the course of a project. In essence, a team creates a work product through the joint efforts of its members. The approach to managing a team depends on the type of group that has been assembled, and whether it is considered to be a high-performance group, or self-directed, or widely dispersed. In this chapter, we deal with a variety of management concerns related to teams.

Types of Teams

There are multiple types of teams, which can be defined by their expected output. The type of team can alter its membership, management, and focus. The types of teams are described in the following sub-sections.

Recommendation Teams

Many teams are assembled for the purpose of making a recommendation to management regarding a course of action. Examples of recommendation teams are:

- How to improve the safety of a manufacturing process
- How to reduce the cost structure of an acquiree
- Whether to expand into a new product niche

A key characteristic of a recommendation team is that it operates under time pressure. There is likely to be a specific deadline by which a recommendation must be made. This is because a particular incident may have triggered the formation of the team. For example, we just noted that this team could make recommendations concerning the safety of a manufacturing process; it is likely that such a team was formed immediately after someone was injured in a production activity.

Because of the time pressure imposed on a recommendation team, it is critical that this group be well-organized from the start, and fully supported by management. Doing so requires the following items:

- *Well-defined direction.* The team must have a complete, well thought-out direction at once. This is needed to ensure that the correct resources are assigned to the team, and that the deadline can be met without time wasted in the exploration of unnecessary paths.

- *Full staffing.* Since the required outcome is needed on an accelerated basis, the team must be fully staffed at once with people having the appropriate skill sets.
- *Full support.* When the team encounters any obstacle that it cannot surmount by itself, the management team must be willing to step in on behalf of the team to eliminate the problem. Otherwise, it will be difficult to meet the deadline.

Once the team has delivered its recommendations to management, its task is not yet over. The biggest problem with recommendations is that they are not enacted, so the team leader also needs to push management to authorize an implementation process. This has two possible outcomes. One is that the recommendation team is then tasked with implementing its own recommendations. The other outcome is that at least some members of the team are tasked with handing off their recommendations to a designated implementation group. In the latter case, it is important to involve the implementation team as early as possible, so it may be necessary to bring these people into the recommendation team before the final recommendations are implemented. By doing so, the implementation team has a hand in the final recommendations, and so is invested in the final work product.

Ongoing Activity Teams

A business may have several self-governing teams that are involved in the improvement of business functions. These teams tend to be in value-added areas, where the intent is to improve service or reduce costs. Examples of the areas in which ongoing activity teams may be found are manufacturing, field service, customer service, marketing, and sales. These teams are especially useful in situations where there are complex problems and the solutions to them are not immediately clear.

An ongoing activity team is not subject to a specific completion date, because its work never ends. Instead, this team is constantly evaluating how to improve performance in its designated area of operations. Despite the lack of a clear deadline, management still places pressure on these teams to perform by assigning ongoing performance measurements, such as cycle time reductions achieved, error rate reductions achieved, or costs reduced.

Ongoing activity teams are more likely to require highly specific skills that pertain to the projects in hand, so it may be necessary to occasionally add people who have the required skills. At a minimum, these teams should include a large proportion of members who have a proven ability to learn new skills, so that they can expand their knowledge as needed to address the demands of the most recent project.

A common feature of an ongoing activity team is that the members work together for long periods of time. A long team duration takes advantage of the slow accrual of trust within the team, as well as their enhanced ability to work together that comes with the passage of time.

An ongoing activity team is constantly spinning off recommendations to management for changes that can be made. However, unlike the recommendations team concept that was noted in the preceding sub-section, an ongoing activities team is more likely to engage in implementations itself. By doing so, there is no risk of a recommendation being dropped as part of a failed handoff to a separate group. Instead, the team formulates recommendations and then immediately rolls into the implementation phase of the work.

Design Teams

A design team is usually involved in the generation of new product designs, or incremental changes to existing products. These teams may stay together for long periods of time, and in that respect are similar to ongoing activity teams. However, design teams operate under highly specific timelines and cost rules. For example, a design team may be tasked with creating a product design in six months that costs no more than $100 to construct. Because of the additional constraints and targets imposed on this type of team, it is important that this group be well-organized and fully supported by management. Thus, a design team contains elements of the characteristics of recommendation teams and ongoing activity teams.

Management Teams

A management team is a group of supervisory personnel that focuses on performance results for a functional activity, program, business unit, division, or even an entire entity. Most management groups are *not* teams, because they are not focused on substantial performance improvements. Instead, most managers simply work together to meet the annual target outlined in the company budget. For a management group to be a team, there should be a stretch goal that requires the group to closely coordinate their activities. For example, a contract program is about to fail, so the responsible management group comes together to examine the cost structure of the underlying contract and renegotiate the contract with the customer, with the goal of reversing the situation. While this stretch goal is being targeted, the management group can be considered a team. Once the goal has been achieved, the group goes back to business as usual, at which point the group can no longer be considered a team.

From a practical perspective, senior executives cannot devote much time to a single topic, and so cannot participate fully in a team project. However, it is possible for a smaller number of executives with a keen interest in a particular goal to set aside the requisite time to see a project through to completion. Thus, it is more common to see very small team sizes in the most successful management teams.

Customer Account Teams

A customer account team is drawn from multiple disciplines within a business, and focuses on the relationship with one key customer. These teams are useful when dealing with very large customers, or customers whose orders have the potential to increase significantly in size. The teams can be used in any industry – for example, for banking services, auditing services, and manufactured goods.

The purpose of a customer account team is to provide a coordinated response to a customer. This response can take different forms, depending on the relationship. For example, if a customer has a problem to be solved, the account team acts as a knowledgeable solution provider. Or, the team could act as a strategic advisor, working to anticipate the future needs of a customer. In both of the examples, the team takes on the role of an expert, which means that it must be staffed with highly experienced and/or highly trained individuals.

Customer account teams may operate under extreme time pressure, since customers can have specific problems that must be resolved at once. However, the problem may not be well-defined, so the team operates under the additional pressure of having to clearly identify the issue and then formulate a solution. In addition, the members of this team will likely remain in contact with the customer throughout any resulting implementation phase, acting as the interface between the customer and the selling entity's functional departments.

Style of the Team Leader

A team leader cannot follow the classic approach of forming a hierarchical organizational structure and then dictating how a team will function. This is because the team members report to managers outside of the team, not the team leader. Given the absence of direct management authority, the team leader must rely upon other techniques.

When it comes to managing a team, there is no ideal management style. Instead, whoever is placed in this role should adapt his or her style to the circumstances. If a team has a mix of domineering and quiescent members, a likely management style will be to coach all parties to adopt a more even level of communication. If a team needs a wildly creative solution, the management style may involve coaching participants to search outside of the team for ideas. If there are seriously deviant individuals in the group, the most appropriate style might be to weed out those causing too much trouble, and shield the remainder from organizational pressure.

It may be easier to define what the management style for a team should *not* be. The manager should not be a domineering sort who immediately imposes solutions on the team and then instructs them to go forth and conquer. This approach merely results in (figuratively) a king and a group of serfs.

If there is any single factor that should be present in a team leader's management style, it is the ability to focus on group processes. One should examine how the team is interacting, whether divergent views are being considered, and so forth, and provide timely nudges to direct the team toward a more optimal outcome.

Though we have just pointed out that no single management style is ideal for a team, there should be an emphasis on defining roles and objectives at the start of a project. The team leader should be very clear about defining the problem to be solved, and working with the team to define the direction to be taken. Then, the leader clarifies the exact responsibilities of each team member. Once these "laying the groundwork" tasks have been completed, the team leader can switch to whatever management style seems most appropriate under the current circumstances.

Collaboration Issues

A team functions best when its members collaborate as closely as possible. The trouble is that people are much more likely to collaborate when they perceive other team members as being similar to them. The "similarity" concept can apply to many factors, such as age, level of education, and nationality. Further, collaboration is even more unlikely when the people assigned to a team do not know each other. Yet another concern is that team members who are specialists tend not to collaborate, instead displaying a strong tendency to support their own views. These blocks to collaboration can be overcome by engaging in the following activities:

- *Minimize the number of strangers*. When selecting people for a team, ensure that a significant proportion of the selected group already knows each other.
- *Train team members*. Provide mandatory training to employees prior to the start of a team assignment, where they receive instruction in conflict resolution, project management, engaging in targeted conversations, and appreciating the views of others.
- *Coach team members*. The team leader constantly monitors the interactions of the team, and steps in to provide coaching when there is a clear lack of collaboration.
- *Define roles*. Each team member should be given a clearly defined role at the start of a project. By doing so, there is less room for participants to bicker over who will be assigned to which task.

A deceptively simple way to foster collaboration is to encourage team members to eat meals together. Doing so substantially increases their time interacting with each other, which is not necessarily what happens when they return to their cubicles and offices after lunch.

Conflict Resolution

A team needs to engage in constructive conflict in order to fully evaluate alternative courses of action. Unfortunately, many teams avoid conflict by settling too quickly upon one outcome. When this happens, they choose a course that may turn out to be suboptimal, or even one that has serious shortcomings.

There are ways to create a working environment in which conflict resolution can be conducted without causing serious interpersonal problems within a team. A mix of the following solutions can create an environment in which alternatives are addressed without causing permanent damage to a team:

- *Set a common goal*. Be sure that the team is entirely in agreement on the goal being pursued. When this is the case, everyone understands that there may be arguments about how to achieve the goal, but they all want to get there. With this focus, arguments are less likely to turn in a personal direction.
- *Argue based on facts*. Collect as many facts about the situation as possible, rather than arguing based on opinions. If there is a conflict that is based on

limited or no information, then pause the discussion until more information is available. If opinions are used instead of facts as the basis for decisions, then arguments will focus on the people supporting an opinion, which quickly leads to interpersonal conflict.

- *Create additional options.* When the team deliberately increases the number of options under consideration, it gives the group a broader range of alternatives, which allows people to spread their support more broadly. When there are only two alternatives, support tends to harden quickly around them, which can lead to politicking in favor of one or the other. When choices are added, the team is more likely to focus on the process of developing alternatives, rather than choosing sides.

- *Have a fair process.* The process used to arrive at decisions must be perceived as being fair. If not, those people whose positions are rejected may perceive the process as being deliberately skewed against them. Unfair decision processes usually involve a strong team leader who autocratically makes final decisions. In this situation, the team is more likely to switch to politics to influence the decisions of the leader. A better approach is to use consensus as much as possible, and to defer to the decision of the most relevant manager when a consensus cannot be reached, and especially when there is a deadline for the decision. This latter approach ensures that everyone on the team can participate in and influence the final decision, even if the actual decision goes against their preferred outcome.

- *Introduce humor.* When a team can include humor in its interactions, it defuses the stress associated with making decisions. It also puts people in a more positive frame of mind, which tends to minimize their levels of defensiveness.

Conflict is a necessary part of a team, since it allows the group to sift through a number of alternatives. The trick is how to handle conflict so that it does no lasting harm to the team members and their relations with each other. When handled properly, team members still feel that they have been given a voice in the process, and so will be more supportive of the direction taken. Further, the decision-making process is more likely to have considered a range of options based on factual information, resulting in better decisions.

Dealing with Counterproductive Behavior

Sometimes, a person is engaged in behavior that is seriously counterproductive to the team. This could involve, for example, a constant stream of complaints, low-quality work, opposing the team plan, or making disruptive outbursts. Since teams are generally small in size, just one person engaged in such behavior can destroy the cohesiveness of the team. While the most obvious solution is to kick the person off the team, the situation may be recoverable by engaging in some intensive listening to see if the individual has concerns that may be valid. While the person's behavior may be quite inappropriate, the underlying reasons could involve issues that are worthy of consideration. For example, if a product design team is proceeding with a design that might contain a safety issue, a team member could become frustrated that no one is addressing his concern, and so elects to oppose further progress on the design by delaying his contributions to the work.

Irrespective of the information found by hearing out the person, the indicated problems must stop. To do so, work with the individual to develop benchmarks for proper behavior, ask if any support can be provided to encourage this behavior, document the resulting action plan, and give a copy to the person. Then have periodic meetings to discuss changes in the person's behavior. These actions may not ultimately convert the person into a productive team member, but in some cases the extra effort can do so.

Internal Conflict Resolution

The team leader does not want to be placed in the position of constantly having to settle conflicts within the team. When this happens, the process takes an inordinate amount of time, and the team members may not be pleased with the resolution, which reduces the authority of the team leader. Instead, consider training the team to settle their own conflicts. Doing so not only clears a large item from the work list of the team leader, but also makes team members responsible for their own solutions. There are several ways to assist in this transition, which are:

- *Teach skills.* Employees are bad at conflict resolution, because they have never received any training in it. This problem can be remedied by going over the basic principles of defining the facts of a situation, mutually laying out possible solutions, and agreeing to changes. It may be necessary to bring in a neutral third party to conduct the training, and to use role playing so that individuals can practice the process.
- *Set an example.* The team leader should strongly favor in-person meetings to text-based communications, and avoid criticizing outsiders or management. This sets an example for the rest of the team, which may emulate this behavior.
- *Coach with queries.* When a team member brings up an issue concerning another employee, do not step in to settle the issue. Instead, coach them with queries regarding how the situation should be handled. For example:
  - Have you listened to the issues that she has? Do you understand them?
  - What steps have you taken to resolve the issue?
  - How would you phrase your concerns to the person?
  - What sort of solutions do you think would be acceptable to both of you?
- *Debrief.* Once a person has been sent off to settle a conflict on his own, ask for a short meeting afterwards to go over how matters went. The team leader may be able to give advice on some aspects of the matter, which can result in a more polished conflict resolution by the employee at some point in the future.

It will require a certain amount of time for these actions to take effect – quite possibly more than the team leader would need to directly settle internal conflicts over the short term. However, the long-term effect is to remove many of these issues from the team leader, while also giving the team more confidence that it can handle them without any intervention.

The High-Performance Team

In rare cases, an organization may need to form a team that is tasked with an extremely difficult goal, such as resolving a prospective lawsuit, fixing a major product flaw, or switching the core technology to a new platform. In these situations, only "A" level experts are used, in order to maximize the flow of ideas. The outcome can be radically different solutions that are delivered within highly compressed periods of time. Despite the potential benefits, organizations usually avoid loading a team up with experts, due to their irascibility, egos, and inability to work with others.

There are ways to improve the odds of creating a productive high-performance team. Given the nature of the team's participants, it is not guaranteed that the following recommendations will work – nonetheless, they create an environment in which great outcomes are more likely. The recommendations are:

- *Select carefully*. An "A" level expert represents a completely different personality type from the normal team member. This individual loves a challenge, wants to take risks, and operates well under pressure. Accordingly, look for these traits when selecting members for a high-performance team. If there are too many "B" level players in the team, they will impede the thought processes of the "A" people by not pushing them along, and by opposing the more radical innovations.
- *Feed their egos*. An "A" level person craves attention, so give it to them. This means publicizing the team's members, giving the group massive amounts of funding, and staying out of their way. By doing so, each person does not feel constrained, and knows that a successful group outcome will improve their reputation.
- *Pack them in*. Keep the team members in close proximity to each other. By doing so, they can continually interact, bouncing ideas off each other in face-to-face conversations. The outcome is a much faster pace of progress.
- *Manage differently*. There are several ways to manage a high-performance team. One approach is to be a perfectionist who demands excellence. Another option is to encourage so many viewpoints that the work environment is continually tumultuous. Under this latter approach, the flow of ideas is so continuous that each person has no time to be locked into his or her ownership of an idea, and so will instead support the best overall outcome. No matter what method is used, the team leader must continually reinforce the time constraints under which the team is working, so that the targeted deliverable will be achieved on time.

Given the intensity with which a high-performance team functions, it is rare for the group to stay together for very long. Instead, they will likely break up as soon as the team goal has been achieved, declining to stay together for other projects. This outcome is even more likely for "A" level experts, who are usually being bombarded with offers to work on other projects. Consequently, no matter how successful a high-performance team may be, do not expect its members to continue together on later projects.

It is quite difficult to find team leaders who can deal in the correct manner with a high-performance team. These individuals are likely to comprise quite a small subset of the total group of team leaders. Consequently, identify which ones are the most capable, and reserve them for use on high-performance teams. Otherwise, an inadequate manager might be assigned to a high-performance team and throw it into disarray.

Leadership Sharing

In the most effective teams, leadership moves among the team members. This is because the formal team leader recognizes that he or she is not always the most effective leader, depending on the circumstances. Instead, someone else may be an expert, and so is the best qualified to lead a discussion and make a decision. For example, if a person is a nationally-recognized expert on tire safety, the decision system for a group might be to designate this person as the one who will make a decision regarding the materials to be used in a new tire design, with input from the other team members. Once this decision has been made, the formal team leader steps back into his role.

As another example, a common team leader role is to negotiate a budget for the team. If someone else on the team is a better negotiator, this person can take over the negotiation role on behalf of the team – irrespective of what her regular job within the team may be.

When the leadership role is shared across the team this also builds more buy-in to the team's goals, since more members are involved in how decisions were reached.

Self-Directed Teams

A self-directed team has no managing team leader. Instead, the team manages itself. Thus, team members are responsible for jointly setting goals, timelines, and work allocations. This type of team still reports to a manager, but that manager is located outside of the team. For example, a self-directed product design team might report to the vice president of engineering.

There are several reasons for promoting the use of self-directed teams. First, there may not be a sufficient number of qualified managers to handle a large number of teams. Or, the members of some teams are so experienced that they clearly have little need for supervision. Or perhaps senior management is promoting a flat organizational structure and sees an opportunity to eliminate another layer by removing managers from teams. Another possibility is the expectation that a self-directed team will not be held back by any restrictions that may be imposed by a manager, and so can generate more creative results.

A self-directed team is more likely to have no termination date. Instead, it has an ongoing mission that may never end. Conversely, few self-directed teams have tight deadlines, since a tight deadline usually calls for the services of an experienced leader who can cajole the team into attaining maximum performance.

For a self-directed team to produce good results, it must have several characteristics that allow it to operate properly. These characteristics are:

- *Involvement*. Team members must be able to participate in the planning process, which means setting their own deadlines and work schedules.
- *Empowerment*. Team members are given a mission and then allowed to fulfill it in any manner they choose. True empowerment only comes with a sufficient amount of resources (in terms of funding, staff, facilities, equipment, and so forth) to do the job properly.

It can be difficult for managers to authorize the use of self-directed teams, since it introduces the nagging suspicion that a team will be unable to manage itself, and so will generate results well short of expectations. Management can overcome this hurdle by giving team members extensive training and advisory support in managing themselves. Also, the concept can be rolled out gradually, so that a team takes on more management tasks over time as it becomes more comfortable with the idea. Here are several ways to gradually assign more management responsibilities to team members:

1. Transfer over those tasks that are already going well. Employees can watch how these tasks are performed, and then mimic the process until they can duplicate the tasks flawlessly. These processes are already fully documented. This approach gives them experience right away with a successful process. Better yet, initially focus on those tasks that will not spark conflicts with others, so that trainees can focus on processes, rather than people.
2. Transfer over those tasks that require some improvement. At this stage, team members are comfortable with the process of taking on new skills, but need to learn about how to improve them, and to document how the altered systems function.

Also, management could limit the concept to its most experienced and mature teams that are most comfortable working with each other. For example, self-direction might only be allowed after a team has worked together for at least a year.

Eliminating a manager does not mean that a business will necessarily save the cost of that manager. Instead, a likely outcome is that the work previously performed by the manager is now spread among the entire team, which reduces the amount of time that they can spend on their assigned tasks. The outcome may be a decline in output or a request to add another staff person to the team in order to make up for the time lost to management responsibilities. The management tasks that a self-directed team must take on include the items noted in the following exhibit.

Management Tasks for a Self-Directed Team

Approving timesheets	Issuing reports
Budgeting	Purchasing services and materials
Developing procedures	Representing the team with outsiders
Disciplining team members	Scheduling work
Hiring new team members	Training team members

In this environment, there is still a need for someone with a team leader title. However, the content of the job has now changed. Instead of having supervisory authority, the team leader is limited to reporting to management, taking instruction from management, and facilitating the implementation of those instructions. Those team leaders who previously acted as managers can have a hard time moving into this more limited role, since they have no real authority within a team and have no experience with this new type of role.

The team leader does not have to be the most senior or the most experienced person on a team. The most important requirement for the job is to have the respect of the team, so they will be more likely to work with the team leader as he or she engages in facilitation activities.

In addition to facilitation work, the team leader in a self-directed team is in charge of managing the boundaries of the team. This can involve dealing with customer issues, problems with suppliers, interfacing with the organization's attorneys over legal issues, meeting with other groups, bringing in technical training, and so forth.

A self-directed team has the following characteristics:

- *Collective management.* The group shares responsibility for management tasks. Thus, budgeting might be assigned to one person, or it could be shared among several people, while procedure development could be taken on by a different person. If the team is not familiar with management activities, this can require the selective use of additional team training.
- *Flat hierarchy.* There is essentially no reporting structure within a self-directed team. Even the team leader is essentially a "first among equals," with no special authority or privileges.
- *Few job descriptions.* The team members have few or no job descriptions, since each person is expected to take on one or more management activities in addition to his or her regular work. In addition, team members are more likely to take on different tasks within this type of team.
- *Broad information sharing.* Since everyone on the team will be involved in its regulation, everyone needs access to the information that would normally only be directed toward a manager. In addition, the entire team must have access to *any* information that can assist them in their task. For example, a product development team might need a comprehensive suite of information about the specifications of competing products, the costs of component parts, and the financial results for the product that is being replaced.

- *Numerous meetings.* A self-directed team needs to co-ordinate its activities frequently, to ensure that the group is progressing together in the same direction. This may require daily meetings. Given the frequency, it is usually not necessary to have overly long meetings – perhaps only enough time to clear up a few issues each day.
- *Self-directed.* As the team name implies, each member of a self-directed team manages his or her own activities, deciding which tasks need to be addressed first, and which can be delayed.

When there are multiple self-directed teams, it is quite possible that each of the teams will experience the same issues. If so, it can make sense to form a committee that is comprised of representatives from the teams. This committee is used to air issues being encountered, and to ask for advice from the other teams. If there are no issues, then the committee does not meet. The only purpose of the committee, then, is to share information across the groups.

If multiple teams are working in the same area, then the purpose of the committee can be broadened to include notifications of work being done. If a change being instituted by one team will impact another team, then the two teams can consult with each other to determine the best way to proceed. This added role gives the committee the task of being a *distributor* of information.

Managing the Dispersed Team

Many organizations are finding that the talent they need is located across broad geographic regions, and cannot be persuaded to move to a single location. Instead, these individuals are collected into teams that work together from their home locations. This is a trend that has accelerated as businesses expand geographically and telecommuting becomes a common work alternative. How to manage a dispersed team is a major issue, since talented employees may be located far away from company facilities. As examples, the following situations may arise:

- A product design team needs deep local knowledge of what customers want in specific markets. This expertise is only available from people based in those regions.
- A software development team needs the expertise of a developer whose skills at working in a specific software language are excellent; the demand for his work is so high that he can work from a log cabin in the mountains, irrespective of where his customers may be.
- A particular type of consumer product requires extensive testing to ensure that it will comply with all government safety standards. An expert in these standards has agreed to work with a product development team on an occasional basis, to provide advice on which features may run into regulatory land mines. Since he is only needed at longer intervals, he will only consult via e-mail and video chats.

In these and other situations, the team manager will find that more problems than usual will arise. Communications will be an issue, since there is no way to have in-person meetings to clarify differences of opinion. Also, if people are spread across multiple time zones, it is more difficult to schedule meetings and hand off projects. The result can be an increasing level of mistrust between the team members, or at least a high level of inefficiency as a team uncovers problems and needs to backtrack to earlier project stages to find alternative solutions. Customers may find that deliverables are completed late, and that the results achieved do not meet their expectations.

In the following sub-sections, we note several issues that can cause problems for a dispersed workforce, and how to resolve them.

Emotional Connection

Teams tend to work together best when there is a strong emotional connection between team members. This connection is highest when members can directly interact to discuss projects, align their needs, and build trust. A dispersed workforce can have quite a difficult time developing a strong emotional connection, since it is hard to foster the necessary social connections. Here are several specific conditions related to the emotional connection problem, and how to resolve them:

- *Disparity in team sizes.* There may be one location where most of the team members are located, with the remaining members scattered among several other locations. In this situation, there is a tendency for the largest group to ignore the input of the few outside members. The team leader can reduce the issue by soliciting and recognizing the contributions of the outside groups, emphasizing the common purpose of the entire group, and spending extra time communicating with the outlier personnel.
- *Large teams.* Some dispersed teams have dozens of members. Given the difficulty of overseeing people who may be based all over the globe, this makes it difficult to make every member clearly responsible for each deliverable. Instead, some employees will have an opportunity to loaf on the job without being detected. In addition, it is more difficult to keep all members of a large team current on the latest information. These problems can be corrected by keeping dispersed teams smaller than the normal team size. The maximum team size should certainly not exceed 10, and many teams function best with half that number of participants.
- *Lack of empathy.* In a properly-functioning team, members regularly have opportunities to engage in informal discussions, perhaps over lunch or in the break room, which allows them to build a sufficiently high level of empathy to allow for productive interactions regarding team-related tasks. Since this "face time" is not readily available to the members of a dispersed team, alternative approaches must be found to build empathy. Possible options are to schedule periodic "in person" meetings with extra time available for social interactions, favoring videoconferencing and phone calls over e-mail (which allows for less interaction), and blocking out time during conference calls for informal "chat" time. "In person" meetings are especially valuable at the start

of a project, since team members can use this time to become more comfortable with each other before the daily distraction of project demands get in the way. In addition, consider quarterly group meetings, perhaps at an off-site location, where everyone can discuss project status and socialize.

- *No prior history.* There may be cases in which every member of a dispersed team is new to every other member. If so, the preceding empathy problems will be exacerbated, since the team is "starting from scratch." However, this may not really be the case. It is possible that some of the team members have interacted with each other during prior projects. If so, they may have already built working relationships that can be carried forward into the current project. If this is the case, the team leader should consider linking up the indicated individuals for some tasks, since they may be more effective when working together. At an expanded level, these pre-existing relationships could be used as the nucleus of a larger group, whose performance is thereby augmented.

- *Uncomfortable team members.* Some members of a dispersed team may be uncomfortable with working on their own, or at least away from the main group of team members. Evidence of this issue is not participating sufficiently in team discussions, requiring constant oversight, and meeting goals late. Though some of the other concepts noted in this section can improve the performance of these people, it is also possible that the only solution is to remove them from a dispersed team environment. In extreme cases, they should be kept in a more structured environment in the future, and not allowed to participate in a dispersed team. Yet another action to consider is to screen all prospective team members with a personality test or behavioral interview to see if they have those characteristics that have proven to work on these types of teams in the past.

- *Late entrants.* It is fairly common for additional team members to be added after a project has already started. If so, these late entrants are operating at a disadvantage, since they never met anyone at the initial kickoff meeting, and instead will probably just be given a brief introduction during the latest conference call or videoconference call. This parsimonious welcome may lead to less interaction with the group, and less weight in decision making. To mitigate this problem, consider flying late entrants to the various work locations to meet the other team members in person. This is especially important if a project is expected to continue for a long period of time.

- *Dispersed decisions.* When decisions are made, it is more difficult to enforce them across all members of a dispersed team, especially when people are located in such different time zones that they do not hear about changes in direction until hours later. This is a particular problem when a project environment calls for continual changes in direction. The manager should reinforce decisions with team members by issuing update memos that list all decisions reached. It is also useful to reinforce decisions by using mixed communication formats, such as initially issuing information by e-mail, and then following up with a phone call. A mix of formats tends to reinforce messages with recipients.

- *Language problems*. When team members use more than one language, there will usually be an agreement to communicate in just one language that is spoken by the largest number of people on the team. If so, this tends to exclude the contributions of those remaining team members whose grasp of the default language is poor. In this situation, encourage those team members using the default language to avoid speaking with slang phrases that are difficult to understand, and to speak at a slow pace. Both changes allow for better comprehension by all team members. In addition, discussions should be periodically paused to verify that all team members understand the flow of the conversation. Further, whoever is monitoring a discussion should call upon those team members not contributing to ensure that they understand the discussion. Finally, encourage all team members to interrupt and ask for clarification if they do not understand what has been said.

- *No physical connection*. Some team members may be located alone and in distant locations. It may not be cost-effective for these people to travel the distances required to regularly visit the home office. The result may be a feeling of isolation, with no real connection to the rest of the team. If so, it can make sense to require the person to initially work at the home office for several months. By doing so, the person gains a much stronger sense of identity with those members of the team who are situated in that location, and begins to understand the values of the team and how they interact. Once this initial period of familiarization is over, the person can shift back to his or her original location. If the term of a project is substantial, it can make sense for these people to occasionally make additional trips to reconnect with the team. If the project duration is shorter, just the single trip may be sufficient.

Forms of Communication

An extremely dispersed team may be located across many time zones, which makes it more difficult to engage in effective communications. The best and most immediate interaction can be achieved with videoconferencing, but this may not be a viable option when some members are working well outside of the normal work hours of the rest of the group. Conversely, e-mail messages may not be answered for hours, which can interfere with work products that are on a tight deadline. These issues can be mitigated by using different forms of communication, depending on the type of communications required. For example:

- *E-mail*. Useful for status updates and the sharing of information.
- *Videoconferencing*. Useful for the clarification and resolution of problems, as well as for presenting a position regarding a decision.

The team leader should reinforce his or her preferred form of communication by using it. Thus, if the decision is to increase the use of phone calls and downgrade the use of e-mail, the manager should reinforce the preference by doing just that.

> **Tip:** When using videoconferencing, have employees give each other virtual tours of their workspaces. Just a simple panning of the camera around a room can alter the opinions of co-workers, once they realize that a person is burdened by working in an open-plan space, or near a busy corridor.

One form of communication that can present particular challenges is the conference call. When many people are listening in on a conference call, it is quite likely that only a few people will be actively involved, which means that everyone else could be engaged in more productive activities. Consequently, the participant list for conference calls should be as short as possible.

A problem with both videoconferencing and conference calls is that, with large numbers of people in attendance, there is a tendency for participants to go along with the consensus opinion, rather than speaking up to address key problems. To combat this issue, assign a senior person the role of probing for unspoken concerns and making sure that these items are discussed at a sufficient level of detail.

Rules

Each member of a dispersed team assumes that the rules of interaction for the team are those that he or she is accustomed to using. For example, one person might have a practice of only responding to e-mail once a day, in order to concentrate more fully on other tasks during the remainder of the day. Meanwhile, another person located elsewhere may be accustomed to receiving immediate responses to e-mails, in order to more quickly arrive at key decisions. These assumptions regarding rules of behavior should be settled when a dispersed team is first formed, so that everyone follows the same rules. Otherwise, it is entirely possible that frictions between the team members will arise that are caused by inaccurate perceptions of the work habits of other people.

Summary

It is difficult to foster an emotional connection among the members of a dispersed team, simply because they cannot interact in person. There are many ways to combat this, including in-person kickoff meetings, the increased use of videoconferencing, smaller team sizes, and a great deal of facilitation work by the team leader.

The Leader of a Dispersed Team

The team leader of a dispersed team is placed in the difficult position of being unable to work directly with team members, instead having to rely on long-distance forms of communication. This means that the leader will have a hard time perceiving any visual or auditory cues that may appear during a videoconference or phone call regarding how team members are feeling. One of the few ways to combat this problem is to appoint people to the team leader position who have an unusually acute ability to detect and correctly interpret these cues. This ability can be enhanced by giving team leaders additional training, but the best scenario is for the individual to already have an innate ability that can then be expanded.

The leader of a dispersed team must spend a large amount of time engaged in facilitation activities, in order to maximize the contributions of everyone on the team. This means that the leader should have extensive practice and training in the art of facilitation. The worst type of team leader for this situation is someone who is accustomed to the command-and-control style of management; this approach would mean that team members would be driven *away* from the team, rather than wanting to support it and contribute ideas to achieve its goal.

Summary

When engaged in the management of a team, a person must be cognizant of many issues, including the physical dispersion of the team, the existence of a deadline, and whether there are any "A" level players assigned to the team. These factors will impact the style adopted by the manager, ranging from a light touch with occasional coaching to full-on participation in every decision. In some cases, it is even possible to dispense with the services of a formal team leader, with the responsibilities for this role being parceled out among the team members. However, when there is an urgent deadline looming, it generally makes sense to have an experienced and active manager running a team.

Chapter 15
Project Management

Introduction

A project is an inherently complex activity that is difficult to organize. Luckily, there are a number of methods available for planning and controlling a project. The project manager can use these tools to track the status of each task, job assignments, and projected completion dates, as well as how this information impacts the project as a whole. By engaging in project management, one can reduce the level of uncertainty associated with a project. A detailed plan also allows for a proper analysis to see if any efficiencies can be produced by tweaking certain aspects of the plan. In this chapter, we describe the work breakdown structure and how to analyze it using several network scheduling tools. The outcome of this analysis is a more tightly focused project that maximizes resource usage while maintaining control over costs and the time required to complete the project.

The Project Planning and Control System

A project planning and control system translates a project objective into a work breakdown structure, which is then analyzed using such network scheduling tools as Gantt charts, the critical path method (CPM), and the program evaluation and review technique (PERT). The outcome of this process is a detailed work schedule and project budget. Once a project begins, hours worked and costs incurred are tracked against the work schedule and project budget. This tracking results in reports that are sent back to the project manager and project stakeholders. Based on this information, the project objective may be adjusted. Thus, the process is a continual loop. It appears in the following exhibit.

Project Planning and Control System

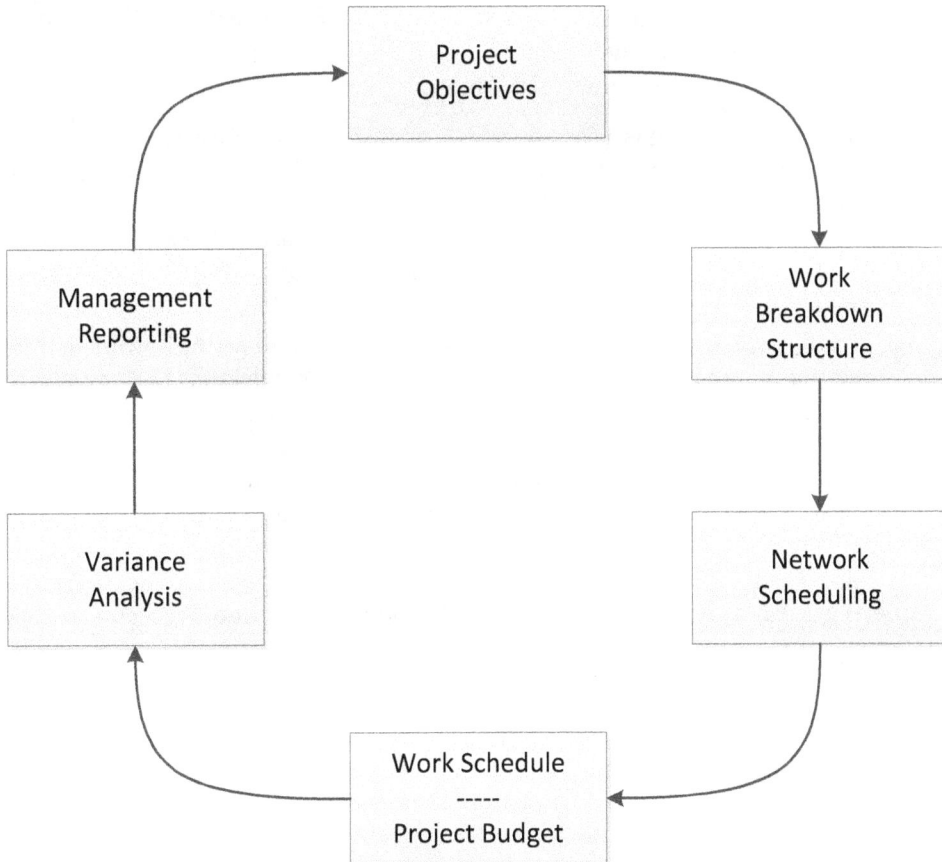

```
                    ┌──────────────┐
                    │   Project    │
            ┌──────▶│  Objectives  │──────┐
            │       └──────────────┘      │
            │                             ▼
   ┌──────────────┐                ┌──────────────┐
   │  Management  │                │     Work     │
   │  Reporting   │                │  Breakdown   │
   └──────────────┘                │  Structure   │
            ▲                      └──────────────┘
            │                             │
   ┌──────────────┐                       ▼
   │   Variance   │                ┌──────────────┐
   │   Analysis   │                │   Network    │
   └──────────────┘                │  Scheduling  │
            ▲                      └──────────────┘
            │       ┌──────────────┐      │
            └───────│ Work Schedule │◀─────┘
                    │    -----      │
                    │ Project Budget│
                    └──────────────┘
```

In this chapter, we focus on the work breakdown structure and network scheduling segments of the planning and control system.

The Work Breakdown Structure

Some projects are inordinately large, making them quite difficult to manage. This issue can be addressed by employing the work breakdown structure, which identifies every task in a project. This process of identification breaks down a project into a cluster of bite-sized pieces that are easier to manage. Each task is listed in an outline format, so that a great many tasks can be clearly stated within a relatively small document. With this information in hand, a project manager can more easily do the following:

- Clearly state all aspects of a project's scope
- Monitor the completion stage of each identified task
- Compile the cost of each task
- Develop work assignments for each task

The work breakdown structure of a project divides activities into *summary tasks* and *work packages*. A summary task describes a set of activities (work packages). A work package is a group of activities for which work is estimated, scheduled, monitored, and controlled. A work package defines work at the lowest level for which cost and duration can be estimated and managed. For example:

- Constructing a shed is a summary task, while laying the foundation, constructing a frame, and building a roof are all work packages within the summary task.
- Installing a purchasing software module is a summary task, while loading the software, porting over existing purchasing data, and testing the new software are all work packages within the summary task.
- Training employees in a new safety program is a summary task, while writing the training materials, training the trainers, and conducting training classes are all work packages within the summary task.

In each of the preceding examples, when all of the work packages are complete, the summary task is also accomplished. A sample work breakdown structure for the construction of a new home appears in the following exhibit.

Sample Work Breakdown Structure for a Home Construction Project

1.0 Design building structure

2.0 Lay foundation
    2.1 Dig hole
    2.2 Build concrete forms
    2.3 Pour concrete

3.0 Construct home
    3.1 Construct frame
    3.2 Add exterior walls
    3.3 Add plumbing
    3.4 Add wiring
    3.5 Add interior walls
    3.6 Add roof
    3.7 Add carpeting and hardwood floors
    3.8 Add windows

4.0 Install lawn
    4.1 Dig trenches
        4.1.1 Have the local utility mark all gas lines
        4.1.2. Identify trench lines
        4.1.3 Rent trench digging equipment
        4.1.4 Dig trenches
    4.2 Install sprinkler pipes
    4.3 Cover sprinkler system
    4.4 Plant lawn seed
    4.5 Plant shrubs

In the preceding exhibit, the top-level activities (noted in bold) are the summary tasks. These are known as *level one* items. All of the indented activities are the work packages. The indented activities can be indented further to denote additional levels of detail, as we noted for the "dig trenches" work package. In that work package, "Dig trenches" was a *level two* item, while "Have the local utility mark all gas lines" was a *level three* item. These extra levels of detail are useful for providing a high level of refinement to a project.

The easiest way to construct a work breakdown structure is to start with the highest-level tasks that are listed on a project's statement of work, and list them as top-tier items (summary tasks) in the work breakdown structure. Then list all tasks required to complete each summary task. It is easiest to state each task beginning with a verb, which denotes that an action is required.

The project manager may find that he or she does not have a sufficiently detailed knowledge of the task steps to develop a complete listing of work packages. If so, consult with other members of the project team who have the requisite skills. In some cases, it may be necessary to consult with outside experts who can fill in any gaps in the plan. When a project is quite large, the project manager may only be able to complete the first level or two of the structure, and must then hand it off to specialists to complete the lower levels.

The work breakdown structure should be fully fleshed-out before a project is allowed to proceed. The reason is that working through the levels of detail required to fully understand a project may uncover areas in which there is uncertainty about what to do. By addressing these areas in advance, the project manager may be able to avoid tasks that might otherwise have caused problems for the project.

Task Relationship Identification

Once a work breakdown structure has been devised for a project, one must then determine how the various work packages within it relate to each other. Certain tasks must be completed before others can begin. For example, pouring a foundation must be completed before constructing the framing for a house, while the framing must be completed before the roof can be added. There are several types of these relationships. One is the *finish-to-start* relationship, where a preceding task must be completed before the next task can begin. For example, a piece of furniture must be stained before varnish can be applied to it. The finish-to-start relationship is the most common relationship. Another relationship is the *start-to-start* relationship, where both the preceding and successor tasks can start when the preceding task begins. For example, in a physical inventory count, received inventory count tags can be verified and tabulated at the same time. These relationships are useful when tasks can be overlapped to compress the duration of a project. Another relationship is the *finish-to-finish* relationship, where the successor task can only be finished when the preceding task ends. For example, a project to prepare a large, multi-course meal requires that the various components of the meal be ready for consumption at the same time – at the end. Thus, one could turn on the oven and begin baking potatoes (the preceding task), and then add a pie to the oven a short time later (the successor task).

When a task is not dependent upon the completion of a prior task, it has no *sequence constraint* – that is, the task can start at any time. Also, it may be possible for several tasks to be addressed at the same time. If so, these are *concurrent tasks*. An example appears in the next exhibit, where the tasks and sequence constraints are described for a project that involves the installation of production equipment.

Sample Sequence Constraint Table

Task Number	Task Description	Predecessor
1	Pour concrete pad	None
2	Position equipment	1
3	Install electrical	1
4	Conduct a test run	2, 3
5	Write an operations manual	None
6	Conduct employee training	4, 5

In the table, note how tasks 2 and 3 can both proceed at the same time, though only after task 1 has been completed. Tasks 2 and 3 have a sequence constraint in relation to task 1, but can be considered concurrent tasks in relation to each other. The full set of relationships is noted in the following network diagram. In the diagram, writing an operations manual is not considered to have a sequence constraint, so it can begin as soon as the project starts. Finally, employee training has multiple sequence constraints, since the trainer needs both an operational machine and an operations manual in order to conduct the training.

Sample Network Diagram

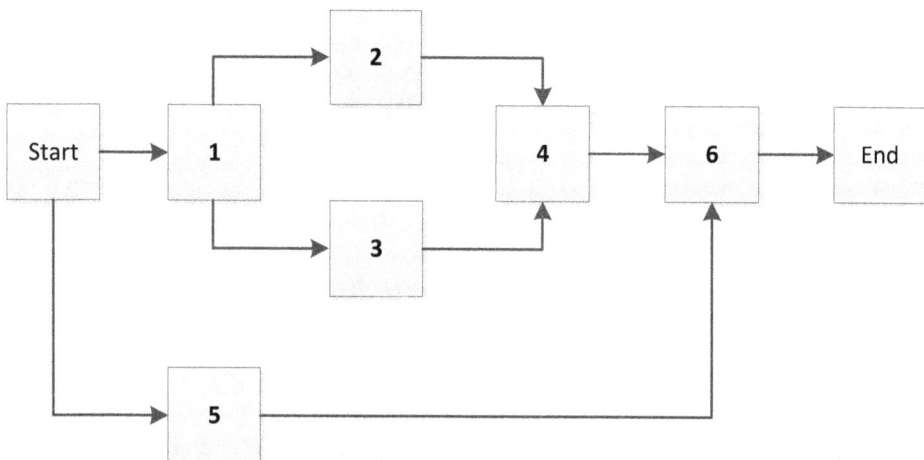

Another possibility to factor into a task relationship analysis is the existence of an *external dependency*. This is an input from an external source that is required before a task can proceed. This dependency frequently takes the form of an approval. For example:

- A government agency must issue an operating license to a power plant before the facility can be turned on. The license is an external dependency.
- A customer must review the progress of a project and give his approval before he will release funds to pay for the next summary task. The approval is an external dependency.
- A building inspector must issue a permit before the wiring for a building will be approved. The permit is an external dependency.

The main concern of the project manager is the existence of sequence constraints, where one task must be completed before another task can begin. If a single predecessor task cannot be completed, it may prevent an entire project from advancing. External dependencies can be particularly difficult to manage, since they typically involve a decision by an entity that is outside of the control of the project manager.

Bottom-Up Estimating

Once a work breakdown structure has been built and task interrelationships identified, one can construct estimates of costs and time requirements for each work package. This work is conducted for each individual work package and then rolled up into a grand total for the project. Because the estimating work begins at the lowest level of detail, it is referred to as *bottom-up estimating*. If these numbers had instead been imposed from above by company management, stakeholders, or the project manager, they would be referred to as *top-down estimating*. Top-down estimating is not recommended, since it is not based on the underlying detail of a project, and so may be wildly incorrect.

The cost estimates for a project must include cost information from all possible sources, including all factors that could ratchet up these costs. For example:

- *Labor cost*. Calculate the labor cost based on the number of hours that will be needed, factoring in the different labor rates for people with higher or lower skill sets. On more critical projects, there is a tendency to use higher-grade people in order to ensure that tasks are completed on time; if so, estimate a higher hourly rate. If additional hours will be needed and people are paid on an hourly basis, estimate a reasonable amount of overtime pay.
- *Contractor bids*. When contractors will be working on a project, include the amount of their fixed-price bids as a separate cost. If they are working on an hourly basis, include their cost in the preceding labor cost category.
- *Materials cost*. A construction project is likely to require a massive amount of materials, while other services-related projects may not require any materials. This cost is derived from the project specifications, not from the work breakdown structure.

- *Equipment cost.* It may be necessary to rent or purchase tools and equipment for a project. If there is an expectation that these may need to be acquired on a rush basis, include rush fees in the acquisition cost. Also include the operating costs required to run the equipment, such as gasoline for powered equipment. Further, include the costs of any tools that will be consumed during the project. If equipment is being purchased for use on several projects, prorate its cost over the projects.

Both time and cost estimates must be compiled for a project with the greatest care. The reason is that cost and time frame are major constraints that directly impact the eventual outcome of a project. If the cost turns out to be higher than expectations, or if the duration is longer than expected, it is possible that the project scope will be reduced. By doing so, the project cost and/or time frame can be reduced back to a level that meets the expectations of stakeholders.

Estimates should be very specific, so that one can evaluate costs and durations at a fine level of detail. In the following exhibit, we note the cost calculation for the personnel needed to complete a few of the tasks noted earlier in the work breakdown structure for a home construction project.

Sample Cost Calculation

Task	Unit	Headcount	Days	Hours	Cost/Hour	Extension
2.0 Lay foundation						
2.1 Dig hole	Staff hour	3	6	144	$40	$5,760
2.2 Build concrete forms	Staff hour	3	4	96	48	4,608
2.3 Pour concrete	Staff hour	2	2	32	60	1,920
			12	272		$12,288

The time requirements developed through bottom-up estimating are worth a careful review, especially when there is a need to complete a task within a short period of time. In a case where there is little time available, the project manager can budget for extra staff or longer working hours to ensure that tasks are still completed on time.

A useful outcome of this analysis is the occasional discovery that adding more staff to a task will not necessarily shorten its duration. For example, when a task requires highly skilled labor for a short period of time, the only way to complete the task may be with those already assigned to it. Adding more staff merely takes time away from the existing staff to train the new arrivals, and so may even extend the task duration. Consequently, this analysis will likely uncover several instances in which there is an absolutely minimum amount of time required that cannot be compressed further.

There may be other instances in which a large number of people can be added to a task, with a reasonable expectation that the outcome will be a significant reduction in the duration of the task. This typically occurs when the required skill level is low, so that the training period is insignificant and a person is fully functional almost at once. For example, in a project to cut back foliage in a fire zone, many people could be added at once with great effect, since the skill level is so low.

Yet another variation on personnel planning is to recognize cases in which a person is being pulled in multiple directions by the demands of several jobs. This is quite common when a person is working on a project while also working on his normal day job at the same time. When a person is multi-tasking in this manner, his efficiency level tends to decline. In this situation, having the person assigned full-time, with no other responsibilities, may be the best way to shorten the duration of a task.

Once estimates of time and cost have been developed, the work breakdown structure and task relationships can be translated into a project schedule. This schedule is commonly presented using a Gantt chart, the critical path method, or the program evaluation and review technique, which are described in the following sections.

Gantt Charts

A Gantt chart is a visual portrayal of the task assignments and task durations within a project. This information is displayed in the form of a horizontal bar chart. The chart can be enhanced with shading to show the level of completion of each task, or a vertical line through the chart that shows today's date. The chart can also show dependencies between the different activities, where one task must be completed before the next task can begin; this means it is relatively easy to identify critical tasks or bottlenecks that might prevent a project from being completed by its planned due date. A simplified Gantt chart that outlines the tasks associated with setting up a production work center appears in the following exhibit.

Sample Gantt Chart

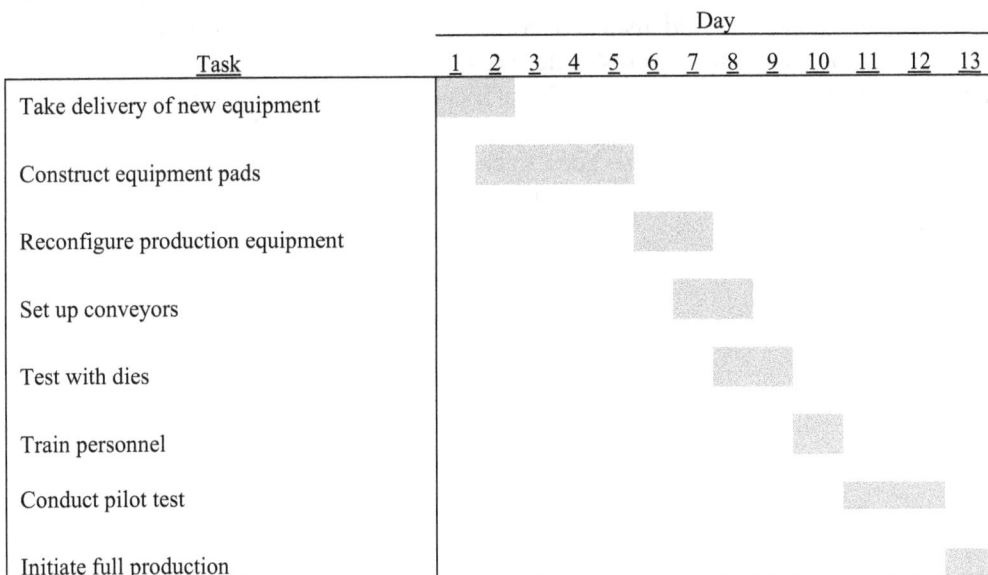

Task	Day 1	2	3	4	5	6	7	8	9	10	11	12	13
Take delivery of new equipment	▓												
Construct equipment pads		▓	▓	▓									
Reconfigure production equipment					▓	▓							
Set up conveyors							▓						
Test with dies								▓					
Train personnel									▓				
Conduct pilot test										▓	▓		
Initiate full production													▓

In the sample chart, note that certain tasks are dependent upon the completion of prior tasks. For example, the reconfiguration of production equipment cannot begin until the equipment pads have been completed. Similarly, employees cannot be trained until the product dies have been tested. These dependencies are critical to project completion, since a delay earlier in the process has a ripple effect that pushes dependent tasks further out into the future. However, other tasks can be worked on concurrently, since there is no dependency between them. There is more likely to be an overlap in the timelines for these tasks. For example, work can progress on setting up conveyors even before the production equipment with which it will be associated has been reconfigured.

The Gantt chart is one of the simplest project management tools, and yet can be quite effective, especially when dealing with a relatively uncomplicated project. Conversely, the complexity of a larger project might instead call for the CPM or PERT techniques, which are described later in this chapter.

Critical Path Method (CPM)

When a project contains many tasks that must be closely coordinated, a better planning technique than a Gantt chart is the critical path method. Under CPM, each task is arranged in sequential order, along with a time estimate for how long it will take to complete the task. An *event* occurs when a task either begins or is completed. This information is then displayed on a CPM chart. This chart is useful for determining how delays will influence the completion of a project, where there is slack in a project, and which tasks are crucial for meeting the project due date.

Slack time occurs when there are activities that can be completed before the time when they are actually needed. The difference between the scheduled completion date and the required date to meet the critical path is the amount of slack time available. The project manager should always be aware of where slack time exists in a project, since this time can be used to reshuffle the schedule to support the critical path. For example, if there is slack time in a task not located on the critical path, resources can be shifted from that task to tasks located on the critical path, thereby bolstering the most crucial tasks. One can also keep track of the trend in available slack time for each task. If the trend is declining, it can indicate that work is taking longer than expected.

EXAMPLE

It takes three weeks to complete a task. The task must be completed in five weeks, which is when it will be needed to support the critical path of a project. The two-week differential is the slack time for this task. The project manager has several options for how to deal with this slack time, including the following:

- Delay the start of the task for two weeks
- Proceed as normal, which leaves the two-week buffer at the end of the task in case something goes wrong
- Reduce the resources assigned to the task so that it now takes the full five weeks to complete

---

A CPM chart is also useful for "what if" analysis, to see where delays are more likely to crop up in a project, and the impact of those delays.

A CPM chart is organized in a specific way, which calls for the use of rules to display information on the chart. Those rules are:

- Each task is represented by an arrow, and each circle represents an event. For example:

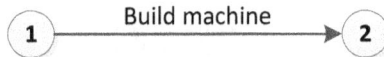

- A linked series of arrows and circles means that the subsequent tasks cannot be completed until the earlier tasks have been completed. In the following example, this means that testing the machine cannot be initiated until the machine has been built.

- The general direction of progress is from left to right.
- When several tasks end at one event, the next event cannot be initiated until all of the preceding tasks have been completed. In the following example, obtaining a construction permit and building an equipment pad are both precursors to testing the equipment.

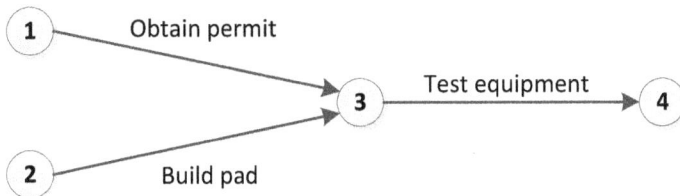

Of particular interest in the chart is that those tasks that could hold up the project are identified as critical. By arranging the chart to focus attention on the critical tasks, one can forecast the time required to complete the entire project. A simplified CPM appears in the following example, to illustrate the concept.

EXAMPLE

The engineering manager of Mule Corporation is planning a design change to the muffler used on the company's iconic "Bad Ass" motorcycle, requiring a reconfiguration of a key work cell. This will call for completion of the following steps:

Step	Task	Duration
A	Design muffler mold	2 weeks
B	Reconfigure muffler work cell to receive mold	4 weeks
C	Acquire tooling and parts for the work cell	3 weeks
D	Install production equipment	1 week
E	Test new equipment with new muffler mold	1 week

The engineering manager shifts this information into a CPM chart, which appears next. In the chart, the bold line indicates the minimum amount of time needed to reconfigure the work cell, which involves steps A, C, D, and E. This is the project's critical path. If the manager wants to shorten the amount of time required to complete the project, he will need to focus his attention on reducing the duration of one or more of these four steps. Step B, reconfiguring the work cell, is not on the critical path, since it requires only four weeks to complete and there are five weeks available. This means step B has one week of slack time associated with it. Conversely, if step A, C, D, or E is delayed, this will increase the duration of the entire project.

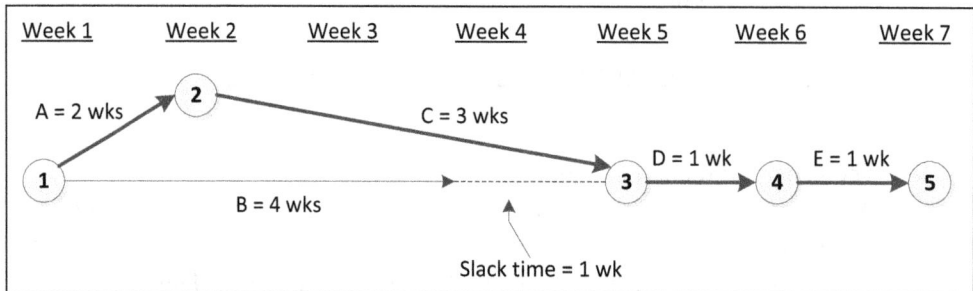

The example presented the concept of the *critical path*. The critical path is the longest path through a network. There is no slack in any task on the critical path, so if there is a delay in any of these tasks, the completion of the entire project will be delayed. Consequently, a project manager's attention is heavily focused on ensuring that each task along the critical path begins and ends on time.

It is possible that there are several near-critical paths associated with a project. If the tasks within these paths become prolonged and their float is consumed, it is entirely possible that one of these paths will become the new critical path, supplanting the original critical path. If this happens, the attention of the project manager is then focused on the new critical path. When there is a near-critical path, it behooves the project manager to watch it closely over time and evaluate the risk that it may become the new critical path.

When a complete work breakdown structure and a CPM analysis have been completed, it is entirely likely that a negative float will be revealed. A *negative float* occurs when the critical path will result in project completion after the mandated completion date. If a negative float is indicated, it should be brought up with the project sponsors at once, which should trigger a negotiation over what should be changed: the completion date, the project cost, or the project scope. Continuing a project with negative float makes no sense, since it is guaranteed to fail (where failure is defined as not meeting the completion date).

The sample CPM chart was based on the conditions present at the start of the project. The durations and types of tasks will change over the course of the project, as well as the relationships between the tasks, so the chart must be continually updated over the course of the project, possibly on a daily basis. By doing so, the project manager has the best idea of where to allocate resources and reschedule tasks.

There is project software available that allows a manager to enter a massive number of project tasks and provide a complete CPM evaluation as output. This software requires a significant amount of time to maintain, so larger projects may have a CPM software person whose full-time job is to maintain the CPM model.

The CPM method works best when a project is well-defined and there are relatively few uncertainties. These conditions make CPM an ideal tool for construction projects. When there is more uncertainty, PERT may be a better tool. It is described in the next section.

Program Evaluation and Review Technique (PERT)

The program evaluation and review technique is a more complicated version of CPM. PERT allows for the inclusion of variable amounts of time for each task. Thus, each task has a most likely, pessimistic, and optimistic duration attached to it. The optimistic and pessimistic durations should have a probability in the 10-20% range. These three estimates are then combined to arrive at a single estimated duration for each task. The calculation of this expected task time is:

$$\frac{(\text{Optimistic estimate} + (4 \times \text{Most likely estimate}) + \text{Pessimistic estimate})}{6}$$

In effect, the calculation gives a heavy weighting to the most likely estimate, but does incorporate the high and low time estimates. A potential problem with this approach is that there may be little historical information on which to base optimistic, most likely, and pessimistic estimates. Conversely, if the project repeats activities that have been completed in the past, then this information may be available.

The outcome of a PERT analysis is placing a focus on where the greatest effort should be made to keep a project on schedule.

EXAMPLE

A project manager at Milford Sound is conducting the preliminary planning for the construction of a new sound stage. One of the tasks is to assemble the scaffolding for the stage. The manager assigns an optimistic estimate of 12 days to this task, 16 days to the most likely estimate, and 32 days to the pessimistic estimate. Using the formula just noted for the estimated task duration, the manager calculates the following expected task time:

$$\frac{(12 \text{ Days optimistic} + (4 \times 16 \text{ Days most likely}) + 32 \text{ days pessimistic})}{6}$$

$$= 18 \text{ Days estimated task duration}$$

The estimated task duration is stated underneath each task description in the PERT chart. For example:

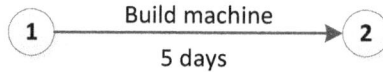

In addition, the early start (ES), late start (LS), early finish (EF) and late finish (LF) times are added to each task. For example:

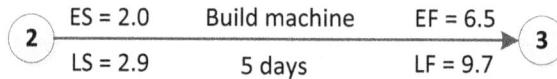

In the preceding example, the assumption is that building the machine is the second task in a series of tasks; this allows for the addition of early and late start information for the task. The project manager knows that the machine building task could begin as early as two days into the project, or as late as 2.9 days. She also knows that the build task should take five days. However, if the early start is achieved, then the best possible early finish will be after 6.5 days. Similarly, if the late start occurs, then the latest possible finish for this task will be in 9.7 days. The concept is extended in the following exhibit, where we follow the early and late finishes for each task through several consecutive tasks:

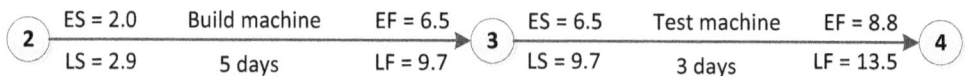

In the preceding example, note how the early finish estimate of 6.5 days for the machine building task becomes the early start estimate for the next task, which is testing the machine. Similarly, the estimated 9.7 day late finish for the machine building task becomes the late start estimate for the next task. In this manner, the project manager can work through the various sequential tasks and estimate high-low values for project completion dates. As the earlier tasks are completed, their actual finish dates are plugged into this model, which results in a different set of estimated early and late finish dates.

When there is a difference between the early start and late start amounts for a task, this means there is slack in the system. In the preceding example for the machine testing task, there is a 3.2 day difference between the 6.5 day early start and the 9.7 day late start. This is the maximum amount of leeway in a task that will not delay the completion of the entire project.

When there is slack in the projections, this means the task is not on the critical path. Critical path tasks have no slack at all, so the early start and late start figures will be the same. Similarly, the early finish and late finish figures will be the same for a critical path task.

The length of a path in a PERT chart is the sum of the expected task times on that path. There may be several paths within a chart, each comprised of a different set of interrelated tasks that must be completed. Whichever path has the longest duration is the critical path, since shrinking this path will compress the duration of the entire project.

The main problem with PERT is the large amount of data that must be incorporated into the planning process. This makes it expensive to maintain, which usually limits its usefulness to larger and more complex projects.

Differences between CPM and PERT

There are several key differences between the CPM and PERT methods. First, the CPM method employs just one time estimate, which represents the normal amount of time in which tasks are expected to be completed. The PERT method uses three time estimates to derive an expected time, which are the optimistic, most likely, and pessimistic durations. Second, the PERT method employs probability in deriving estimates, since three-time estimates are used to derive durations. Third, the PERT method is used on projects in which it is difficult to determine the completion percentage, except when completion milestones are reached. The CPM method is more likely to be used on projects where the percentage of completion can be derived with some degree of accuracy. Thus, the essential difference between the two methods is the ability to incorporate a primitive probability distribution into a PERT analysis, thereby making it the more useful method when there is a higher level of uncertainty.

Project Management Constraints

Projects have a strong tendency to run longer than their expected due dates. In order to keep a project on track to meet its due date, this usually means that the project manager must cut back on some of the deliverables or be willing to incur extra costs.

However, a close examination of the constraints built into a project can be used to not only bring a project in on time, but even ahead of schedule.

The main problem causing difficulties in project management is that each person given a task in the chain of project activities is also given a due date. That individual is quite likely to delay starting the assigned task, knowing what the due date will be. This has two effects:

- Because the person has delayed starting the project, there is no possible way to accelerate the assigned completion date; or
- The person may find that unforeseen difficulties cause the deliverable to be completed later than expected.

In short, any task in a project is likely to be completed either on time or too late; it is nearly impossible to complete a task early. When the time periods associated with each task in a project are aggregated, this means that the inherent nature of the scheduling system will result in delayed completion dates.

There are several ways to deal with this problem. The key step is to not issue a due date for each task. Instead, the people working on a task are encouraged to complete it as soon as possible, so that they do not delay the start date of the work.

An additional improvement is for the project manager to maintain a large time buffer for the project as a whole, which is positioned at the end of the project timeline. When a delay does arise in an individual task, the time overage is taken from this general buffer. By taking this approach, the manager is constantly aware of the amount of excess time still available for delays before the project will run past its scheduled completion date. The concept appears in the following illustration, showing before-and-after representations of a project timeline where time buffers are shifted out of individual project steps and into a general buffer.

Individual Time Buffers

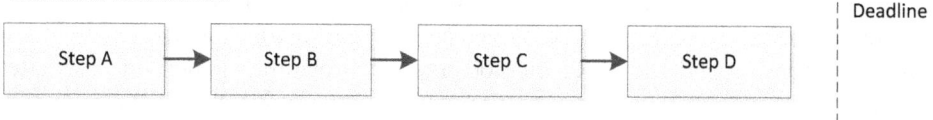

Step A → Step B → Step C → Step D

Deadline

General Time Buffer

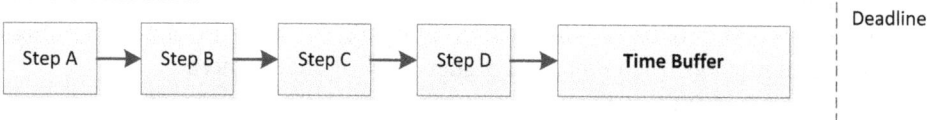

Step A → Step B → Step C → Step D → **Time Buffer**

Deadline

A typical project has a critical path of activities that must be completed on time for the project as a whole to be completed by its scheduled due date. A constant problem that the project manager encounters is when outside activities feeding into the critical path are completed late. When this happens, the critical path is also delayed, thereby extending the completion date of the entire project. A solution is to create a time buffer at the end of each of these feeder activities. As noted earlier, employees are not given due dates for any activities, but are instead encouraged to complete work as soon as possible. If a person is still running late, the time overage is taken from the time buffer established for the feeder activity. Doing so minimizes the amount of time by which a feeder activity is likely to run over, thereby keeping delays from interfering with the critical path. The concept appears in the following illustration showing before-and-after representations of a project timeline where time buffers are shifted out of individual feeder activities and into a general buffer at the end of each sequence of feeder activities.

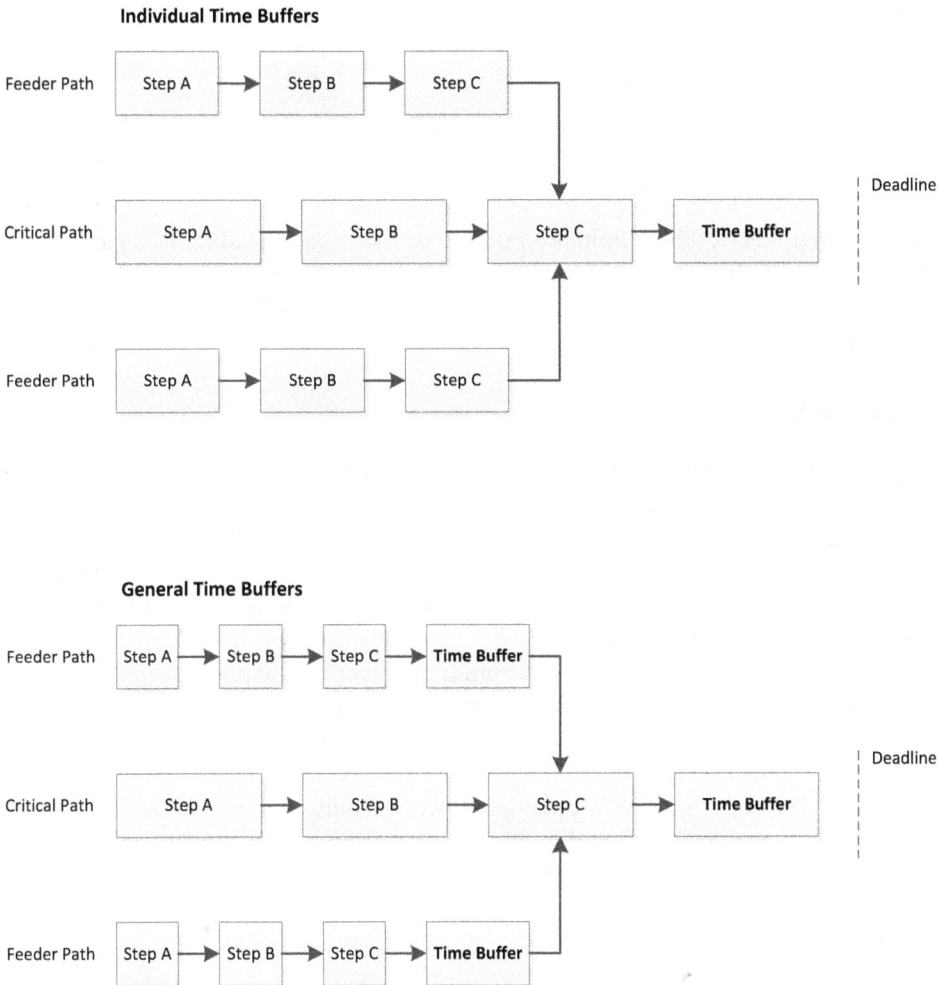

Individual Time Buffers

Feeder Path	Step A → Step B → Step C
Critical Path	Step A → Step B → Step C → Time Buffer	Deadline
Feeder Path	Step A → Step B → Step C

General Time Buffers

Feeder Path	Step A → Step B → Step C → Time Buffer
Critical Path	Step A → Step B → Step C → Time Buffer	Deadline
Feeder Path	Step A → Step B → Step C → Time Buffer

The problem with assigning due dates to project activities can be a particular concern when dealing with outside contractors. These entities conduct business by issuing deliverables as of a specific due date, so they are also likely to fall into the trap of either delivering on time or late – but never early. The problem can be mitigated by offering to pay a higher fee to contractors in exchange for giving company business a higher priority. The offer can be sweetened by awarding more work to those contractors willing to assign a higher priority to company activities.

A final concern with project management is that certain individuals involved in a project may be tasked with different deliverables for different sections of the project at the same time. For example, a software quality reviewer may suddenly find herself being required to tackle reviews for four different modules of a software project at the same time. To get around this scheduling conflict, it is necessary to delve deeper into the project schedule to determine exactly which individuals will be involved in all activities (both on the critical path and in the feeder activities). Instances of multiple work assignments can then be spotted, for which either of the following actions can be taken:

- Bring in additional staff to increase capacity when there are scheduling conflicts
- Alter the schedule of activities to avoid conflicts

In short, constraint management concepts can be used to vastly improve the outcome of long-term projects. The elimination of due dates from individual tasks and the selective use of time buffers simply recognize the existence of constraints on a process, and are used to compress the total amount of time required to ensure timely completion of a project.

Resource Leveling

Many of the preceding planning techniques can assist in completing a project on time. However, they may not optimize the use of people and equipment while doing so. Instead, there may be tasks that require an inordinate amount of effort to complete within a short period of time, which can result in overtime charges and burned-out people who will then work at suboptimal levels or require time off. Or, a mass of temporary workers are brought in to work intensively on a few tasks for a short period of time, after which they are dismissed from the project. These people must be trained, and the value of that training is lost as soon as they leave the project.

A better approach is to maintain a high level of efficiency by keeping the same people working on a project for as long as possible, avoiding the use of overtime and excess staff. By doing so, the project gains from having a smaller number of well-trained and experienced personnel who work on it from start to finish.

An additional consideration is that certain types of equipment may only be available for use within narrowly defined time periods. For example, construction equipment may only be available to be leased for a few months, after which someone else has reserved the equipment. If so, the schedule needs to accommodate these restrictions.

Another possibility is that personnel or equipment may be underutilized on a project. When this happens, there is a risk that an individual or key equipment will be shifted off to another project. Or, an employee might be laid off from the company. When this happens, it may be difficult to get these resources back at a later date, which could interfere with the timely completion of the project. By being cognizant of these issues, the project manager may be able to compress work for valuable resources, so that they are fully employed for a reduced period of time, after which their work is done and they can leave for other projects.

To engage in resource leveling, identify the peaks in resource usage that are clearly excessive. Then follow these three steps:

1. *Delay tasks.* During the period in which there is excessive resource usage, delay noncritical tasks. The amount of this delay cannot exceed the float for those tasks – otherwise there is a risk of extending the duration of the entire project. This delay shifts work out of high-usage periods. The adjacent periods to which the work is being shifted may also have a fairly high amount of scheduled resource usage, which may in turn call for shifts further along the timeline – thus, resource leveling can have the effect of ripples spreading out through a schedule.

2. *Adjust resources.* The preceding step may still leave a number of resource peaks that are clearly excessive, or declines in resource usage that might normally call for the elimination of resources. When there is a resource usage spike, add resources to the plan (such as more employees). When there is a decline in resource usage, schedule fewer resources. For example, if two people have been scheduled for a month and there is not enough work for them, would it instead be possible to schedule just one person for a longer period of time?

3. *Extend completion date.* If the preceding steps do not result in an adequate amount of resource leveling, the remaining option is to extend the completion date. Doing so allows for more time in which to complete tasks, thereby spreading the resource load over a longer time period.

These steps will likely require multiple iterations before a reasonable amount of resource leveling can be achieved. It is possible that the outcome will involve having several tasks that have considerably reduced floats. This can be a dangerous situation, since there is now less buffer built into the schedule that is available for absorbing unforeseen problems. When the amount of residual float is small, it may make more sense from a risk management perspective to retain the float and add more resources, even though this entails some additional cost.

EXAMPLE

A project manager at Norrona Software is planning an upcoming project for the development of a warehouse management system. She notes that a volume testing task is currently scheduled to require 80 hours of staff time in one week, with one person assigned to the task. This task is not on the critical path, and so has a float of an additional two days. The project manager could expand the task by two days, thereby greatly reducing the employee's hours of work per day. However, an analysis of project risks indicates that there is a 30% chance that the software will fail the volume test and so will require additional testing. Given this risk, the manager wants to retain the float. Instead, she chooses to assign an additional person to the task. Doing so eliminates the resource spike and preserves the float, though at the cost of the additional person.

Resource leveling is especially useful when there is no particular rush to complete a project, since tasks can be readily stretched to accommodate overloaded resources. Leveling is also a useful option when there is pressure to keep the project cost low, since overloaded resources tend to increase costs.

Summary

The planning process is essential for even the smallest project, since it provides a baseline for evaluating progress and is an excellent tool for scheduling resources. At a minimum, a work breakdown structure must be created, along with the identification of task relationships and the use of bottom-up estimating. This information is needed to gain a clear grasp of the flow of activities for smaller projects. When there are many tasks to be completed and the level of project uncertainty is low, the critical path method can be used to clarify where the project manager should be focusing the bulk of her attention to ensure that the project is completed on time. In a very complex and uncertain environment, the program evaluation and review technique can be employed. In these latter situations, it may be necessary to employ a full-time project planning staff to keep the model up-to-date, since there will be changes every day as a project progresses.

Chapter 16
Managing a Start-Up

Introduction

A start-up business must develop a new product or service and insert itself into a market niche, and do so with limited funding, if any. This is an extremely difficult environment for the manager, who needs a different skill set from what is used in a more established enterprise. We cover the unique aspects of managing a startup in the following pages.

Types of Start-Up Managers

The process of starting up a new business can be energizing, but also involves long hours of work and a real risk of losing the initial investment. What kind of motivation is needed to manage this type of business? One possible motivation is that a manager is deeply committed to the type of product or service that the new business is targeting. Others are driven by an ownership stake in the business that could eventually turn into real wealth. Another possibility is that managers are tired of working in large, bureaucratic organizations and want to have a more meaningful impact on a day-to-day basis. And finally, some managers love to be involved in every aspect of a business, from product development to shipping goods out the door. No matter what the underlying motivation, the manager of a start-up needs to be willing to deal with a flood of problems at all hours of the day or night, which calls for a high energy level.

Criteria for Success

Not all managers are able to function successfully within a start-up business. A new organization requires certain attributes in a manager that greatly increase the odds of success. A selection of these criteria are:

- *Cash tracker.* A good start-up manager knows the company's cash position at all times and likely cash flows in the near term. This information makes it easier to predict when more cash will be needed, or when to cut back on expenses. Those who do not track cash assiduously are far more likely to go out of business.
- *Familiar with the market.* Though it is possible to succeed in a market with no prior knowledge of it, the road to success is easier if the manager has a background in the market that provides enough familiarity with the situation to avoid the more obvious mistakes. Thus, someone who has self-published in the past is more familiar with the writing process when she starts up her own magazine, and so is better able to deal with authors.

- *Flexible.* When one option does not work, the ideal start-up manager re-orients the business in a different direction to see if that will work. This means not being wedded to the initial approach taken by a business; instead, it may be the third, fourth, or fifth iteration of the business that finally takes off.

- *Hard working.* It is obvious that the manager of a start-up needs to be hard working, but the extent of the work required can be a shock. The work simply never ends, so it is entirely possible that every waking moment is spent at the office. Some managers even set up temporary sleeping facilities where they work. The trouble is that the company must be set up from scratch, so *everything* must be assembled – locating facilities, finding employees, developing products, selling to customers, and so forth. This is a particular concern in the product development area, where a complete suite of products must be developed for the company's selected niche.

- *Perseveres.* Most start-up businesses will struggle to survive. This may involve working in overcrowded spaces with second-hand equipment, funding the business with credit cards, raising money from family and friends, and so forth. The ideal start-up manager will always find a way to keep the business moving forward, no matter how difficult the obstacles may be.

- *Practical.* The manager of a start-up is able to deal with problems as expeditiously and cheaply as possible, though doing so while keeping in mind the long-term strategy of the business. Conversely, a start-up manager does not pursue the theoretically perfect solution if doing so will take too long or be too expensive. For example, if the office is overheating, a practical solution involves a quick trip to a store to obtain a fan or a window air conditioning unit, not an extensive office upgrade to install central air conditioning.

- *Self-confident.* The manager of a start-up needs to be massively confident that she can master every aspect of the business, knowing that it will eventually flourish. Without this core level of confidence, doubt sets in and the manager begins to question whether she is on the right path.

- *Untroubled by ambiguity.* A new business represents a completely untrodden path, where the manager can head off in any direction at all. A great start-up manager relishes this ambiguity as a wonderful opportunity. However, many managers who are comfortable in a bureaucratic organization will flounder in a start-up, because they are uncomfortable with the lack of certainty.

- *Willing to share.* A manager might start a new business in order to operate autonomously, but this does not work in the long run – in most cases, it is impossible to expand without sharing the work load with others, accepting the fact that a successful business may require her to step aside from the dominant management role in the business.

A person should possess a substantial proportion of these attributes in order to offset the very high risk of failure associated with a start-up business.

Start-Up Strategy

The preceding list of success criteria will not be sufficient if a start-up manager is not able to come up with a unique strategy that will provide the business with a profitable niche market. It is not sufficient to simply identify the initial strategy idea – the manager must be able to translate the strategy into a detailed plan for how to proceed, and then execute the plan. This is hardly a one-time planning process. On the contrary, it is quite possible that there will be ongoing adjustments to the strategy as the manager learns more about the industry in which he is operating, quite possibly resulting in changes to the plan on a monthly, weekly, or even daily basis.

Where does the start-up strategy come from? Many opportunities are spotted because they are in the same industry in which a manager already works. These possibilities tend to have a higher likelihood of success, since the manager already has a firm knowledge of the industry, and has a reasonable idea of how to make the strategy succeed. A variation on this approach is when an opportunity is spotted in an area in which a manager has a hobby; in this case, the manager's knowledge of the industry may not be so high, but the passion to enter the industry may be greater. Another possibility is that an opportunity is spotted in an area entirely outside of where a manager works or has a hobby. In this case, the odds of success are somewhat reduced, since the person has no prior knowledge of the industry. However, this can also mean that the manager is not constrained by what are considered to be the standard operating rules of the industry, allowing for a completely "outside the box" solution that blindsides competitors. Despite the last example, the more successful strategies tend to align with a manager's existing skill set.

Start-Up Planning

As just noted, the strategy of a start-up may change continually. If so, is it necessary for the start-up manager to devise a detailed new plan for every iteration of the strategy? This is not a small issue, since some people have a tendency to wallow in the planning stages of a business, never emerging from the process to actually do anything. This "paralysis by analysis" can be avoided by setting a strict limitation on the depth of planning used. Thus, planning should include a clear, one-line statement of the corporate strategy, followed by monthly revenue and expense projections for each product that extend out to a reasonable planning horizon (perhaps only a few months), as well as the administrative expenses of the business for the same planning horizon. A cash flow forecast should cover the same period. This level of planning detail can be easily updated, perhaps in less than an hour. The point is to provide sufficient detail to affirm that the new strategy could work, thereby allowing one to proceed immediately to implementing the plan.

Pitfalls to Avoid

Start-up businesses can fail for many reasons. A canny manager should be prepared for the following pitfalls:

- *Inadequate financials.* A manager needs to know the financial status of the business as soon as possible. When this is not the case, the manager has no idea which products are earning a profit, or how well the business is doing as a whole. Avoiding this trap requires a one-day closing of the books at month-end, followed by the immediate release of financial statements. Better yet, the manager should insist on a daily flash report that itemizes the critical financial and operating metrics for the business, such as cash in the bank, daily sales, cash collected from customers, and the size of the customer order backlog.
- *Inadequate staff.* It can be quite difficult for a start-up business to attract the absolute best staff, so the organization may be burdened with a large proportion of underperforming people. A manager needs to be cognizant of performance issues, and be willing to fire anyone who cannot meet expectations.
- *Operational failures.* Customers can be unusually critical of failures in a start-up company's customer service, which may involve product failures, safety concerns, slow order fulfillment times, or an inability to deal with complaints. A manager needs to constantly monitor any processes that can be experienced or seen by customers, so that operational issues can be dealt with promptly.
- *Overexpansion.* An initial success with a start-up may drive a manager to expand the concept too quickly, resulting in new store locations before the concept has been completely locked in, or weak controls in new locations, or expanding into niche products that are less profitable than the original product. A classic example of overexpansion is when a business builds up a massive amount of inventory and customer receivables to support its sales growth, resulting in working capital requirements soaking up its excess cash, to the point where it runs out of cash and collapses.
- *Poor skills alignment.* If the firm is lacking in a key skill area, identify it as soon as possible and start looking for the necessary talent (which may be obtained from a contractor, rather than a direct hire). For example, a start-up software company finds that it has a critical shortage of sales engineers who can run product demonstrations with prospective customers, so it begins an immediate hiring and in-house training program to obtain the necessary talent. As another example, a fledgling company finds that it does not have the relationships needed to raise money, so it hires a chief financial officer who has the necessary connections with local bankers and investors.
- *Inadequate cost and price controls.* The reporting of costs and product margins tend to be quite weak in a smaller business, so that the manager does not know if prices are being set at levels that will generate a profit, or if costs are being maintained at levels that will minimize the outflow of cash. This is a particular problem when sales are increasing rapidly, since the absence of cost and price controls can result in mounting losses. The best solution is to

constantly monitor these issues as soon after month-end as possible. It can be helpful to track costs on a monthly trend line, to see if there are ongoing cost increases that need to be addressed.

- *Fraud.* A start-up company is at a higher risk of fraud than a more established business, since it tends to have fewer controls. This is a particular problem in the accounting area, where just one or two people may have control over the accounts, and so are better able to hide the theft of assets. This risk can be reduced somewhat if the manager is willing to be involved in selected accounting activities on an ongoing basis, as a monitor.

Late-Stage Issues

The manager who survives the early years of a start-up must confront a new set of challenges in the later stages of the business. Now, the firm occupies a relatively solid niche, is growing at a steady and predictable rate, and has adequate financing. In this situation, the manager needs to decide whether it makes senses to move away from running the business, perhaps handing over operational control to a professional manager. It is quite possible that a successful start-up manager is *not* a successful late-stage manager, where priorities tend to shift toward the development of consistent and reliable products, services, and financial results. These goals are entirely valid, but are based much more on organizational, procedural, and training improvements than was the case in the early days of the business. In short, the manager's skill set may no longer fit the business.

In rare cases, a business will take off like a rocket and grow at an extraordinary pace. In this case, life centers on locating enough funding to ensure that a lack of cash does not trip up the rate of growth. The manager will also spend an inordinate amount of time searching for, interviewing, and training new employees, since the demand for employees will be rapacious. An inevitable side effect of this influx of new employees is that the manager must delegate large portions of her job to others, which can be a wrenching experience. Also, the manager needs to support a basic set of cost controls, to ensure that funds are not frittered away on unnecessary activities.

As sales begin to slow down after a few years, the manager will need to push the pace on innovation, to keep the business from becoming stodgy. This can involve abandoning the chief executive officer position in order to personally direct the product development staff, or directing a disproportionate amount of funding toward product development, as well as trying to maintain a vibrant culture that still attracts the best and brightest new employees. It can be difficult to keep a start-up culture as a business matures, given the increasing number of employees and the many company locations at which they may work.

Start-Up Risk Management

Starting up a new business is unquestionably risky, since there are no products, no customers, and no cash coming in the door. However, there are a few ways in which a manager can reduce these risks, as noted in the following bullet points:

- *Partner with another company.* It may be possible to enter into an arrangement with an established firm, usually where the partner either buys the products of the start-up or acts as its distributor. If the concept proves to be successful, the partner may also provide financing or make an offer to buy the business. For example, a start-up drug research firm could partner with a large pharmaceuticals firm, which provides the funding for drug trials in exchange for the right to market any resulting drugs.
- *Outsource selected functions.* When all functional areas of a business are kept in-house, a business is adopting a relatively high base of fixed costs. When a company is in its infancy, it can make sense to outsource as many of these functions as possible, thereby keeping the monthly sales breakeven point quite low. For example, a bookkeeping service could maintain the accounting records, while a contract manufacturer produces the company's goods.
- *Acquire an existing business.* A significant amount of risk can be eliminated by acquiring a business that has an existing product line and recurring customers. However, the buyer also acquires the firm's reputation, which may be in need of repair, and may spend more than the business turns out to be worth.
- *Buy a franchised operation.* The risk reduction points just noted for an acquired business also apply to a franchise, where the buyer gains access to a brand name, standardized processes, management support, and the right to sell the goods and services of the franchisor. However, the franchisor charges a periodic franchise fee and a percentage of sales, which can be a significant amount of money. Another downside is that the franchisor sets prices and can mandate that the franchisee continue to invest in the business. Thus, the franchising option offsets reduced risk with a reduced amount of control.

Summary

It takes a unique kind of innovative and risk-tolerant person to manage a start-up company. If a person has not been involved in a start-up in the past, it can be worthwhile to consider the demands of this type of business before taking the plunge. At a minimum, one should possess a great deal of determination, in order to fight through the innumerable obstacles that will inevitably arise. A second critical characteristic is the ability to minimize expenditures of all types for as long as possible, in order to keep the business alive long enough to prove itself. In short, grit and prudence are essential characteristics of the start-up manager.

Chapter 17
Manager Ethics

Introduction

Ethics refers to the moral principles that guide a person's behavior. Ethics act as a benchmark for deciding whether an action or decision is good or bad. Managers find that they routinely have to make decisions that require ethical judgments, since many decisions can potentially harm others. Unfortunately, some managers do not consult their moral principles when making decisions; instead, they simply assume that if an action is not prohibited by specific laws, it is acceptable to proceed. In this chapter, we address many ethics-related topics, including practices to improve ethical behavior, codes of conduct, and ways to incorporate ethics into decision making.

Ethical Infrastructure

Various structures can be installed within a business that make employees more aware of the ethical practices that management wants to promote. When these structures are routinely placed in front of employees, there is a much greater tendency to follow the entity's stated ethical practices. Examples of this infrastructure are:

- *Present clear expectations*. A code of conduct is included in the employee manual, discussed with new employees, and routinely reinforced by messages from management. This code clarifies expected behavior. Further, the board of directors and the management team routinely communicate their expectations, stating clearly what is desirable and undesirable activity.
- *Have role models*. Every person in a supervisory position acts as role model for the employees, showing through their actions the expectations for proper ethical behavior.
- *Set reasonable goals*. When employees are given achievable goals, there is no temptation to break the rules to achieve the goals. Conversely, stretch goals that can only be attained through inappropriate behavior are to be avoided.
- *Respect employees*. When the organization shows a proper level of respect for and interest in its employees, they are much more inclined to treat the business in the same way. In this situation employees are more likely to actively pursue the ethical goals of the business, reporting any lapses to management.
- *Impose penalties*. The penalties that will be imposed on employees who break the code of conduct are clearly laid out in the employee manual. These penalties must be actively enforced, so that employees understand why they must follow the ethical standards set by management. See the comments in the following sub-sections regarding detection theory and the punishment of unethical behavior.

- *Be open to comments*. The structure of the business should allow for open discussions of employee concerns, so that ethical problems can be brought out and debated. The result is usually mutual agreement on how to handle specific situations. See the comments in the following sub-section regarding letting off steam.

- *System of controls*. There is a robust system of controls within the company. These controls are intended to minimize the number of situations in which employees will be tempted to engage in activities to steal from the firm. However, the beneficial effects of a system of controls reverses when there are too many controls. When the system is clogged with controls, it is perceived as being dysfunctional, which may draw reactions from employees to circumvent it.

The last item, the system of controls, is worth additional discussion. When a firm has a large number of controls, with tight oversight of all employee activities, the message being sent to employees is that they are not trusted. When employees feel that this is the case, they are more likely to engage in unethical practices. In effect, they are meeting the expectations of management that they are not to be trusted. This finding conflicts with the increasing mandate for more controls in a business, on the grounds that more controls always result in reduced errors and asset losses. It is possible that a better approach is to concentrate the use of controls in areas where there is a significant risk of major loss, and maintain a lower level of control over other operations. The net effect may be that employees respond to the perceived change in expectations by performing to a higher standard.

Another important item was the presentation of clear expectations. When employees are routinely reminded of the ethical values of the organization, it reminds them to think of the meaning and significance of honesty at the point when they are tempted to make an incorrect decision. By routinely presenting a picture of an honest person to employees, they are more likely to emulate that image.

The ethical infrastructure works best when applied to a younger organization, where no one is accustomed to any other system (or lack thereof). Conversely, when a new manager is hired into an older organization, he or she has a more difficult time breaking up the existing calcified systems and replacing them with a more robust and ethical infrastructure.

Detection Theory

Detection theory states that the probability of a transgression decreases as the probability of detection goes up. In other words, when a person is contemplating committing an ethical breach, he first takes into account the probability of being caught. If there is a low risk of being found out, then the person is more likely to proceed with his plans.

Clearly, detection theory points us in the direction of creating circumstances in which there is a high probability of detection. For example, we can document all transactions so that there is a clear record of activity, have people work in teams so that someone else can see a transgression, and routinely audit transactions. An excessive number of these controls can make it appear that management does not trust employees, so be prudent in selecting controls.

Punishment of Unethical Behavior

It is not sufficient for management to talk about ethical behavior. It must also have a system in place for punishing anyone who breaks the organization's code of conduct. Otherwise, employees will realize that the code is empty words and so will have no reason to follow it.

There are a number of possible punishments for an ethical breach, ranging from suspension while an investigation is conducted to termination of employment and even prosecution. Organizations have an unfortunate tendency to gloss over these issues with nothing more than a verbal warning. When this happens, a message is being sent to the entire organization that an ethical lapse is really just a minor issue that has no significant repercussions. The reverse approach of issuing a significant punishment in a timely manner makes it quite clear to everyone that ethical lapses will not be tolerated.

EXAMPLE

As part of a routine audit, a company finds that its sales manager has been stealing money by submitting inflated expense reports. Over several years, this has resulted in overpayments to the sales manager of $50,000. The employer not only fires the sales manager, but also chooses to prosecute to the full extent of the law.

A beneficial side effect of prosecution is that other employees see how the company reacts to being defrauded. Because the sales manager is being pursued vigorously in court, employees understand that there is a greatly reduced opportunity for fraud within the company, and so will be less inclined to engage in it. Further, when the company pursues restitution for the amounts stolen, this reduces the perceived gain that others might see from engaging in fraud.

The punishment level for fired employees can be enhanced by maintaining an ineligible for rehire list. This list is maintained by the human resources department and prevents someone from being rehired by any subsidiary of the company – ever. As soon as a person is fired for an ethical breach, they are entered on the list. All subsequent job candidates are matched against the list before they can be hired.

Letting off Steam

A business may be going through a difficult time, in which case it is necessary to lay off staff or cut pay. In this type of situation, employees are more likely to steal assets from the business to show their frustration. Management can mitigate the amount of asset theft by allowing employees to blow off steam – usually by spending a large amount of time explaining the situation to them and spending yet more time to answer any questions posed by employees. If management instead simply informs employees of the situation without allowing them an avenue for letting off steam, there is a strong risk that theft levels will increase.

Fairness of the Decision-Making Process

Employees are much more likely to act in an ethical manner when they feel they are being treated fairly in the decision-making processes of the organization. When there is a fair process, employees are more likely to accept its outcome, especially when they have input into the process and they understand the reasoning behind the outcome. A fair decision-making process has the following components:

1. Employees can give input before a decision is made.
2. The rules for making decisions are clearly laid out and logical.
3. The persons making decisions have a history of doing so based on objective information and appropriate decision criteria, instead of their personal biases.
4. The decision-making process is applied consistently over time.
5. Decisions are communicated politely, taking into consideration the feelings of the recipient.
6. When decisions are made, the persons making the decisions state how they arrived at the outcome. Better yet, the organization periodically highlights the consistency in decision making to show that bias does not exist.

When employees are treated with the dignity and respect inherent in the preceding ideal decision-making process, it should be no surprise that they are much more likely to respect and admire the management team, which makes it easier for managers to require a high level of ethical behavior from their staff.

The Role of Managers in Ethics

The managers of a business can have a profound impact on the ethical behavior of employees. A manager should routinely demonstrate the best possible behavior through his actions and promote this conduct through personal communications with the staff, general corporate communications, and the general example given by his actions. The ideal manager is seen as being honest and principled, making fair decisions, setting a high ethical standard, and working to show subordinates the implications of their own decision making. The last point is of particular importance. The ideal manager is a counselor, helping employees work through their own decision-making processes.

When a manager is respected and admired by employees, they are more likely to emulate the person's behavior. This means they will copy the manager's decision-making processes, while also avoiding counterproductive work behaviors of which they do not believe the manager would approve. Thus, a manager can exercise an inordinate amount of influence over an organization by molding the thinking of employees.

Molding the thinking of employees does not mean that the management team can (or should) attempt to alter the moral values of employees. Most people have a strong idea of what is right and wrong already, and will not alter their perceptions just based on a mandate from the company president. However, management can coach employees in the decision-making processes that can be used to arrive at a reasonable decision. Employees then use their existing moral values to evaluate situations.

A manager is not necessarily just the person granted the title of chief executive officer. There may be many other managers within an organization, some without any identification as such on the corporate organization chart. These informal managers may have gained some degree of authority due to their social skills or experience; as such, they can have a profound effect on the ethical behavior of employees. Given their outsized influence, the senior managers of a business should be aware of who these people are and make a strong effort to counsel them regarding ethical decision making. Focusing on this group of managers gives senior management an unusually strong level of influence over the organization as a whole.

In a situation where management elects to follow a course that employees believe to be ethically incorrect, employees are more likely to undermine management's efforts and will certainly not go out of their way to be of assistance. Thus, there needs to be a significant amount of overlap between the ethics of the management team and the employees in order to arrive at a reasonable working relationship between the two parties.

When managers are routinely promoted from the employee ranks, these individuals have been steeped in the behavioral norms of the employees, and so are likely to continue to apply those norms as managers. This is fine when an organization already has high moral standards, since those people who have been internally promoted will likely perpetuate the current situation. However, if the organization does not have a highly ethical culture, a habit of promoting from within is more likely to maintain the status quo – each new group of managers is just the same as the group it is replacing.

The Effect of Unethical Managers

It can be instructive to look at the negative effects of management when there is an unethical person in a position of authority. Employees have a tendency to follow orders, even when those orders are clearly wrong, so when an unprincipled person is issuing orders, there is a possibility that those orders will be carried out – even if employees consider the orders to be reprehensible. The reason is that the employees do not feel responsible for the action because they are not the ones who initiated it. Also, they may feel that protesting will put them at risk of being fired.

This effect is especially pronounced when the person has a strong aura of authority. This aura can be conveyed when a person has a large amount of experience, a very senior title, a doctorate, dresses well, and so forth. Consequently, there is a serious risk that just a few of these "bad apples" within an organization could cause widespread ethical lapses.

A reasonable way to minimize the effect of these managers is to tell employees that it is quite acceptable to question dubious orders, without fear of consequences. This approach will only work if there is a method in place to route information to an ethics office, so that the board of directors is made aware of situations in which managers are causing problems.

Signs of an Unethical Manager

What are the indicators of an unethical manager? One sign is that the person is more aggressive, continually snapping at and belittling subordinates. This is an indicator because the person is clearly showing that he does not want any discussion – he only wants to be obeyed. And, because the dictatorial signal is being sent so clearly, employees are more likely to obey his demands. Further, those employees more likely to make a stand will probably be forced out, leaving a group of employees sufficiently cowed by the manager's behavior to implement whatever demand is made.

Another indicator of an unethical manager is someone who consistently violates the rules that are applied to other employees. For example, a company president prohibits the charging of personal expenses on expense reports and then proceeds to do so himself. Or, the president advocates a strong nepotism policy and then hires family members into key positions. This type of person places himself above the rules that apply to others, and so is much more likely to engage in ethical lapses on a recurring basis.

The Code of Conduct

Many organizations create a code of conduct, which contains rules of behavior that guide the decisions made within a business. This code is intended to set standards for employees, frequently in areas that have caused ethical debates in the past. The topics covered may include:

- Conflicts of interest
- Harassment
- Marketing practices
- Political gifts
- Public disclosures
- Confidential information
- Compliance with laws

An abbreviated sample corporate code of conduct appears in the following exhibit.

Sample Corporate Code of Conduct

Company employees are expected to act lawfully, honestly, and in the best interests of the company. The following code provides some guidelines for business conduct by our employees:

1. *Conflicts of interest.* Employees are expected to use their judgment to act in the best interests of the company, and so should avoid actual or apparent conflicts of interest. A conflict of interest exists when personal interests interfere with the best interests of the company. For example, employees must obtain prior approval before beginning any employment relationship with another company, serving on a board of directors, or receiving gifts from a client or business partner.

2. *Relationships.* The company does not prohibit dating among employees. However, if a relationship involves two people in a direct reporting relationship, it must be disclosed to the human resources department. When a significant other is within one's chain of command, a manager cannot be involved in any decisions regarding the person's compensation, promotion, discipline or termination.

3. *Harassment.* The company does not tolerate harassment of its employees. If this has taken place, employees are encouraged to provide a written complaint or call the company's whistleblower hotline.

4. *Confidential information.* Employees are required to use the company's confidential information for business purposes only, and must always keep this information in strict confidence. This responsibility includes the confidential information of third parties that was received under non-disclosure agreements.

5. *Compliance with laws.* Employees are expected to act within the bounds of applicable laws, rules and regulations. Specifically, all employees must comply with all laws pertaining to anti-corruption, international trade, lobbying, campaign finance, and anti-trust activities.

If you learn about a violation of this code, promptly report it to your manager, the human resources department, or the legal department. If you are uncomfortable about reporting in this manner, consider doing so anonymously.

When a code of conduct is rigorously followed by management, it can represent a significant basis upon which to build a highly ethical corporate culture.

Many retailers impose a code of conduct on their suppliers, possibly because bad practices on the part of suppliers could reflect poorly on them. When fully implemented, such a code of conduct can be extended through the entire supply chain, including sub-contractors. These parties are more likely to follow the imposed code of conduct if they know that the retailer will sanction them at once if any failures come to light. An example of a supplier code of conduct appears in the following exhibit.

Sample Supplier Code of Conduct

The company's supplier code of conduct defines standards for fair, safe and healthy working conditions and environmental responsibility throughout our supply chain. All suppliers must commit to adhere to the following code of conduct:

- *Child labor.* No person shall be employed under the greater of the age of 16 or under the age of completion of compulsory education. Juvenile workers (up to age 18) shall not perform any work that may compromise their health or safety.
- *Discrimination.* No employee will be subject to any discrimination in any aspect of their employment, including hiring, compensation, work assignments, and promotions.
- *Environment.* Our suppliers must comply with all applicable environmental laws and agree to be monitored by our representatives to ensure compliance with those laws.
- *Forced labor.* There will be no use of forced labor. Suppliers are required to monitor any third party that assists them in recruiting or hiring employees, to ensure that no people seeking employment have been compelled to do so.
- *Harassment and abuse.* Every employee will be treated with respect, and shall not be subject to any physical or psychological harassment.
- *Health and safety.* Our suppliers will provide a safe and healthy workplace in order to prevent employee accidents or health problems.
- *Hours of work.* Our suppliers will not require their employees to work more than the regular and overtime hours allowed by local laws, and shall not exceed 50 hours per week. Suppliers will not request overtime work on a regular basis.
- *Law and code compliance.* Our suppliers are expected to comply with the relevant laws and regulations of the country in which workers are employed.
- *Overtime wages.* Employees must be compensated for overtime hours at the legally required rate. Where no legally required rate exists, overtime must be paid at a rate of 125% or more of the standard wage rate.
- *Quality.* Our suppliers must have a clearly documented quality system and quality improvement plan that includes audits and procedures that meet our quality standards.
- *Subcontracting.* We do not permit subcontracting without our prior written approval. Our direct suppliers must monitor approved subcontractors and sub-suppliers for social and environmental responsibility.
- *Traceability.* We require all suppliers to continuously monitor all locations in their supply chains and provide information about all factories and other sites that are involved in the production of our goods.
- *Wages and benefits.* We favor suppliers who progressively raise employee living standards through enhanced wages and benefits that exceed legal requirements. Every employee has the right to compensation for a normal work week that is sufficient to meet that person's basic needs and provide some additional discretionary income.

The Dangers of Anonymous Feedback

In the preceding sample corporate code of conduct, we noted that employees may report violations anonymously. The most common approach is the suggestions box, while hotlines and surveys may also be employed. While anonymous feedback can be useful, there are several problems with it, which are:

- *Witch hunts*. When comments are anonymous, managers may engage in witch hunts, searching through the organization to find out who made a comment.
- *Irresponsible behavior*. Because the system is anonymous, employees bear no responsibility for their comments, and so are more likely to make comments that are harmful to their fellow employees, such as backstabbing remarks.
- *Difficulty of corroboration*. When there is no attribution associated with a suggestion, it is quite difficult to corroborate the issue. This is a particular concern when the issue being raised involves alleged improper behavior.

Given the problems with anonymous feedback, it is better for a manager to engage in different behaviors that will encourage employees to directly contact him or her with their concerns and suggestions. Here are several possibilities:

- *Move the office*. Employees may be deterred from visiting the boss when this entails walking to a different floor and negotiating a way past several executive assistants. Instead, situate the office where employees are located, preferably right in the middle of them.
- *Move to an adjacent seat*. A manager's desk is an instrument of power, especially when it is large and formidable-looking. When such a desk is situated between the manager and an employee, the employee is much less likely to make suggestions. A better approach is to take a seat next to an employee to discuss an issue.
- *Give guidelines*. Employees may put forward suggestions on a wide range of issues, which are too broad or non-strategic to be worth further action by a manager. In this case, employees make comments but see no management action, so suggestions dry up. A better approach is to ask employees for suggestions in specific areas that correspond to the needs of the business, so that management is more likely to address them – which creates a positive feedback loop.
- *Walk around*. Employees will generally not seek out a manager to ladle out advice, since doing so takes them away from their home turf. To counteract this tendency, routinely walk around the business and engage with employees. By shifting to their territory, people are more willing to open up about problems and opportunities.
- *Ask for feedback*. The manager should routinely incorporate a request for feedback into every discussion with employees. After a while, employees will become so accustomed to the request that they will be more likely to make suggestions.

- *Go outside the core group.* The manager should look outside of his immediate group for the most valuable suggestions. The core group probably has the same background and knowledge, and so is least likely to come up with unusual ideas. In particular, seek out people who are new to the company, since they may have a fresh perspective on how tasks are done in other companies.
- *Be seen to take action.* Employees will not make suggestions to a manager who does not fight on their behalf, since there is no point in doing so. Instead, the manager needs to be seen pressing forward on their behalf with senior managers. Only then will employees feel that their concerns are being addressed, in which case they will continue to come forward with suggestions.
- *Discuss results.* Some employee ideas will be shot down by senior management, which can make employees feel that their immediate supervisor did not address their concerns. The supervisor can counteract this impression by discussing with them the actions she took, and the issues that then arose. Doing so may encourage them to keep making suggestions.
- *Assign credit.* When a person's suggestion leads to an improvement, publicly assign the credit to that person. Doing so makes it clear that suggestions are appreciated, and will likely trigger more comments.

Profits versus Stakeholder Considerations

A CEO is told by shareholders at the latest shareholder meeting that profits are unacceptably low. The next day, she is confronted with a decision to spend millions of dollars to keep groundwater contamination from occurring at one of the company's production sites. If she spends the money, there will be no water pollution issues for the local community, but profits will be obliterated for the rest of the year. This issue highlights a core problem with the modern corporation, which is that it can become excessively beholden to the demands of its shareholders, putting profits above all other considerations. This creates a short-term performance bias, where decisions are made that continually benefit shareholders at the expense of other stakeholders in the business, such as employees, customers, suppliers, lenders, and the local community. Instead, the manager needs to consider the needs of each group of stakeholders, such as:

- Customers, who expect an adequate level of product quality and goods that are safe to use
- Employees, who expect a safe working environment and reasonable compensation
- Local communities, which expect the firm to not pollute the area or cause safety issues, and to contribute to the overall quality of life in the area
- Regulators, which expect the firm to meet or exceed their minimum regulatory standards
- Special interest groups, such as environmentalists, which expect the firm to adhere to their performance standards
- Suppliers, which expect to be dealt with fairly and paid on time

The situation is exacerbated by the pervasive use of stock option grants for senior managers, who can profit handsomely from a run-up in the corporate stock price. These temptations not only focus attention on the need for more profits, but can also lead to fraudulent financial reporting in order to drive up share prices even further.

Given these concerns, it should be no surprise that managers are more inclined to engage in the following practices to enhance profits:

- Creating an unsafe work environment [harms employees]
- Deceptive sales practices to land customer orders [damages customers]
- Depressing wages and benefits [harms employees]
- Falsifying financial statement information [damages creditors and lenders]
- Going bankrupt in order to void a union contract [damages employees]
- Overstating customer invoices [damages customers]
- Reducing the quality of materials in products [damages customers]
- Selling confidential information [damages customers]
- Taking unwarranted discounts when paying invoices [harms suppliers]
- Violating environmental regulations [harms the community]

In short, the lure of personal gain through short-term profits can lead managers to take ethically dubious stances in many parts of a business.

A better way to make decisions is to identify all stakeholders in a business, noting their expectations for what the firm can do for them, and their ability to influence the company. When a stakeholder can cause significant trouble for a company and the firm has the ability to meet the demands of the stakeholder, it can make sense to proactively reach out to that stakeholder and create an arrangement that works well for both sides.

EXAMPLE

Quest Clothiers, maker of rugged outdoor wear, has most of its apparel manufactured in African countries. A nonprofit organization monitors working conditions in Africa, and brings substandard working conditions to the attention of Quest's management, which the nonprofit threatens to take public. After meeting with the nonprofit, they come to an arrangement where the nonprofit identifies problem suppliers for Quest and also recommends suppliers that provide better worker treatment. This arrangement meets the goals of the nonprofit, while also allowing Quest to develop a reputation for ethical sourcing of its production.

A good way to deal with the concerns of stakeholders is to focus on the *triple bottom line*, which refers to the financial, social, and environmental results of a business. Each of these results focuses on a different activity – generating a financial return for investors, having a positive impact on people, and having a positive impact on the planet. The intent behind this manner of reporting is to make corporate managers more aware of their responsibilities outside of the more traditional focus on returns to investors. A problem with this more comprehensive reporting method is the difficulty encountered in quantifying results for the last two measurement areas.

Corporate Social Responsibility

An extension of the concept of assisting stakeholders is corporate social responsibility, which is the viewpoint that a business should be more aware of its impact on society and the environment. The intent is to deliver positive outcomes for all stakeholders in the business that result in long-term sustainability, rather than focusing on just a positive return for its shareholders. The actions taken should extend beyond the narrow interests of the firm, exceeding the basic requirements of the law. There are many aspects to corporate social responsibility, including the following:

- A low carbon footprint, perhaps coupled with actions to clean up the environment.
- Dealing with employees in the most ethical manner possible.
- Engaging in philanthropy, especially in those local areas where the firm has facilities.
- Engaging in volunteer events, perhaps by allowing employees to do so on company time.

Not only does this approach result in an improved environment, it also enhances the image of the organization with its stakeholders, who will then be more likely to support it. Further, people may be more willing to work for such an organization, which enhances the quality of its employees.

The corporate social responsibility concept can be broken down into several stages of performance. At its most basic level, a company still has to earn a profit, since it will otherwise go out of business and so will be unable to address its other responsibilities. The next most basic stage is for the organization to obey the law. Thus, it cannot engage in illegal activities and must abide by any regulations that apply to it. These two stages are the most essential core requirements for the basic operations of a business. At the next stage, the firm should be keenly aware of its ethical responsibilities, which go beyond the basic requirements of the law, forcing managers to pursue those actions that "do the right thing." And finally, the highest stage of performance is discretionary responsibility, where management voluntarily makes social contributions that are not required by any economic interests, regulations, or ethical responsibilities. For example, a business may choose to offer its employees paid time off to engage in non-profit activities, or it may send assistance to people located in a disaster area, or even assign its staff to nonprofit activities for extended periods of time.

The Complexity of Ethical Issues

Not all situations represent clear ethical choices that every person would answer in the same way. For example, here are several instances in which the ethics of a decision are murky:

- At what point should a company stop gathering information about its customers? It is generally considered reasonable to accumulate past purchases information in order to predict future buying behavior, but is it reasonable to buy additional information from third-party data aggregators to build a more comprehensive profile of each customer? To make the decision more difficult, competitors have decided to buy this additional information, and so have gained a competitive advantage over the company.
- How far down the supply chain should a company be responsible for safe working conditions and child labor laws? Does responsibility stop within the company, or at its first level of suppliers, or the suppliers of the suppliers?
- A business is about to go bankrupt, and it is questionable that the firm will survive the bankruptcy process. Knowing that this is the case, should a salesperson conclude a service agreement with a potential new customer and take an advance payment from the customer? The advance could provide critical funding for the company, but if the firm ends up being liquidated, the customer will likely lose the advance.
- A paint manufacturer has developed a new type of quick-dry paint, but the local regulatory authority has not approved it for sale, due to the presence of trace amounts of a suspected carcinogen in the paint. A neighboring country does not conduct such rigorous testing. Should the manufacturer sell the paint in the neighboring country, or shut down the project entirely?

Decision Making Approaches

Given the difficulty of making some decisions where there are ethical considerations (as noted in the preceding section), a manager can employ a variety of decision-making techniques. For example:

- *Distributive justice.* Make decisions based on justifiable criteria. By using this approach, promotions will be based strictly on the qualifications directly associated with a job, and not on arbitrary decision criteria, such as a person's age, gender or race.
- *Moral rights approach.* Assume that people have fundamental rights that cannot be taken away by a management decision. Thus, the best decision alternative is one that enhances or does the least harm to the rights of those impacted by it. By using this approach, a manager would be more inclined to respect the privacy rights of employees by not inspecting the websites they access while on company time.

- *Practical approach.* Make decisions based on the prevalent standards in the profession and society at large. By using this approach, a manager will make decisions that she would be comfortable seeing publicized to the community.
- *Procedural justice.* Make decisions based on fair administration of the rules. By using this approach, a manager would state her expectations for how employees should treat each other, and will consistently impose penalties on anyone who does not meet her expectations.
- *Utilitarian approach.* Make a decision that results in the greatest good for the largest number of people. By using this approach, a manager would be more inclined to pay for pollution controls for a production facility, since doing so results in reduced health problems for the people living in the surrounding area.

Most managers will make ethical decisions using these techniques, but also while being influenced by the rules and inter-personal pressures imposed by an organization. Thus, if there is an ingrained history of upholding the law (common in a long-term, more bureaucratic organization), then managers will be more likely to closely adhere to the rules of the business. However, a few stronger-willed managers have developed their own opinions about what is right, and how to treat other people. These individuals are more likely to violate the rules of an organization if they feel that those rules are incorrect, even if doing so will have adverse consequences for them. This latter group tends to be more supportive of their direct reports, and so tend to be highly regarded by their subordinates, though not necessarily by their superiors.

The Ethics Committee

When management finds that it has to continually deal with ethical questions regarding how it conducts business, it may be time to convene an ethics committee. This is a group of company employees that provides rulings on how to deal with questionable issues. Its rulings have the force of law within the company, and so should be used as the basis for dealing with similar issues.

An ethics committee should also take responsibility for disciplining any employee that violates the firm's code of conduct. There should be a standard set of disciplinary actions that can be taken, so that the committee is seen to be consistently dealing with similar types of violations.

The ethics committee may be a relatively informal group that meets infrequently, or one that uses a structured meeting process and regularly scheduled gatherings, depending on the size and nature of the business. A large firm may choose to be even more formal, appointing a chief ethics officer and staff that is responsible for providing ethics training, advising management, and dealing with problems. In the latter case, an ethics committee may still be empaneled, primarily to advise the ethics department.

Whistle Blowing

An employee may go to an outside agency, such as a newspaper or regulatory division, to publicize improper behavior within a business. These whistle blowers frequently do so out of a sense of frustration, when their attempts to bring up these issues within the firm are stonewalled. Rather than dealing with whistle blowers as an annoyance, management should take the reverse course and set up confidential hotlines to encourage this sort of behavior. Doing so may bring up issues such as employee fraud that management was completely unaware of.

Hotlines are most effective when any leads generated are routed directly to a committee of the board of directors. Doing so ensures that complaints cannot be squashed by managers who may be complicit in the issues being brought up.

There is a strong tendency for whistle blowers to be driven out of an organization, because they have gone against the established culture in order to point out wrongdoing. Combatting this tendency calls for strong support by senior management to protect whistle blowers, ensuring that they are not marginalized within the company. Otherwise, employees will see the negative effects on whistle blowers, and so will be less inclined to report any problems that they see.

Summary

Managers are responsible for creating an environment in which employees are more likely to engage in the most ethical and socially responsible behavior. The typical manager has a significant multiplier effect on the level of ethics practiced, by working in an honest and fair manner that employees will want to emulate.

Engaging in ethical behavior might be considered an incidental activity for a manager, since there is no direct impact on profits – but this is not the case. When there is a strongly ethical environment within a firm, employee turnover is reduced and stakeholders are happier, which enhances the reputation of the organization. This tends to support a long-term increase in sales and profits, as outsiders are more willing to do business with the firm, insiders are more willing to support it, and higher-quality job candidates are attracted to it.

Chapter 18
7 Habits of Effective Managers

Introduction

A manager may be as busy as possible, fully engaged in her work and apparently succeeding in all areas, and yet does not meet the performance goals set for her or reliably make the correct decisions to improve her area of responsibility. The trouble is that a manager's job can appear to be overwhelming, making it difficult to ascertain the key factors that are most likely to result in success. How do we decide which aspects of the job will make a manager more effective? A highly effective manager is one who always does the right thing. In essence, this means that the actions of a manager result in a business achieving its intended goals. Few managers are truly effective, since many of them are waylaid by insignificant issues, or incorrectly place a premium on being excessively efficient.

Being *effective* means that a person has a strategic mindset, always ensuring that the organization is deploying its resources correctly. Being *efficient* is more of a tactical issue, where the organization is maximizing its productivity. The trouble with an excessive focus on efficiency is that the organization may be highly efficient in activities where the business should not be engaged. Consequently, a strong focus on effectiveness results in a more financially viable business over the long term.

EXAMPLE

A new regional sales manager of Optimistic Corporation is trying to be as efficient as possible, and so decides to eliminate his executive assistant position, thereby saving his company a total of $60,000, which includes the cost of the payroll taxes and benefits related to the position. Because the executive assistant is no longer available to schedule the manager's time, he forgets about a lunch appointment with a key customer. The customer thinks that Optimistic no longer cares about his account, and moves his business to a competitor. The net present value of the customer's likely business over the next five years would have been $150,000. In this example, the manager was focusing on being overly efficient from the perspective of the administrative staff budget. From the perspective of the entire company, this action resulted in a net loss of $90,000. Thus, effectiveness trumps efficiency for a manager.

A key part of the following recommendations is that each one is described as a *habit*. This means the manager engages in the activity on a regular basis, to the extent that it is hard to give up. Ideally, the manager gives these habits an extremely high priority, so they are always addressed before less critical activities. By maintaining a tight focus on the following seven recommendations, the manager is maintaining a high level of effectiveness on a continuing basis.

Habit #1 – Live Among the Staff

An essential element of management is communication, and a manager is in the best position to do so when parked in the midst of his staff. Thus, a production manager should have a desk on the production floor and a controller should be situated in the midst of the accounting department. This also means removing any blocks to communication, such as a closed office door or a receptionist who demands an appointment. Instead, employees need to feel as though they can walk in at any time and discuss any issue. This impression can be enhanced by going into active listening mode as soon as an employee arrives, in order to obtain every possible scrap of information that the person is trying to convey.

Living among the staff does not mean just being available to passively receive information. In addition, the manager should routinely walk among the employees, actively chatting with everyone. Doing so makes it much easier to obtain information on the spot, or at least to encourage employees to come to the manager's office later for a more private talk. Further, arrange for lunches with employees as frequently as possible, thereby giving them more opportunities to discuss issues.

Living among the staff conveys a powerful benefit, which is early notice of problems and opportunities. As soon as something happens, the manager is likely to hear about it, and so can take action. This can result in incipient problems being fixed before they become larger, as well as strategic and tactical shifts as soon as an opportunity arises. For example, a credit manager hears from her collections staff that a key customer may have just filed for bankruptcy protection, and so can immediately contact the shipping department to stop all subsequent deliveries to that customer, thereby saving the company a significant bad debt loss.

Habit #2 – Be Aware of Your Demeanor

Employees are constantly watching their manager for signs of anything at all, such as annoyance, anger, fear, or frustration. They may then make all sorts of inferences about these observations, such as to steer clear of the manager today because she is on the warpath, or that she is showing unusual favoritism to someone who does not deserve it, or perhaps that she is planning a layoff. Any of these inferences can negatively impact employees. An effective manager is much better at displaying a calm, even-tempered demeanor. When employees see a cool, unruffled manager who can listen to issues, ponder the options, and make considered judgments, they are much more likely to be supportive and work together to achieve key goals. Thus, a composed manager has a multiplier effect on her staff, who are more likely to behave in the same way.

Habit #3 – Offload Decisions

A new manager can be overwhelmed with the number of possible issues that require decisions on an ongoing basis. When this happens, there is not enough time to deeply consider the options and risks associated with each one, resulting in the manager constantly making suboptimal decisions. A better approach is to critically examine all decisions and decide which ones can be offloaded to subordinates. These offloaded decisions are routine items for which there are only a few possible decision outcomes, and which are generally low-risk. Shifting these decisions away leaves more time to consider the more critical decisions that the manager must still make, while also empowering employees to take more control over their jobs. The main downside to offloading decisions is that an employee might make an incorrect decision. This issue can be corrected with proper training, as well as by setting up decision rules for employees to follow.

Habit #4 – Correct Recurring Problems

A manager's time can be consumed by problems – listening to complaints, tracking down causes, and making short-term fixes. Addressing these problems can leave little time for other activities, to the point where a manager never seems to be getting ahead and actually making any improvements. The solution is to make a list of the problems arising over a period of time, and to then categorize them by frequency and the time required to correct each one. Then focus on permanently correcting the recurring problems that consume the largest part of the manager's time. By doing so, it is possible to rapidly advance down the list of problems, as more time becomes available to deal with lesser issues.

Habit #5 – Reiterate Plans at a Medium Level of Detail

A manager typically deals with a fluid situation over the course of a year, as problems arise, employees leave and are replaced, and senior management imposes any number of strategic or tactical changes. An effective manager adjusts for these changes, making continual updates to the planning that applies to her area of responsibility. This may involve changes in spending for assets, hiring plans, promotion plans, and so forth. These plans should be considered an effective tool for management, not as an annoying burden that consumes the manager's valuable time. The trick to turning planning into an effective tool is to only plan down to a medium level of detail, where changes to a plan can be completed in an hour or two. When the planning is driven down to an additional level of detail, where expenses are planned by month for every possible expense category, the manager will find that the time required to maintain the plan massively increases, while the resulting plan provides little additional useful information. In short, a modest amount of planning is cost-effective, but too much planning is a burden.

Habit #6 – Focus Attention on a Few Changes

Managers are certainly judged on their ability to implement changes within an organization. Because of this pressure, a manager may be tempted to implement a blizzard of changes all at once. The trouble is that almost any change will have its detractors who slow down the process, while unexpected problems will delay implementation and require additional funding. And furthermore, the organization may resist a change for a long period of time, effectively reverting back to the old way of doing things once the manager is no longer focused on it. The best solution is to identify just one or two really crucial changes, and then unwaveringly focus on them for an extended period of time. The best outcome is when every possible aspect of a change has been thoroughly addressed, and a measurement system is in place that will warn the manager if there is any backsliding in future periods that warrants her attention. This more focused approach results in fewer changes, but those changes are more thoroughly implemented.

Habit #7 – Develop Employees

The preceding habits were targeted at short-term and medium-term improvements in manager effectiveness. This last habit is much longer-term in nature. The manager should constantly review the readiness of her employees for new responsibilities, assigning them to training classes, cross-training them in different positions, and promoting them when they are ready. Doing so results in a department in which *everyone* is operating at maximum effectiveness, not just the manager. There is also a strong chance that employee turnover within the group will decline, since their satisfaction with their positions and pride in their group should increase.

This habit will mean that the manager is grooming a number of people who could eventually take over her position. A less self-confident manager might consider this to be a threat, but a better view is that the manager is setting herself up for promotion to a more senior position, where she can deploy these seven habits again.

Summary

When a new manager wants to be effective, the most critical of the habits noted here is the first one – it is essential to wade into the crowd and find out what is going on. Without that information in hand, every other recommendation listed here is useless. The next most essential habit is to drive decision making as far down into the group as possible, in order to create enough time for the manager to deal with the most difficult issues. And finally, focus on just a few changes at a time, in order to achieve more enduring results. A likely result of implementing these habits is a much more focused group of employees that is more responsible for their actions and which has developed a firm belief in their abilities to get work done. An effective manager could not ask for more.

Glossary

A

Authority. The power to give orders, make and enforce decisions, and commit resources.

B

BCG matrix. A system for classifying a portfolio of companies into dogs, stars, cash cows, and question marks.

Bottom-up estimating. When estimating work begins at the lowest level of detail.

Brainstorming. The process used to come up with creative new solutions by engaging in an open group discussion.

Budget. A document that forecasts the financial results and financial position of a business for one or more future periods.

Bureaucracy model. The use of a high level of organization within a business, using clear job definitions, a hierarchy of authority, and rules and regulations.

C

Chain of command. The official order in which authority is delegated down from top management to employees.

Coaching. A set of training methods that focus on the needs of specific individuals, including feedback about how to improve their performance.

Code of conduct. Rules of behavior that guide the decisions made within a business.

Constraint analysis. The monitoring of bottlenecks within a business.

Contingency planning. The development of plans to deal with emergencies.

Corporate culture. The group of beliefs, values, and norms that determine how employees interact with each other and process business transactions.

Corporate social responsibility. The viewpoint that a business should be more aware of its impact on society and the environment.

Critical path. The longest path through a network. There is no slack in any task on the critical path, so a delay here will delay an entire project.

Critical path method. A visual portrayal of tasks that are arranged in sequential order, along with a time line for how long it will take to complete each task.

D

Decision making. The process of selecting an alternative from a range of possible options.

Delegation. The transfer of authority and responsibility from a superior to a subordinate.

Detection theory. The concept that the probability of a transgression decreases as the probability of detection goes up.

Divisional structure. The use of separate organizational structures to service different product lines or geographic regions.

E

Effectiveness. The extent to which an objective is attained.

Efficiency. The completion of a task while using a minimal amount of resources.

Emotional contagion. When one person's emotions and related behaviors trigger the same emotions and behaviors in others.

Emotional intelligence. The ability to recognize one's own emotions and those of others, and to manage emotions to enhance performance.

Empowerment. The practice of giving employees an increased amount of information and decision making responsibility.

Ethics. The moral principles that guide a person's behavior.

External dependency. An input from an external source that is required before a task can proceed.

Extrinsic reward. A tangible form of compensation or recognition given in exchange for achieving something.

F

Functional structure. An organizational structure in which a business is broken up into departments, so that each area of specialization is run by a different manager.

G

Gantt chart. A visual portrayal of the task assignments and task durations within a project.

General administrative theory. A set of 14 principles of management, as set forth by Henri Fayol.

H

Hierarchical structure. An organizational structure in which decision making is concentrated at the top, with lower levels being told how to implement those decisions.

Hierarchy of needs. A categorization of an individual's needs, as classified by Abraham Maslow.

I

Income statement. A financial report that summarizes the revenues generated, expenses incurred, and any resulting profit or loss for a reporting period.

Intrinsic reward. The sense of satisfaction gained when performing a task.

J

Job enlargement. Increasing the number of tasks associated with a job.

Job depth. Increasing the level of authority and responsibility associated with a job.

L

Leadership. The act of inspiring others to engage in the tasks needed to achieve a goal.

M

Management by exception. The practice of only bringing up issues with management if results represent significant differences from the expected amount.

Management by objectives. The assignment of objectives to employees, usually tied to a system of rewards, to ensure that a plan is achieved.

Management by walking around. The concept of informally interacting with employees to discuss their work.

Manager. A person who is in charge of one or more tasks, usually with several people reporting to him or her.

Matrix structure. The assignment of multiple responsibilities to employees across multiple functional areas.

Mintzberg's managerial roles. The concept that managers are engaged in interpersonal, informational, and decisional roles.

Mission statement. A written statement of the core purpose of an organization.

N

Negative float. When a project's critical path will result in project completion after the mandated completion date.

Networking. The creation and active maintenance of a group of acquaintances for the mutual benefit of the group.

O

Onboarding. The process of helping new employees understand a firm, including how it functions, the people working within it, and their interactions.

Open book management. The practice of giving all employees access to an organization's financial and operational information.

Operational plans. Detailed plans that focus on those specific processes and tasks needed to achieve tactical goals.

Organic structure. A flat reporting structure, in which a manager's span of control covers a large number of employees.

Organization chart. A visual representation of the corporate hierarchy.

Organizing. The process of assembling resources in such a way that specific objectives can be achieved.

P

Performance appraisal. The process used to evaluate an employee's on-the-job performance.

Performance dashboard. A data presentation that shows the key performance indicators and measurements that are essential to the accomplishment of a plan.

Power. The ability to make things happen.

Program evaluation and review technique. A variation on the critical path method that allows for the inclusion of variable amounts of time for each task.

R

Responsibility. The obligation to perform a task.

S

Scenario planning. The derivation and examination of a set of distinctly different future viewpoints.

Scientific management. The careful study of a job to determine the best possible procedures for conducting it.

Silo mentality. A condition in which there is very little information sharing between departments.

Slack time. An interval that occurs when there are activities that can be completed before the time when they are actually needed.

Span of control. The average number of people managed by each supervisor in an organization.

Strategy. A plan of action that is targeted at achieving a major aim.

Summary task. A description of a set of activities.

SWOT analysis. An investigation of the strengths, weaknesses, opportunities and threats associated with a business.

Synergy. When two things work together to create an effect greater than the sum of their individual effects.

T

Tactics. The detailed means by which strategy is carried out.

Theory X. The concept that employees must be coerced to engage in work.

Theory Y. The concept that employees are capable of being self-directed in accomplishing tasks.

Time and motion study. The analysis of the exact motions required by a person to complete a task.

Top-down estimating. Estimates that are imposed from above by company management, stakeholders, or the project manager.

Total quality management. The ongoing elimination of process errors, as well as the streamlining of operations.

Transactional leader. One who defines the supporting structure beneath a vision, covering required roles, tasks, schedules, and reward systems.

Two-factor theory. The concept that certain factors directly relate to employee satisfaction, while other factors relate to employee dissatisfaction.

V

Variance. The difference between an actual measured amount and a basis, such as a budgeted amount.

W

Work breakdown structure. The identification of every task in a project.

Work package. A group of activities for which work is estimated, scheduled, monitored, and controlled.

Index

www.ingramcontent.com/pod-product-compliance
Lightning Source LLC
Chambersburg PA
CBHW080522220326
41599CB00032B/6171